CREATRIX

(Creātrix – Noun – Female Creator)

WISDOM • INSIGHTS • PRINCIPLES
SHARED BY THE MOTHERS OF SUCCESS STORIES IN SPORTS, BUSINESS AND CULTURE

Blake Gunther

Mary Fischer-Nassib & Chris Mueller

Copyright © 2021 Gunner Publishing

Editing and copy editing by Blake Gunther and Devin Wenzel

Cover design and chapter icons by Kate Desiderio (@artnsoul.studios)

www.Creatrix.blog

ISBN # 978-0-578-75532-8

To my family and friends - for all the help ranging from proofreading, copy editing, design feedback and the countless conversations in regard to this project - thank you. Special thank you to my mom for her proofreading help. Thank you, Drew Gunther, for brainstorming the original idea for this on our flights to and from California. Love you.

To Devin Wenzel, thank you for your unconditional help and support throughout this entire process. Couldn't have gotten this done without you. I'm proud to call you a great friend.

-Blake

A portion of this book's proceeds will be donated to these special causes -

- Good+Foundation (@goodplusfdn) - Founded by Jessica Seinfeld, Good+ pairs goods with innovative services to dismantle multi-generational poverty for under-resourced families.

- Believe and Achieve Foundation (@believeandachievefoundation) - Providing access to basic needs, making a difference in the lives of children and families. The Believe and Achieve Foundation functions under the premise that strong community partnerships and quality outreach programming will make a positive and lasting difference in the lives of our youth.

- Sow Good Now (@Sowgoodnow) – Sharing time, talent and treasure through the sports we love. Sow Good Now teaches athletes to recognize their own personal gifts and use them to give back for the common good.

CONTENTS

Part I. Athletes

Part II. Business & Culture

Introduction

When the Good Lord was creating mothers, He was into His sixth day of "overtime" when the angel appeared and said, "You're doing a lot of fiddling around on this one." And God said, "Have you read the specs on this order? She has to be completely washable, but not plastic. Have 180 moveable parts...all replaceable. Run on black coffee and leftovers. Have a lap that disappears when she stands up. A kiss that can cure anything from a broken leg to a disappointed love affair. And six pairs of hands."

The angel shook her head slowly and said, "Six pairs of hands.... no way."

"It's not the hands that are causing me problems," God remarked, "it's the three pairs of eyes that mothers have to have."

"That's on the standard model?" asked the angel. God nodded.

"One pair that sees through closed doors when she asks, 'What are you kids doing in there?' when she already knows. Another here in the back of her head that sees what she shouldn't but what she has to know, and of course the ones here in front that can look at a child when he goofs up and say, 'I understand and I love you' without so much as uttering a word."

"God," said the angel touching his sleeve gently, "get some rest tomorrow…"

"I can't," said God, "I'm so close to creating something so close to myself. Already I have one who heals herself when she is sick...can feed a family of six on one pound of hamburger...and can get a nine-year-old to stand under a shower."

The angel circled the model of a mother very slowly. "It's too soft," she sighed.

"But tough!" said God excitedly. "You can imagine what this mother can do or endure."

"Can it think?"

"Not only can it think, but it can reason and compromise," said the Creator.

Finally, the angel bent over and ran her finger across the cheek.

"There's a leak," she pronounced. "I told You that You were trying to put too much into this model."

"It's not a leak," said the Lord, "It's a tear."

"What's it for?"

"It's for joy, sadness, disappointment, pain, loneliness and pride."

"You are a genius," said the angel.

Somberly, God said, "I didn't put it there."

— **Erma Bombeck, When God Created Mothers**

HOW TO GET THE MOST OUT OF THIS BOOK

Consider for a moment the myriad of moving parts required to bring a new human into this world and ensure it grows into a thoughtful, productive contributor to its community. "It takes a village to raise a child," as the adage goes. But as the leader of that village, mothers are faced with the challenge of influencing their children's passions and education, shaping their values and nutritional habits, supporting them through life's most demanding moments and instilling the self-confidence required to achieve their utmost potential. This book aims to explore how 38 mothers of highly exceptional individuals handled these monumental, yet underappreciated responsibilities.

Creatrix is meant to be read like an anthology. Open up to any chapter, at any time, and you will find gems of brutal honesty, eternal wisdom and transformative inspiration. However, only when it is taken as a whole can the reader identify the most useful patterns of motherly advice. That's the advantage of having 38 unique stories. Each individual account is valuable and entertaining, but it's the entire collection that reveals the universal parenting philosophies in which our subjects simply do not waver.

If you are a parent or soon to be parent, this book is for you. It will provide you with practical skills for raising children from a wide range of disciplines and backgrounds. The next time you start to criticize, pressure or coddle your child, you might reflect on something you took from this book. If you feel like parenthood is consuming your life, this is a chance to assess and reset. At least one of the subjects in *Creatrix* has dealt with similar struggles to your own and they will be the first to tell you that no one is perfect. Fortunately, raising children is a lifetime commitment, so the best thing you can do is enjoy the process.

This book is also meant for young adults, of any age, to learn to sympathize with their parents' impossible responsibility. When we are young, we do not understand what it is like to be responsible for another living, breathing human being. We cannot yet comprehend the depth of parental anxiety nor the stress of transforming an infant into a happy, responsible, stable adult. Every decision, every rule, every suggestion can have tremendous, unexpected influence on an evolving mind. In order to achieve more, we must understand the perspective of those advising us. Not every parent is perfect. Maybe you feel as if yours are toxic and detrimental to your development. Maybe they are extremely supportive and honest. Either way, this book will help you avoid unnecessary turmoil, improve your perspective and help prepare you if you yourself decide to take on the responsibility of parenthood someday.

There are no predetermined steps to follow here, just principles. We encourage you to go through these questions with your loved ones and answer them yourselves. You will be surprised at the amazing conversations they ignite!

WHY WE WROTE THIS BOOK

Blake is fascinated by human psychology. He has an obsessive curiosity over why people say what they say, react the way they react, behave the way they do, or end up how they end up. It emerged by questioning how his own mother and father raised four children with different interests and dispositions into lively, successful adults. How much of an effect did their solid foundation have? What tactics did his mom use to instill strong values in her children? He also saw this in how his grandma, Eleanor, raised his father. She provided a strong foundation and instilled in him the belief and confidence that he could achieve anything. What was her secret? Once Blake got this idea in his head, he had to bring it up in every conversation. The results were amazing discussions about the impacts of various parenting styles. The idea continued to morph until Blake recognized that so many other people could find value in what he was discovering and *Creatrix* was born. Blake believes a quote that best sums up what his mom and grandma taught him about the essence of motherhood, or parenthood in general, comes from Mother Teresa - "Intense love does not measure, it just gives."

As the sixth of twelve children and mother of five, Mary

co-authors this book in honor of her mother, Helen Fischer, and for the chance to delve into the minds and lives of these unique mothers whose children have reached high levels of success. Mary believes you can be anything you want to be, but you can't be everything you want to be, and motherhood always comes first. She is passionate about elevating the work that mothers do to serve as a foundation for the children they raise. Mary's mother made raising a dozen children seem fun and effortless. As a child, Mary was often asked how her mother did it. Mary thought to herself, "Did what?" It wasn't until she had her first child that she finally noticed and laughingly wondered, "how DID my mom do it!?" To Mary, mothers make invisible sacrifices every day for their children and their success by putting their needs above their own. There is no road map and every child is unique so the chances of hitting the mark on every child raising issue is unlikely. However, being honest and being present is what counts. Mary hopes this book will help all mothers feel less alone and more confident in the many roles they play in shaping the lives of their children.

Chris has a unique perspective on motherhood. Both of his parents died by the time he was 5 years old. His mom passed away in a high-speed car accident on the Pennsylvania Turnpike that he and his older sister miraculously survived. After the accident, he was adopted by his Aunt Julie, one of his mom's two sisters, who raised four children on her own as a single mother. It was her perseverance, guidance, empathy and compassion that empowered him to overcome the cards he was dealt and never allow his circumstances to dictate his life's outcome. Because of her impact on his life, Chris is passionate about spreading awareness on the value of a mother's influence and hopes that this book can foster more "Aunt Julies" for future children facing unfortunate situations.

THE PROCESS

We approached our subjects for several reasons. Namely, they can explain their child's behavior on a subconscious level that they alone understand. They had a front row seat to, and in many cases a strong influence on, the series of choices that put their child in a position to achieve uncommon success in their chosen field. Before the children highlighted in this book became success stories, they were just innocent kids trying to navigate the ups and downs of life. Before Myles Garrett grew to be 6'4 and exploded as an NFL star, he was just a kid from Texas who stood up for his boy scout friends and worried about maintaining good grades to meet his mother's standards. Before Maya Gabeira was surfing 73-foot waves and breaking world records, she was the teenage girl who wasn't taken seriously as a surfer because of her gender. Before James Harris was one of the world's top real estate brokers, he was the kid with ADHD getting kicked out of schools for being a poor student.

To access stories like these, we spent nine months conducting dozens of interviews. It was peculiar timing. The world had just shut down due to the Coronavirus pandemic and our project came to a halt. But we quickly realized that total quarantine actually catalyzed peoples' willingness to spend hours answering questions from us.

Each perspective and story you are about to read is a piece of clay cultivated by experience and time. This book aims to mold these pieces of clay together to create a blueprint for you to nurture a life of success for you and your children or future children. Just as our understanding has evolved from compiling these pages, we hope yours will from reading them.

Part I

Athletes

A mother is the chef. The chauffeur. The ball girl. The cheerleader. The dry cleaner. The motivational speaker. The ankle taper. The sideline prayer. The late snack maker. The believer.[1]

---

[1] Theathletesparent.com

"The only thing I would do differently is appreciate the time more when they were young, to enjoy each moment. They're so fleeting as they age and we darn near push them to the next steps. *Hurry and walk, hurry and talk.* All those things, rushing to the next big stage in life. Then, they move out. It's over, and you want them to be little again. So, live in the moment, savor it. You won't regret it."

> **Myles Garrett**
> IG: @Flash_Garrett

Audrey Garrett is the mother of Myles

Garrett, the former No. 1 overall pick of the 2017 NFL draft who now stars at defensive end for the Cleveland Browns. Audrey grew up in Newport News, Virginia in the 1970s, where she overcame any and every obstacle that arose in her path. From her unstable upbringing with an alcoholic father, to the challenges of living with a widowed mother in a wheelchair and three other siblings, Audrey never allowed herself to become a victim of her circumstances. She had dreams of a better life to chase.

Audrey attended college at Hampton University and graduated with a degree in Mass Media Communications. But she wasn't done there, later earning a Master's in Marketing and Public Relations from Southern New Hampshire University and currently on the path of earning a Doctorate in Strategic Leadership. Gifted with the pen, she took up a career in technical writing after school until her path led to Arlington, Texas. It was there in Texas, a place where faith, family, and Friday Night Lights became fixtures of everyday life, the place where Audrey nurtured her four children – Myles, Sean, Tiffanie and Brea – into the successful adults they are today.

While each child is a standout athlete in their own right, with Sean being a first-round pick of the New Jersey Nets of the NBA draft in 2011 and Brea the 2014 National Champion in the weight throw, it was Myles, the youngest of the four, who was rated the nation's No. 2 overall prospect in high school and received NCAA All-American honors twice during a decorated three-year collegiate career at Texas A&M and then was the first overall pick in the 2017 NFL draft. Since then, Myles has compiled 42.5 sacks in 52 games for the Browns as a team captain and is a key component of the franchise's future. He signed a 5-year, $125 million contract with Cleveland in July 2020, which made him the NFL's highest paid defensive player at the time. He finished the 2020-2021 season with 12 sacks, 18 QB hits and four forced fumbles – landing him on the NFL's first-team All-Pro list. Off the field, he has partnered with numerous charitable organizations ranging from the National Multiple Sclerosis Society, an ode to the disease that put his grandmother in a wheelchair, to the Chris Long Foundation, providing water for communities in Africa.

In the following chapter, Audrey provides an inside look into her remarkable story, describing her journey from Newport News to raising one of the NFL's most dominant, yet misunderstood, players.

Did your mother inspire you in any way? What kind of values did you take from her and instill in your own life as a mother?

My mother and I were the only mothers in my immediate family. None of my siblings ever had kids so our relationship was extra special. I am not particularly like my mom but we had the best time laughing and enjoying each other's company. She was able to encourage each of us to go to college and lead productive, positive and responsible lives. She is my absolute role model for womanhood.

What kind of dreams and goals did you have when you were a kid? How much did they influence where you are today?

I initially wanted to be a lawyer, then a writer. I ended up being a technical writer. I thought I would be a sports reporter like Jane Kennedy. While I did not become a reporter, I did have a career as a writer in general.

When was the earliest indication that you thought Myles might have extraordinary talent?

Never even thought about it. We were focused on schoolwork. If you wanted to play sports, then you had to keep your grades at Bs and above. Myles was not necessarily always a dominant figure growing up. He had surgery when he was 11 and 12 because he had flat feet. He laid on the couch for six months to heal one foot and then had to do the same thing for the other foot, so he was pent-up on the couch for 12 months. Before that, he wasn't really much of an athlete but after that he came out turning into the freak Myles Garrett. What he is now is from sheer hard work on top of natural talent. He never took his talent for granted. He never coasted.

Did you have to do anything to foster Myles' talent or was he always self-motivated?

Nope! We made it clear if you wanted to be the best at

anything, you had to work and want it for yourself more than we could want it for you. We can't do it for you. We're here to support you and that's important, but we can't do it for you.

Did you put any systems in place for Myles to build the habits that lead to his success?

The reward was being able to stay in our dang house. I am not going to reward a child for doing what they are supposed to be doing. You got two jobs, be a student and mind your parents. If you can't or won't manage those, find somewhere to stay cause nothing else is acceptable under our roof.

How did you handle Myles' accomplishments and keep things in perspective?

My kids did not start competing in sports until junior high school. Their accomplishments were academic. Due to the age difference between siblings, they saw sports could be rewarding in many ways and they pushed one another to do better than they did. Not aggressively, but in a supportive way. We never said we are going to see a game to see a sibling compete. We always said we were going to support the activity that the other sibling was involved in.

If you were heavily involved, how did you make time for yourself?

There was no time for myself. I completely lost my identity in being my children's mother. I was either Sean's mom, Brea's mom or Myles' mom. I still get introduced as, "This is Myles' mom", but I am now comfortable correcting people by adding, "Hi my name is Audrey. I am…."

Once they all grew up, I learned to be myself again. I had to learn about and discover new passions and things I was interested in because my kids are starting to move to their own lives and they remove that invisible umbilical cord faster than you could ever imagine. Even while you're still supporting them, you start to find some things that you want to be passionate about and that's what I did as soon as Myles started going to college. I'm now super into crafts, glass etching, embroidery, sublimation, etc. I just made a few baby bibs for Mary's granddaughter :)

What would you say were important qualities to possess to be the mother you were?
Patience, love, listening, not being judgmental, discipline and setting and keeping boundaries for what was acceptable and what was not.

What were things you think you may have handled differently?
I hate to say it, but nothing. I was blessed with how my children came out. Though not perfect, they are perfect for me. The only thing I would do differently is appreciate the time they were young and to enjoy those moments. They are so fleeting as they age and we darn near push them to the next steps. "Oh, hurry and walk, hurry and talk, I can't wait until they start school." All those things rushing to the next big stage in life. When they move out it's over and you want them to be little again.

What is your relationship like now with Myles?
I talk to Myles probably one to two times weekly. We still talk about anything and everything. Even though he is an adult, if we're ever talking about something where I want to jump into mother mode I will always ask, "Do you want me to listen or do you need my advice?" When I'm listening, I'm being your friend. When you want some commentary, I'm being your mother.

If you could name one characteristic you believe Myles inherited from you, what would that be?
His heart. He has the heart of a giver and service to assist

those less fortunate. Myles has tremendous compassion. I've always tried to model that for him. I am always more impressed when people come up to me and talk to me about the man Myles is versus the football player he is. The bigger and greater vision for Myles is being there for the people who are less fortunate, seeing the greater picture for his love of humanity and animals is better to me than seeing him as an athlete or what he does on the field. Playing football is a job. When that job ends what are you going to do for the rest of your life that's going to leave an impact? What will your legacy be? I don't want it to be hitting (Pittsburgh Steelers QB) Mason Rudolph over the head. I want it to be that he brought life to the world. The strongest strength of character is doing things when no one's watching and when you don't get credit or don't get patted on the back.

What is something you think the media or public has wrong about Myles?
That Myles is a dirty player. He always tries to play fair and within the rules. The helmet altercation was a mutually bad decision and reaction to a player who was dead set on aggressively confronting Myles after the play was over. Myles bore the brunt of the punishment for protecting himself. That night, he called me and said, "Mom I really want to call (Mason Rudolph) and check on him. I hope he doesn't have a concussion or anything."

After that incident, my first thought the next day was Mason's mom. I felt like I should also reach out because my son could have really hurt her son, and mother to mother, I just felt like I should reach out. But there are times when "I'm sorry" just does not cover it. It's a moment that changed both of their lives in a way that no one could have guessed before it happened.

Did your relationships with friends and family change at all after Myles "made it"?

I was disappointed at a few who felt entitled to ask for things because they were family, but we started early telling people it is not our money or our career. We also limit who has access to him via communication methods. Both his father and I have no problem putting friends and family in their place when folks get out of line and start asking for "things."

Did any times of adversity set you up for later success?

I failed in some capacity EVERY day! There is no roadmap to be the perfect parent. I always talked to my kids to make sure we both got better in this thing called family. I had to learn that each child is different and had to be parented differently while loved the same.

How did you respond to situations that made you feel overwhelmed?

I drank wine, plenty of wine – white and red. But really, I prayed and still do to this day.

Can you offer any advice to young or soon to be mothers/parents?

Do not be your child's friend, set boundaries, LOVE them and show them love, lift them and encourage them, model the way, be your own child's playbook for life. Talk to them daily, eat dinner with them, let them express themselves respectfully yet make sure they know you make the rules. This is not a democracy; you are in charge.

Do not curse at your kids, do not deny them the other parent if you are not together if that parent is fit. Your kid needs both of you. Your kids are not your spouse or partner in the household. Do not burden your kids with the responsibilities of adults. What I mean by this is that there are parents that make these kids the man of the house or the provider for the family even before they have gotten a contract or a job. They burden them with the responsibilities that they should have themselves to manage the household and financial issues, holding on to the desperate expectation that the kid steps into that role and provides. Let them be kids. They will have plenty of time to be adults. If you take care of them, they will take care of you. Again, model the way.

Do not be afraid to ask for help. I needed my mother when I had kids more than I ever needed her in my entire life! I needed someone with experience. There's nothing that can prepare you for a baby in your house more than a parent who's done it already. Even when Myles came around, I still called my mom all the time. It's a fountain of information when you allow a seasoned woman to help you and give you advice with your babies.

Appreciate every moment. I was so busy pushing everyone to the next milestone that I think I missed some great things. If I could go back, I think I would have slowed down and smelled those individual moments like individual roses.

Looking back, what would you say was the greatest gift you gave to your kids?
I would say the gift of the power of prayer. Understanding that sometimes you will need to have a talk with God and that he does answer prayers while the answer may be no or even not right now, having a relationship with God and understanding that Jesus will sustain you in your darkest hour!

If you could tell the world one thing, what would it be?
Be willing to extend grace and mercy to all you meet because at the end of the day, we are all just walking each other home!

"I would say my greatest gift that I gave to my kids was my presence. They have no concept of us not being there and that's just the way we wanted it. A true, unwavering support system."

Cam Reddish
IG: @CamReddish
TW: @CamReddish
Zanthia Reddish
IG: @DrZReddish

Zanthia Reddish is the mother of Cam

Reddish, an NBA player on the Atlanta Hawks who formerly starred for Duke University's highly decorated 2018–19 team. She was raised in Norristown, PA, an urban community located 30 minutes outside of Philadelphia and began working various jobs at age 14 before eventually becoming a first-generation college graduate. She holds five degrees, highlighted by a Doctor of Education from Immaculata University (PA). Zanthia served as an elementary school principal in the Methacton School District for the past 18 years before moving to Atlanta in 2019 after Cam was drafted to the NBA.

Along with her husband, Bob, Zanthia ran Cam's top-tier AAU team for several years and guided him through an intense Division I basketball recruiting process. Now, in addition to parenting her younger son Aaron, she manages Cam's business affairs and oversees Impoweredd, a consulting firm founded by the Reddish family that provides mentorship, resources and support for the families of young athletes as they transition through education and sports.

Under his parents' tutelage, Cam quickly rose to

basketball stardom before he even stepped foot on Duke's campus. As a 6'8" forward at Westtown High School, he was rated as the No. 3 overall prospect in the Class of 2017 by ESPN and later earned McDonald's All-American honors following his senior season. He chose Duke over the likes of Villanova, University of Kentucky, UCLA and UConn to join a highly touted Blue Devils squad, featuring two other top prospects: Zion Williamson and R.J. Barrett. In 2019, Duke became just the second college program in the modern basketball era to have three players from the same team – Williamson (No. 1), Barrett (No. 3) and Reddish (No. 10) – get selected in the top 10 of the NBA Draft. Cam averaged 11 points and 4 rebounds per-game as a rookie with the Hawks and has flashed significant progression during his second season in the NBA.

In the following chapter, Zanthia talks about her experiences as a mother, student, educator, administrator and life coach, along with the story behind her decorated son's drive and determination.

Did your mother inspire you in any way? What kind of values did you take from her and instill in your own life as a mother?
I had a good relationship with my mother. Although, we went through typical drama when I was a teen, but nothing too major. My mother did the best she knew how. She always provided for us and handled her business. We always lived in a nice home, never had bill collectors call and never went to sleep until my sister and I were home. While she didn't give me specific lessons on financial literacy, she led by example. She always owned her home and was fiscally responsible and she transferred that trait to me.

When was the earliest indication that you thought Cam might have extraordinary talent?
We knew when Cam was a toddler that he was gifted with a ball. It was confirmed by a prophecy when he was 8 years old. We, as parents, knew that he was special when he was in high school.

Did you have to do anything to foster Cam's talent or was he always self-motivated?
Cam was intrinsically motivated to play ball. He has always been laser focused on basketball. We talked about the importance of continuing to work hard because he was so immensely talented, that it was often effortless for him to play. We also encouraged him to rest sometimes, because young people don't always realize how important rest is to one's growth and production.

How did you handle Cam's accomplishments and keep things in perspective?
We congratulated Cam, but we really didn't make a huge deal of his accomplishments in sports. Cam never really liked the spotlight; he just wanted to play.

How did you make time for yourself?
I enjoy being at the games, practices, etc., so I was heavily involved. I was the administrator of his AAU team and my husband was one of the coaches (he stopped coaching Cam in eighth grade). Outside of basketball, I have a close relationship with my friends and have plenty of opportunities to pamper myself.

As a mother, what were you good at saying no to?
I really didn't have to say no to Cam that much because I always trusted his judgment. However, my younger son would say I said no too much! I often forced myself to say yes on purpose because I understand how important it is as it relates to child development.

What would you say were important qualities to possess to be the mother you were?

I'm very driven. I'm a get-it-done type of person. I'm also very social, confident and articulate. I try to use my strengths to help others.

What were things you think you may have handled differently?

I was very intentional in my parenting practices because I am well-trained in child development. One thing I would do differently, however, is focus on intentionally teaching a mindset that encourages resiliency and growth. Helping my children focus on effort, rather than achievement, would likely have helped them avoid perfectionistic tendencies.

What is your relationship like now with Cam?

Cam and I are very close. I manage his business affairs; however, I do not manage him. I oversee his team and run his LLC. I moved to Atlanta where he was drafted and live about 20 minutes across town. We do not talk every day; we mostly text a couple times a week. I am cognizant that developmentally, he is at the age and stage where he wants and needs to feel independent. So, I give him some space, but I am close enough if he needs me. I am strategic in our interactions in an effort to maintain our positive relationship. It seems that our relationship continues to evolve and get better with time.

If you could name one characteristic you believe Cam inherited from you, what would that be?

My drive. We are both focused on being the best we can be, especially at our craft. Sometimes, we both work too much, but we definitely have been successful because of our strong work ethic.

Any stories of adversity that Cam faced?

Cam has dealt with his share of adversity, including major surgeries that have caused him to miss time from playing basketball. He has dealt with that mental and physical anguish and it has helped him to be in a better position to deal with the situation we are currently dealing with as we learn to adjust to the COVID-19 pandemic.

How did you respond to situations that made you feel overwhelmed?

I am a certified life coach, so I employ several strategies I have shared with others over the years. One of the biggest things I do is educate myself. Not knowing information stresses me out. It's really easy to be stressed if you have no idea what to expect out of certain situations. It's actually one of the major things Impoweredd does – we help teach our clients what to expect and that helps tremendously.

Another point of emphasis is to talk to a therapist. You need to talk to someone who truly gets it. Using mindfulness strategies is a great way to learn how to stop your brain long enough to not freak out over things you didn't know or couldn't change. I really had to do the work with a therapist to settle my spirit and learn to be present. I encourage folks to work with professionals. I got Cam a sports psychologist years ago when he was in high school. Not just for him, though, but for the family too. We're all going through it together.

Can you offer any advice to young or soon to be mothers/parents?

I encourage moms to learn as much as they can because parenting a professional athlete at this level presents many challenges. Learn from those who have been where you are going. I am happy to help any and all that reach out. At Impoweredd, we support families as they transition through education and sports.

Also, pray a lot and trust God as it relates to your

child. Stay involved and encouraged, but most of all, be informed and strategic in your interactions.

Looking back, what would you say was the greatest gift you gave to your kids?

I would say my greatest gift that I gave my kids was my presence. They have no concept of us not being there – and that's just the way we wanted it. A true, unwavering support system.

If you could tell the world one thing, what would it be?

Nothing can thwart the will of God – every promise He has made will come true. We are witnesses and are forever grateful for His favor in our lives.

"I think an important quality was being fun. Nothing was too serious in our house; life is hard enough. We let the kids have fun. Sure, we had structure like bedtime, homework, dinner, but it was a fun home. I remember laughing and playing a lot."

Joc Pederson
IG: @YungJoc650

Shelly Pederson is the mother of Joc

Pederson, a Major League Baseball outfielder who currently plays for the Chicago Cubs. Shelly grew up in a small-town north of San Francisco. She was the youngest of two daughters and spent most of her childhood living a typical upbringing. Although just before her senior year of high school, Shelly's father passed away at the age of 48. It flipped her entire family's world upside-down. Around that same time, Shelly met her husband, Stu.

Shelly and Stu started dating a year later and remained together through college while she studied athletic training at Arizona State and he played baseball for the University of Southern California. After school, they eventually married in 1985 and pursued Stu's professional baseball career until 1993. Shelly was a devoted full-time mom focused on raising their four children – Champ, Tyger, Joc and Jacey.

All four are unique in their own rights and have succeeded in various forms and fashions. Champ, first and foremost, is an integral part of the Pederson family. As the oldest, Champ has been an invaluable influence on the rest of his siblings while serving as a source of inspiration for all who encounter him. He has down-syndrome but has never let his disability hold him back in life, competing as a Special Olympics athlete and even giving a pre-game speech to the Dodgers before Game 5 of the 2015 NLDS. Tyger, the second oldest of the bunch, played three years of minor league baseball and is now a hitting coach in the St. Louis Cardinals organization. Jacey, the youngest in line, played women's soccer at UCLA and was a former member of the U.S. Youth National Team (2012-2016).

And then there's Joc. He was born in Palo Alto, California the year before Stu retired. And even though their father was done playing, the Pederson boys grew up in a baseball culture. Following in the footsteps of Tyger, Joc starred for Palo Alto High School's baseball team, batting .466 with 20 stolen bases during his senior season. He was a hot prospect coming out of high school and had committed to play at USC, but he was selected in the 11th round by the Dodgers and signed with the organization instead of playing college baseball. After four years in the minors, Joc made his MLB debut in 2014 and was named an opening day starter for the following season at 22 years-old making him the youngest player to do so for the organization since 1969. His six-year career in the big leagues has featured its fair share of highs, but none higher than the Dodgers' 2020 World Series title. Joc had four hits in 10 at-bats in the series, highlighted by a home run in Game 5. Joc has been to the World Series three times and to go along with that, he was an All-Star his rookie year and he has been in the home run derby twice. Joc entered free agency and decided to sign with the Cubs in January 2021.

In this chapter, Shelly talks about the most important aspects to raising young athletes and how she approached guiding her children through sports.

Did your mother inspire you in any way? What kind of values did you take from her and instill in your own life as a mother?

Growing up, I remember my mom not being all that interested in being a mom that much. She was raised as an only child, as was my dad, so that meant no aunts or uncles on either side. We had no cousins, so holidays were spent with family friends or grandparents on my mom's side. I don't have any real memories of traditions or family get-togethers. Extended family wasn't anything I was familiar with.

My mom was pretty occupied with doing her thing and just not that interested or emotionally able to raise a couple girls. We did not discuss anything that involved emotions or personal issues. She wasn't a bad person; it just wasn't her nature and I didn't know any better. One thing I did know is that more than often, she was busy and didn't want us to bother her. I remember making a mental note, that when I had kids, I would never put them off like she did to my sibling and me.

Once the grandkids came around, she was a HUGE presence in our lives. It was like the switch went on and she couldn't get enough. For that I am grateful – the kids had this loving, doting grammy and nothing but fond memories of her.

When was the earliest indication that you thought Joc might have extraordinary talent?

One of the first times I understood Joc was different, I was volunteering in his third grade class and was working with a group of boys (that I knew played baseball). We were chatting and I asked them what teams they were on and if they had a game that afternoon. They all answered, "No, only Joc has a game today because he plays at a higher level." It then dawned on me, Joc was different than these boys and they admired his abilities. But it made him different that they didn't always include him with after school playdates and such. Elementary school was tough for my kids, I'm not sure why.

The kids always enjoyed sports, all of them, but Joc, at an early age, developed a love for baseball more than anything. In our garage, Stu hung a ball from the rafter just so Joc could go out and hit it on his own. When he was 3 years old, I would often find him sleeping with his bat tucked away under his arm. He loved to play. Because he was younger, his age prevented me from signing him up for teams or camps, but once coaches saw him, they allowed him to play with them. It went like this through high school. Our rule was that if he played up on the varsity team, he should be there to play. He's not going up for the status of being on the team at a higher level. The goal was to actually be playing and bettering himself.

Did you have to do anything to foster Joc's talent or was he always self-motivated?

We raised our kids to be fair, play hard and do things the right way. Joc was a rule follower. He used to play a game at recess where you shoot a basketball and if you miss you go to the end of the line. One afternoon, I got a call from a mom, she told me Joc had punched her kid in the stomach. I agreed with her, punching was not okay and said I'd speak to Joc. I asked him what happened with the kid, he told me he kept cutting the line, so Joc told him to get back in line. The kid didn't, so Joc pushed him, not punched. I believed him and let it go. I was on great terms with the principal and office staff, so they always let me know if the other parent was a little out of touch, overreacting, or if something needed to be corrected.

We supported and encouraged them. We had expectations for them and playing sports was something we wanted them to do. But they also had to fulfill other duties and school was the priority. We had what we called the B-rule. Anything below that and they would have to sit out of sports until they brought the grade up. It never happened. We didn't expect perfection, we wanted our kids to have a high school experience they could enjoy and not the rigorous academic load that many of the kids in Palo Alto were enduring. The stress levels at this particular high school ran so high, there was so much academic pressure, kids were overachieving and stressed out. Parents put so much pressure on their kids, that they were compelled to apply only to the Ivy Leagues and other top ranked universities. I knew I didn't have Einstein's or Ivy League bound kids, so I wasn't going to make their high school lives miserable by forcing them to take accelerated AP classes. If they chose to, that was on them. I think Jacey made that choice. I'd have friends tell me that I was making a mistake and cutting their chances by not having them take more rigorous courses. I guess I firmly believed they would be okay, and to this day, I wouldn't change that.

How did you handle Joc's accomplishments and keep things in perspective?

One time, Joc was playing little league in a playoff game. He was pitching and Stu was the coach. A ball was hit and the fielder bobbled the ball. Joc did something that showed he was upset with his player. Stu saw the body language, called a timeout, and took Joc off the field, explaining to him that you never show your teammate up. Stu's other coach kept insisting that Joc had learned his lesson and it was time to put him back in to help the team win, but he insisted this was a lesson Joc needed to learn. And now, to this day, I think Joc is probably one of the best teammates. It's hard to be tough on your kid, but if not us, who was going to do it? I don't think our kids would say today we were mean or too tough, we just tried to make them aware and have consequences.

Another thing we tried to teach was, "There will always be someone bigger, better and faster than you. You just do your best and that's all you or anyone can ask for!"

As a mother, what were you good at saying no to?

Not a lot! Really, things that were more impactful on what I felt involved the physical safety of my kids. I can remember when Joc (age 12 or 13) was playing in a summer all-star league. The venue was like an hour and a half from our home. Most families traveled back and forth with their boys for the games. One family thought it was a good idea to get their son a hotel room near the field by himself. Joc thought it was a good idea to stay with that boy. Definitely no, on my part. Joc did his best to try and convince us it was okay for him and his friend to stay in the hotel by themselves. He was really angry with us, but it wasn't okay. We all remember that one, because the car broke down on the way home, which really aggravated Joc more. We laugh now of course!

Every year in high school, they had a senior cut day where the kids will go do something together. During Tyger's senior year, they were going to the beach which required driving over a freeway that we were not comfortable with the boys driving on. Having a car packed with boys was out of our comfort zone. We did offer to drive them to and from the beach. Tyger's group went along with that. So, it was more irrational kid stuff that I said no to. They had a pretty long rope and made good choices.

What would you say were important qualities to possess to be the mother you were?

Stay true to who I am. I am very easy going and I don't expect much in return, but I always demanded the truth. I am not interested in having a relationship with someone that can't be forthcoming. We all make mistakes, and they can be fixed, but lying just impacts the whole thing and I don't have time for that. I always told the kids, "I don't judge you and what you do, my concern is that you're safe and making good choices." I tried to impart to the boys how to be stand up young men, do the right thing and help those that might not be able to help themselves.

They didn't always appreciate that I would sometimes involve myself with others, and they'd say, "Mom don't!" or, "Mom don't say anything, don't get involved." The stubborn part of me felt like I needed to.

Maybe now they appreciate that about me, I don't know. Other qualities would be:

- I had to be the best advocate I could be for Champ. I was very clear on what his capabilities, strengths and weaknesses were. I had to make sure he had the best opportunities for his development. It wasn't always easy but standing up for the rights of your child proved to be the best route for us. Champ is successful today because I didn't let him just be placed in a class for kids with special needs. It is not generic; each child should have the opportunity to be challenged to succeed.
- Unconditional love – that's a given, I guess.
- I think another quality was fun. Nothing was too serious, because life is hard enough. We let the kids have fun. We had structure like bedtimes, homework and family dinners, but it was a fun home. I remember laughing and playing a lot. The kids are more serious now, but they still have fun. I'm probably the least serious of all the family.

What were things you think you may have handled differently?

Maybe telling the kids I loved them more. I know they know I loved them, but I didn't necessarily say it. We say it now, but it's still a bit uncomfortable as it wasn't something my parents or my husband's parents did. We have physical love hugs, but hearing it is nice too.

As far as handled differently, I wish I'd been more intuitive about Joc's anxiety. Maybe it would have helped him cope a little earlier or something we could have begun working on sooner rather than later for him. I hate to think that anyone would suffer silently. I have experienced anxiety in my 50s and now that I know what he was going through at such a young age, it pains me. If someone has never dealt with anxiety, the stress, fear and angst is so overpowering. No one should have to wonder what is happening. Education is definitely needed, starting in elementary school.

If you could name one characteristic you believe Joc inherited from you, what would that be?
Joc is keenly aware and observant of others, from feelings to obscure things, as I am too. I also think he and I are on the impulsive side. He's more guarded now about things that he says or reacts to. He is also more thoughtful. I am a work in progress with trying to think before I speak. But again, I am who I am!

Joc is fun natured and definitely more relaxed during the off-season. He is very focused and driven during the season. It always makes me smile and happy when I see him having fun and laughing with the guys in the dugout. Having his family is such a joy for me to see that he has something to distract him from baseball, it only enhances his life, and he recognizes that.

Any stories of adversity that Joc faced?
Joc had lots of challenges in school starting early, and as he got older in middle school, he struggled more academically. Early on, he was diagnosed with a cognitive learning disorder. Reading was extremely difficult for him and he struggled in that department. He learned by listening and observing and could tell you what was said, but if he had to read, comprehend and write it down, that's where the difficulty was. School wasn't taught in such a way that worked with his style. He received extra help as he had an IEP (individual education plan), we were already very familiar with this, as Champ being in Special Ed also had a plan.

Another time was when Joc decided to sign with the Dodgers and not go to USC. I was a bit disappointed, as he wouldn't have the college experience. However, before he reported fall training with the Dodgers, he went to visit several friends who were freshman in college. He texted me that weekend and said, "Mom, I know I made the right decision, there are just way too many distractions going on." We ultimately had him make the decision to sign or go to school. The night the deadline to sign came, he had been back and forth with his agent and they were negotiating with the Dodgers. We went to a going away BBQ for Joc and his classmates that were all heading off to college. The agent was on and off the phone, the pressure was high, as it was the deadline night. Joc asked us what he should do, and the answer was he needed to make the decision and we'd support his choice. Stu said, "I don't want to make the decision for you and have you come back one day to blame me that it wasn't the right one." He finally got on the phone with Logan White, the Dodgers' player personnel scout. He asked Joc, "Do you want to be a Dodger?" Joc said, "yes sir, I do." The next day, we drove to LA for Joc's physical and signing the paperwork. Just like that, my boy was a professional baseball player. He was sent to Arizona later that fall and then the next spring he headed to low-A ball. He wasn't having much success there, so on Father's Day, he was sent to rookie ball. When I spoke to him, he was more disappointed that he let Stu down on Father's Day. Of course, I told him that was not the case, and we are proud and love him no matter what happens. From that season on, he worked hard and moved up the levels pretty quickly. I can say it wasn't always easy and there was frustration. Stu and I would take turns visiting him. We tried to go monthly, as we know that lifestyle and how hard it is to be alone and in a city that's not home.

How did you respond to situations that made you feel overwhelmed?

I think it's impossible to be a mother and not feel overwhelmed at times. I was/am fortunate enough to have a very practical husband. One thing he always said is why worry? Whatever happens, we will handle it, but don't spend time worrying until there is something to worry about. Stu has always been there, no matter what. He might not have the exact advice I want/need, but he's there for me and always has been. He's my rock!

Can you offer any advice to young or soon to be mothers/parents?

I've often had people ask how we made our kids successful. What did we do? My answer was always the same, we didn't do it for them or make them do it. My kids reached this level because they had a passion and love for the sport. You can't make someone want to practice. It's on them to do it. Obviously, we supported them and were there for whatever they needed, but we didn't coddle our kids. We weren't overly tough either. We tried to make them responsible for their actions and to take care of their things. We often would see parents carrying their kids' sports bags or backpacks. That was a no for us. That was their sport and they needed to take care of their stuff. The kids all learned to do their laundry and, this way, I wasn't responsible when they didn't have a clean uniform or couldn't find some article of clothing. Stu taught them early on and they did it. I hear from the boys now, they either had girls do laundry for them in college or pro ball. Now, Joc pays someone, but that's all good. I think it's fair to say he's earned it.

Looking back, what would you say was the greatest gift you gave to your kids?

Unconditional love and sit-down family dinner's every night. We were what we believed to be positive role models. We made our kids our top priority. Everything we did was family centered.

Also, I had an open heart and a very open home. We often hosted and sometimes housed friends and teammates that maybe needed a home environment they didn't get or have at their own home.

If you could tell the world one thing, what would it be?
Be you. Stand up for what you believe and stand up for others. Don't be afraid to fail, learn from it. Be kind and do what's right. Do what makes you happy and have fun.

"What works for one mother may be a complete disaster for another because children are so different. Enjoy your children above anything else. Children prefer your time over the things you buy them."

Daniel Ochefu
IG: @DanielOchefu32

Elizabeth Ochefu is the mother of Daniel

Ochefu, the starting center on the 2016 Villanova NCAA championship team.

A native of Cameroon, Elizabeth spent her early childhood and teenage years between Africa, Paris and London due to her father's successful business career. After high school, she relocated to the United States and eventually raised her four children in Maryland, just north of the Washington D.C. area. Elizabeth guided her family from a tiny, one-bedroom apartment on the 10th floor of a downtown high-rise back to Nigeria. After nine years, they finally returned to the U.S. and settled in West Chester, PA—a 30-minute drive from Villanova's campus—where she's lived ever since.

In order to provide a stable life for her family, Elizabeth worked a handful of jobs in numerous industries ranging from a facility manager, hotel manager, network administrator, IT trainer, systems analyst and nurse. Her story is a reflection of perseverance, self-motivation, hard work and a dedicated willingness to achieve success.

Elizabeth instilled those very same qualities into her

son at an early age. Daniel played both soccer and basketball growing up. Once his talent for the game flourished, he transitioned to solely focusing on basketball.

Daniel arrived at Villanova in 2013 and made an immediate impact on and off the court. Going from a fringe player in his freshman year, Daniel played a fundamental role during his senior year when Villanova won their first NCAA Championship since 1985. He earned an All-Big East Honorable Mention in his final season after averaging 10 points and 7.5 rebounds per game.

After short stints with the Washington Wizards, Boston Celtics and NBA G League, Daniel now plays professional basketball overseas in Japan. Daniel is also an entrepreneur with his hands in real estate, finance, media and philanthropy work, where he helps provide scholarships for students in Nigeria. Elizabeth discusses her journey from Africa to the United States, the trials and tribulations she experienced throughout her life and her strong mother-son relationship with Daniel.

Did your mother inspire you in any way? What kind of values did you take from her and instill in your own life as a mother?

My mother was a very passionate and strong-willed woman. She was highly motivated, very stylish and was a strong influence in my life. She embodied feminism in a very subtle way and exuded a lot of sophistication.

In our culture, women are very subservient. My mother was different in that respect. She wanted to succeed in a man's world. She taught me to be a high achiever and to work hard to achieve my goals. My mother was a perfectionist, but she was also patient, compassionate and had the most generous heart. We were very close; she was my confidante and my idol.

As a mother, she taught me to embrace life to its

fullest. She taught me to not only work hard but to work smart. I'll never forget when my mother came to visit one day, and I gave her Daniel so I could focus on things around the house. I was rushing all over, cleaning the living room, running to scrub the bathroom, and she looked at me and said, "I'm so disappointed in you. You're working hard, but you're not working smart. Why don't you make a plan? Clean specific rooms on specific days. If you're hoping to complete a task, lay out a plan of action. A lot of people start but very few finish."

My mother embraced the challenges of life in a positive way. She taught me that life is full of curveballs, but with the right attitude, I could achieve anything I put my heart into. My mum taught me to be generous and kind to those around me. She taught me to expect more of myself and less of others. I took all these values from my mum and instilled them in my personal life as a mother and wife.

Any stories of adversity?
Being a mum is the hardest job; it feels like you face adversity every day. When I go to work, I put on my nurse's coat. When I'm done, I can take that coat off. Being a mum is like a second skin that you can't take off. You can't just take time off from being a mum like you can from your 9 to 5 job.

When was the earliest indication that you thought Daniel might have extraordinary talent?
When Daniel was in first grade, we were called in to his school. His teachers told us they thought he should be on medication for ADHD because he was so disruptive in class and had no attention span. We took him to a child development program to get him tested. After several tests, someone was assigned to follow him around class and recess for a couple weeks. After all that, they brought us in and showed us the results. He had the brain equivalent to that of a college student. At that point, we

knew he was very intelligent.

As for his athletic side, Daniel loved soccer until he became too tall to be on the soccer field. It was around this time when he started to have an affinity for basketball, but there was no organized basketball in Nigeria for young kids, so he would play basketball with grown men on concrete. He had the height for it but not the power – he was still just a boy. One summer, we sent him to America for a Philadelphia 76er's overnight basketball camp. When he came back, the director of the camp told us he was very good and that he needed to come to Westtown school to play for him. So, we did just that, and it worked out wonderfully.

Did you put any systems in place for Daniel to build the habits that led to his success?
He was unusually self-motivated. We taught him the importance of self-discipline and encouraged him to believe in himself. We also ensured that he explored different opportunities and taught him to have a very worldly outlook on life.

Everyone faces self-doubt, did Daniel ever want to give up on things, and if so, how did you go about handling that?
Daniel is extremely tough. I don't recall a time when he wanted to give up on any of his goals. Once he made up his mind, he forged ahead and worked relentlessly to achieve them. Not that he never faced adversity, he most certainly did. He would talk about challenges he faced and pick himself up to start again from a different perspective. He set the bar high for himself and worked hard to attain his goals.

Life in the United States can be hard, especially hard for a black family that isn't in tune with the culture here. America is a culture of extreme freedoms but also with extreme prejudice. Daniel had to learn how to adjust to fit into a mold that he had no control over and make the best out of life. Sports can be that bridging point to help lessen the divide that comes from being from different cultures and different socioeconomic backgrounds and that's exactly what basketball did for Daniel and our family.

How did you handle Daniel's accomplishments and keep things in perspective?

We always tried to keep him within his age range and not to have these larger than life, unattainable expectations. He was so tall that people would always expect him to act much older than what he was. I think we were very humbled by his accomplishments and we never made a big deal of them. We encouraged him to see them as a blessing and a special gift from God. We encouraged him to understand the importance of being a part of a team. We kept him grounded by making him understand that he should never feel arrogant because of his talent. We always made sure that he remained a child and enjoyed the life of a child outside of his talent.

I tried to make sure everything wasn't about the sport. It's hard, especially when you're dealing with sports in the U.S., where the focus is mainly on the sport and not so much about having fun. More pressure is put on winning and aspiring for a scholarship or championships. Having three other children helped with this too. Daniel's talent and his lifestyle had to fit in with the rest of the family dynamic. You miss out on so much of your kid's life and the growth of your child if you focus on just sports. So, I always tried to focus on things outside of basketball for that exact reason.

If you were heavily involved, how did you make time for yourself?

Being a mother of four, I learned through the years to appreciate those little moments to catch a nap here and there, read a book between games, treat myself to sleeping in on Sundays after church and just knowing how to skip some games.

There were times where I would sit in the parking lot in my car while one of his games was going on because I was so exhausted and I just wanted to sit in the car and listen to a book on tape. I remember one time it was a very cold day and I had the heat running the whole time. I dozed off to sleep and when the game was over, the kids came out and woke me up saying, "Let's go mom!" but the car battery was dead! Oops!

As a mother, what were you good at saying no to?
As a mother, I learned to say no to any request that made me neglect or favor one child over another. If Daniel had games that conflicted with activities his siblings had, I made sure that I gave as much attention to everyone in equal measures. Having a student-athlete is so demanding, especially when you have other kids. It seems like the whole family's schedule revolves around the student-athlete's schedule. It was very important to me to be able to draw balance there and realize that I must take care of the needs of the other kids in this family. We all enjoy going to his games, but we also had to make time for other people's interests, so that was an instance where I said no a lot.

What would you say were important qualities to possess to be the mother you were?
Not taking things too seriously, embracing successes and learning from failures. Being very organized and making time to spend with my kids doing fun things. Listening to my kids. Nurturing a sense of self and disciplining when necessary, but also rewarding with love and encouragement. Above all, having faith in God that in the end, it will all be alright. For me, my faith has always been a strong part of my life, so I think that's what's helped carry me and my family on for a very long time. Because of that, I always have a positive outlook on life.

What were things you think you may have handled differently?

I think I would have taken time to savor each step of the experience. If I could go back, I'd try not to get caught up in the hustle and bustle. I would try to simply enjoy every moment and remember that the time spent with my kids is more important than anything else. Childhood flies by – it's an overwhelming experience that's supercharged with activity.

There's so much power when you and your child are together in the present moment. Cherish those times together. You're not going to get those moments back, so make the most of them while you still can!

What is your relationship like now with Daniel?

Our relationship has evolved to one of mutual respect, friendship and parental love. We're in contact now every day and talk about anything and everything with great ease. I am very proud of Daniel because I see now that all the years invested in teaching him the values that I learned from my parents were not in vain. He has grown into a responsible caring adult: astute in his financial portfolio, a leader among his peers and a good role model to his siblings.

Over the years, we've shifted from mother and son to good adult friends with respect for each other. The relationship has evolved into one where we both listen to each other's views, agree to disagree and embrace our differences in opinion. Daniel now appreciates the fact that even though I may not be an athlete, I bring a lot of life experiences to the table that have been beneficial to him. He still asks for my opinion, but I will not make decisions for him. Outside of basketball, he has a lot of business ventures. He's an active real estate investor and he also does a lot of philanthropic work, such as providing basketball expertise and playing opportunities to kids in Nigeria.

Did your relationships with friends and family change at all after Daniel "made it"?

I surround myself with genuine people and am upfront with them that my son's success is his to enjoy. I obliged with autographs and pictures as much as possible but also respected my son's privacy when he came home.

When Daniel got cut by the Wizards, I told him, "Now, you'll know who your real friends are." I don't think it's bad for someone to have to go through that. It was a good lesson for Daniel and it helped him learn who his true friends were. I think all professional athletes and their families would agree that you have to learn how to manage your relationships.

How did you respond to situations that made you feel overwhelmed?

If I find myself overwhelmed, I pray like there's only prayer to save the day. I take a much-needed rest and change activities so I can regenerate and regain focus. I also listen to classical music to relax. Afterwards, I can tackle the issue from a different perspective.

Can you offer any advice to young or soon to be mothers/parents?

Motherhood is an amazing journey and a lifelong learning experience. There's no simple formula for success. What works for one mother may be a complete disaster for another because children are so different. Enjoy your children above anything else. Children like your time more than the things you buy them. Spend quality time with your children and prepare yourself from day one for the day they leave home. Be true to yourself and know that your children learn from watching you. If you do not pray, learn fast how to pray, for you will need divine intervention at times to deal with the challenges of kids as they grow up. Pray to have the stamina to survive the burst of energy required and constant alertness that is a must for a mother to have.

I would also say ignore anyone who says motherhood is easy and a bed of roses, it's constant hard work. I would also ignore anyone who tells a mother that she is a friend to her child before being a parent. Children need boundaries and need to understand respect. You are not their friend. When you put yourself at their level, there's a very great chance that chaos will ensue. Of course, I want my kids to like me, but we're not mates. There are certain things you can't say to me because I am your parent and there's a line that I drew in the sand to make sure that was understood. There's ample time to be friends when they become adults.

Unconventional advice is to remember effective disciplining is important to keep body and soul together when bringing up a child. And the operative word here is effective, as discipline should never be abuse of any form and discipline does not have to be corporal punishment. There are more effective ways to discipline without causing emotional or physical harm. For Daniel, it was taking basketball away. That was his love, and as soon as basketball was in the balance of being taken away, he straightened up immediately!

Looking back, what would you say was the greatest gift you gave to your kids?
I think the greatest gift to my kids is their faith. This helped them to become young adults with a strong sense of responsibility and integrity. It forged in them the belief that there is more to life than immediate gratification.

If you could tell the world one thing, what would it be?
Do not be afraid to embrace life. You live once, so make the most of your time on earth and find happiness within yourself. Then, touch someone else's life in a positive way.

"The greatest gift that I gave to my kids was true love and confidence. They grew up in a family where everyone listened to each other's voice and we tried to build a space of dialogue and calmness. Both of my daughters could choose their own path knowing they will always have my love and support."

Maya Gabeira
IG: @Maya
Mayagabeira.com

Yamê Reis is the mother of Maya Gabeira, a

world-record setting surfer widely considered as one of the best female athletes in the history of her sport. Yamê, a native of Brazil, was born in São Paulo, raised in Rio de Janeiro and still calls Rio home today. She grew up in a small residential neighborhood within the city, where she attended Catholic school before eventually studying sociology in college. After school, however, Yamê strayed away from the conventional path and shifted careers into fashion design. She went on to earn an MBA from Fundação Getulio Vargas in Brazil and a Certificate of Achievement for sustainability from the London College of Fashion while climbing the Brazilian fashion industry ladder. Yamê is the current CEO of Green Fashion Consulting, a sustainable fashion consulting agency based in Rio. She is involved in several other fashion sustainability initiatives like Rio Ethical Fashion, which she founded in 2019 as the first international sustainable forum in Brazil.

Yamê had Maya in 1987 while married to her ex-husband Fernando Gabeira, a famous politician, author and journalist most known for his role in co-founding Brazil's Green Party in the 1970s. Maya and her older sister, Tami, were raised in Rio, but the divorce of their parents in 1999 caused internal strife within the family that directly affected Yamê's relationship with her daughters. After two years of rebelling against her mom, Maya decided to live with her father in order to have more freedom. She eventually moved to Australia by herself through a student exchange program. That's where her journey to surfing stardom first began.

Today, Maya currently holds the world record for the largest wave surfed by a female after conquering a 73.5-foot wave at one of the world's most iconic surfing locations in Nazare, Portugal. She set the record in February 2020, breaking her own previous record of 68-feet from 2018. Throughout her historic career, she has won six total Billabong XXL Global Big Wave Awards for Best Female Performance and has received both an ESPY and Teen Choice Award for Best Female Action Sports Star. Among other notable accomplishments, she was the first woman to surf the Alaskan Sea, California's Ghost Trees and Tahiti's Teahupoo. The 2016 documentary *Return to Nazare* chronicles her comeback after suffering a terrible near-death accident at Nazare in 2013.

Yamê and Maya reconciled their relationship in Maya's early 20s after Maya started traveling worldwide. In 2007, they co-founded a company called Maya Gabeira Eventos to help manage Maya's sponsorships and business ventures. The two have remained close ever since. While times weren't always perfect, the ups and downs of their relationship ultimately shaped their unwavering bond today.

Did your mother inspire you in any way? What kind of values did you take from her and instill in your own life as a mother?

My mother, besides being a very beautiful and fashionable woman, was also very gifted as an artist and pianist, although she worked as a teacher. When I was 9, she started college and graduated with a degree in Sociology. She's always been my inspiration.

The most important values I got from her were my independence as a woman, the sense of social justice and the value of believing in myself and who I want to be.

What kind of dreams and goals did you have when you were a kid? How much did they influence where you are today?

My childhood dream was to have the power to decide everything about myself and my life. Children are very limited on realizing their wishes and I remember my suffering and dreaming of growing up and being empowered as an adult.

When was the earliest indication that you thought Maya might have extraordinary talent?

She was a very gifted ballet dancer from an early age. She loved dancing and spent the entire day dressed in ballet clothes waiting for the classes. It worked out that a lot of the benefits you get from ballet – balance, lower body and core strength – translate very well to surfing.

She was introduced to surfing around the age of 13. She asked me if she could go with some boys to a remote beach and surf. I said yes, reluctantly, and she came back saying she didn't have fun because all the boys went out onto the water and left her on the beach to watch. Next time they asked her to go she said she would go only if she gets a board and can join them. The rest was history. She was quickly better than all the boys and never looked back!

Did you have to do anything to foster Maya's talent or was she always self-motivated?
Maya was very self-motivated. She had a strong sense of discipline, concentration, focus and organization. Those are qualities that belong to her personality.

How did you handle Maya's accomplishments and keep things in perspective?
This was always very hard because she was very sure about her goals and feelings and not so willing to negotiate. She did not want to go to school anymore, all she wanted to do was surf! She viewed school as something that took her away from her passion. I believed she was good enough to make a living surfing but I did not want her to pursue full time until she had finished high school. I thought that studying whatever she likes should be a goal for her, as we are not an upper-class family. In my mind, college is always the right way to find a career path that suits you.

If you were heavily involved, how did you make time for yourself?
Moms rarely have time for themselves, so we learn how to engage children in our activities and be part of it playing together and helping in a special way. You have to negotiate a lot of the time.

Any stories of adversity that Maya faced?
Maya started traveling globally at a very early age, around 15 years old. She was a girl traveling by herself or with boys to remote beaches, sometimes with no connections and not good conditions in places such as Sumatra. It was a hard time to spend many days with no news from her.

What would you say were important qualities to possess to be the mother you were?
Love above everything. Trusting in my child. Being open to dialogue. Listening to her. Being resilient. Motherhood

is not a smooth road all the time.

What were things you think you may have handled differently?
I think I could have been more flexible in small little things and fight just for the big things. Not worrying about silly things such as the "don't do this or don't do that" that moms feel like they have to say. Try to enjoy life more.

What is your relationship like now with Maya?
The long time we were apart (when Maya was 15 to 20 years old) led us to admit how important our relationship was. By her 20s she had proved how vital surfing was for her, that this was really a life choice and that it was not possible turning back. We are very close. I used to travel a lot to spend time with her whenever I could. We founded a company that I've been managing so we are professional partners and I take care of her business affairs in Brazil.

If you could name one characteristic you believe Maya inherited from you, what would that be?
She is hard-working and a very intuitive person. I like to think she gets that from me.

How has Maya grown from the adversity she has faced?
Maya spent three or four years recovering from accidents. It was a very hard time feeling pain every day, with a very uncertain future ahead. In 2013, off the coast of Portugal, Maya got swallowed up by a 60-foot wave. She almost drowned. The damage to her lungs and body was so severe she did not even realize she also broke her ankle until a couple of days later when the bulk of the pain resided. She already had an existing spine problem (before the accident, which she knew was going to need surgery eventually) but no doctors in the U.S. wanted to operate

on her because of her current fragile condition. But thank God we met a doctor in Brazil who agreed to operate on her. She ended up coming back to big wave surf and realized her biggest dream ever, breaking the female world record in 2018 by surfing a 68-foot wave in the SAME place as her horrific accident off the coast of Portugal.

How did you respond to situations that made you feel overwhelmed?

I breathe, pause and let time put things into perspective. I avoid reacting in fright, which is much easier said than done. This behavior came to me with maturity.

Can you offer any advice to young or soon to be mothers/parents?

The biggest learning lesson I've got from my daughter is to follow my dream, no matter what – listen to my heart, listen to your child's heart and let it go!

Looking back, what would you say was the greatest gift you gave to your kids?

The greatest gift that I gave to my kids was true love and confidence. They grew up in a family where everyone listened to each other's voice and we tried to build a space of dialogue and calmness. Both of my daughters could choose their own path knowing they will always have my love and support.

If you could tell everyone in the world one thing, what would it be?

Follow your dreams no matter what.

"Have high expectations of your kids but understand they are not perfect, they are kids. There is no right or wrong way to do things as long as there is love, patience, understanding and laughter."

Kerri Walsh Jennings
IG: @KerriLeeWalsh
Margie Walsh
IG: @Waymaijoe

Margie Walsh is the mother of Kerri Walsh Jennings, a highly decorated professional beach volleyball player and four-time Olympic medalist who still competes today. Margie is from Saratoga, California, a small town in the San Francisco Bay Area just west of San Jose and the Santa Clara Valley. She was one of eight siblings and the daughter of two loving parents, both of whom worked tirelessly to provide for their family of 10. Unfortunately, Margie's father suffered a massive heart attack when he was 42 and died eight years later of an aneurysm, which forced her mother to take up a larger role within the household. She always admired her mom for her strength and resilience amid those times of turbulence, two redeeming qualities that influenced the mother Margie would become.

After college, Margie married her high school sweetheart, Tim, and began working as a real estate agent. She's still a realtor to this day, and has four children – Marte, Kerri, Kelli and KC – all who went on to lead successful lives in their own right. The Walsh's were a family of athletes while growing up in Scotts Valley and

Saratoga, CA. Kerri was introduced to volleyball at age 10 and ran with it, eventually becoming the Gatorade National High School Player of the Year in 1996 before playing collegiately at Stanford. She won two national championships in college and began her professional beach volleyball career immediately upon graduating in 2001.

For most of Kerri's career, she played alongside Misty May-Treanor. The dynamic duo earned three gold medals together in 2004, 2008 and 2012 Summer Olympics and had a 112-match winning streak from 2004 to 2008. When it was all said and done, Kerri and Misty went down as one of the greatest beach volleyball pairs of all time. Following her partner's retirement in 2012, Kerri teamed up with April Ross and later set the career record for most wins by a female professional volleyball player. Kerri and April won a bronze medal at the 2016 summer Olympics in Rio de Janeiro. Now, Kerri is preparing to compete at the 2021 Tokyo Olympic Games.

Before Kerri solidified herself as a legend in the professional volleyball ranks, she was just Margie's daughter. This chapter provides an inside look into those days through the eyes of her mom. From managing four children with hectic sports schedules and weathering some rocky teenage years to raising a world-renowned Olympian, Margie's unique perspective on motherhood provides invaluable advice for navigating life's ups and downs.

Did your mother inspire you in any way? What kind of values did you take from her and instill in your own life as a mother?
Being one of eight kids, I had much respect, admiration and love for my mom. She did it all, loved us all and was tough on all of us. She was a great role model that you can have it all with hard work and love.

She inspired me with a never-ending passion for life

and commitment to family. She taught us to work hard, never quit, do your best, be kind and take responsibility.

What kind of dreams and goals did you have when you were a kid? How much did they influence where you are today?

I think my dreams were to have a good job so I could enjoy my life and family. I also wanted a good husband and I got that. Tim and I met at 15 years old and have been married 44 years so far. We have great kids – I feel like we overachieved there. I always wanted to stay close and be a part of all my brothers' and sisters' families and Tim's. My other dreams were to be happy but keep moving, stay motivated and get a little bit better as a person each day. I think I have it all!

When was the earliest indication that you thought Kerri might have extraordinary talent?

Kerri was always a natural athlete, both sides of our family are pretty athletic. From ages 6-10, she played on her older brother's teams. She always held her own even though she was a year younger than everyone else. At 10, she started volleyball at school. She picked it up quickly and loved it. She worked hard, played hard and was eager to learn and get better. She was asked to try out for a club team, and she made it. She took off from there, getting better, working harder, learning more and loving it. It was the start of something special in her life. Extraordinary at 10? No, but natural ability, great worker, eager to learn and a desire at this young age to be one of the best, yes.

Did you have to do anything to foster Kerri's talent or was she always self-motivated?

She was surrounded by athletes and sports in our family. We fostered healthy competition and love of sports. She was always motivated to be the best at whatever it was she wanted to do. We taught her to start with the basics and to build a good foundation for any sport. We wanted her to learn to do things the right way and not to take shortcuts.

How did you handle Kerri's accomplishments and keep things in perspective?

We praised and celebrated her accomplishments, but always as part of a team. We reminded her to do her best and help the team and to take it seriously but have fun. Perspective was important. Kerri was good but we always encouraged her to work at getting better. Lots of people were better than her but I always emphasized to keep working at getting better as a player, teammate *and* person. It helped that she wanted to do all of those things.

Was Kerri interested in dating in high school? How did you handle her romantic relationships if the person she was attracted to did not seem like a good fit based on your motherly instincts?

Kerri was a busy girl, and she loved her social life. She and her brother had the same circle of friends, so they had fun. She had close girl friends who were also on her volleyball teams so that was good. Kerri loves love so it was always in her heart. Her dad and brother were a bit of a loving obstacle to her dating as no one was good enough. I knew Kerri could take care of herself. Her dad and I totally blew her relationship when she was in her 20s. It was her life, her choices, but we didn't think who she was dating was the best for her. We were strained for a couple of years. It broke her heart and ours. It was her life, her choices, not ours. We learned from that.

What would you say were important qualities to possess to be the mother you were?

Love, listening, understanding and patience. I always put the kids and family first and guided them to be better people. I encouraged them to do their best and then a little bit more.

What were things you think you may have handled differently?

I'm happy about how we did as a family. Most likely, I could have listened better, could have trusted them a bit more and recognized that they were/are good, strong and capable people who need to make their own choices. I said my thoughts and still do – but it's their life – not ours.

What is your relationship like now with Kerri?

Kerri and I love each other very much, we always have. I guess we have even more respect for each other's life choices now. I continuously grow more in awe of her life, her work ethic, her dreams, her family. She's pretty amazing, loving, passionate, relentless, successful, humble and grateful.

If you could name one characteristic you believe Kerri inherited from you, what would that be?

Her relentless nature.

How did you respond to situations that made you feel overwhelmed?

There were and still are times I would feel overwhelmed. What I do is simply pray. It works every time!

Can you offer any advice to young or soon to be mothers/parents?

Put family first. Life is not fair. Don't keep score. Listen and have high expectations of your kids, but know they are not perfect. They are kids. There is no right or wrong way to do things as long as there is love, patience, understanding and laughter.

Looking back, what would you say was the greatest gift you gave to your kids?

Faith in God and family. Faith that He is always with you and you are never alone.

If you could tell the world one thing, what would it be?
Smile, it makes everyone's day better.

"Becoming a mom (or parent in general) is the most significant transformation in your lifetime. Embrace it with confidence. Motherhood is a blessing. Cherish it through the good and bad days. You'll end up being best friends for life."

Emily Batty
IG: @EmilyBatty1

Cindy Batty is the mother of Emily Batty, a

Canadian cyclist, Olympian and cross-country mountain biker. Cindy was born into a large family that lived in a small town off the northeast coast of Nova Scotia. Her parents did the best they could to make ends meet, but money was often scarce with seven children to provide for. So, when Cindy was 8, the family packed up and moved across the country to Ontario for a new life. Cindy attended high school there, which is where she met her husband Rick. They've been married for 43 years and have four children together – Eric, Mark, Emily and Charlotte.

By marrying Rick, Cindy married into a farming family. Her journey through motherhood started while living on the same farm she calls home today. The children were raised there, often riding their bikes around the trails that surrounded the property. The "mountain-bike crazed" family was tight-knit, hard-working, active and, above all, self-motivated.

That's where Emily developed her roots. She was first introduced to biking by her older brothers at age 10. The two wheels quickly became a passion for her, which turned into a career of choice that made her a national name. Emily started professionally racing in 1999 and was competing in the Canada Cup series by 2001. She competed in her first World Championships in 2005, and then made her Olympic debut at the 2012 London Olympic games, where she still competed despite breaking her collarbone three days before the race. She earned a fourth-place finish at the Rio Olympics in 2016.

Emily's other notable career highlights are as impressive as they come. In 2014, she was a Silver medalist at the Commonwealth Games and won Gold at the Toronto Pan Am Games in 2015. In 2016 and 2018, she won Gold at the Mountain Bike World Championships and Bronze at UCI Mountain Bike World Cup overall series. She also took home Gold medals at the Canadian National Championships in 2016, 2017, 2018 and 2019. Emily is still an active member of Canada's Olympic Team as well as the Canyon MTB racing team and is also a Red Bull athlete.

This chapter provides a valuable learning lesson for mothers who are raising kids through an important phase in their life - whether it's an entrance into preteen years, transitioning through high school or navigating college. Below, Cindy explains why parents must allow children to develop their own "will to succeed."

Did your mother inspire you in any way? What kind of values did you take from her and instill in your own life as a mother?

Ma (we always referred to her as "Ma") was a great woman, mother, matriarch and my best friend. Cooking, cleaning, laundry and baking were just a few things a stay-at-home mom tends to. Her baking was like no other. Ma was a kind soul, strong and a hard worker. She never complained.

When my time came, I wanted to be a great mother,

just like mine was. I wanted to be there for my kids. I wanted to be involved in what they were doing. I wanted to be there to hear their stories at the end of a school day. Our kids did the usual stuff like soccer and baseball, but all four ended up in competitive cycling (mountain biking and road cycling). I was the chief cook and became the queen of bottle washing. Rick and I attended every race they competed in. We loved it. I think it is one of the reasons why we are so close today as a family.

When was the earliest indication that you thought Emily might have extraordinary talent?
Emily has two older brothers and one younger sister. They had a typical sibling relationship. They would banter at one point and be best friends the next. It was our oldest, Eric, that first got into mountain biking, and it snowballed from there. When it was Emily's turn to get behind the tape, it became clear very early on that she had a talent for racing her mountain bike.

   All of our children had an incredible thirst to compete and I think there was a silent competition between them as to who could come home with the most medals. One crisp cold sunny day, their dad took the four kids snowshoeing. Emily was 6 or 7 years old. When they returned home, dad said there is something unique about Emily. Her older brother Eric is, and always has been, a real goer. And on that day, she was consistently on Eric's tail and he would try to drop her but couldn't. That is something only a parent can understand.

Did you put any systems in place for Emily to build the habits that lead to her success?
Emily was always very self-motivated about her racing. She was committed to the training and programs that her coaches built for her. At first, their dad would ride with them to build the endurance required around competing. As she got older, we invested in having her work with a professional cycling coach to help her bridge the gap to

get to a higher level of competition. We also ensured that she would have the opportunities to be involved in training camps and programs to excel in her career early on. She knew that this sport requires hard work and dedication and was determined to make it happen.

How did you handle Emily's accomplishments and keep things in perspective?

After an event, whether it went well or not, we looked at how she could improve for next time and celebrated the hard work paying off.

If you were heavily involved, how did you make time for yourself?

Although I was heavily involved with Emily's cycling career, and the other kids, I managed to take some time for myself. I have a few hobbies I enjoy and mostly enjoyed them over the off-season from racing.

Any stories of adversity that Emily faced?

Emily's greatest challenge as a young athlete was dealing with the cycling body's politics - from a provincial to international level. Due to rules and regulations, athletes are prevented from progressing based on age. Emily had an incredible thirst to compete at the highest level.

The most significant adversity that Emily faced was the 2012 Olympics. Three days before the Olympic race, she crashed while training, resulting in a broken clavicle and ribs. Her upbringing taught her to pick herself up, brush herself off and get back on the bike. Broken and bruised, she still competed. It was far from the performance that she had been anticipating after years of training to get to that point, but she proudly competed so she could still represent her country. Like with most careers, there are highs and lows. Another year Emily went months with less-than-ideal results only to realize that she had mono.

What would you say were important qualities to possess to be the mother you were?
- Setting boundaries and rules.
- Teaching the kids at an early age to be respectful (it goes both ways).
- Being supportive in all areas of life.
- Love them unconditionally.
- Sacrifice - my kids always came first and were my priority.
- Patience - this goes without saying.

What were things you think you may have handled differently?
When one refers to the hockey mom, it was somewhat difficult not to become one but let the kids pursue this passion at the level they wanted to and not force them to as it would make them bitter and possibly leave the sport or anything they wanted to achieve. The will to succeed has to come from their heart, not ours as a parent. We did learn that everything has to come from within them to be truly successful. You cannot push them to have any long-lasting success.

In a perfect world, you could make improvements to what we did, but we didn't know what the perfect thing for training that worked for her was. Emily has never been a paper person and she approached training the same way. She didn't like highly structured training but wanted to put a lot of fun into her training. Training and learning have to be fun for a young athlete to be truly successful and it can't seem like a burden or an overload.

What is your relationship like now with Emily?
We hear from Emily regularly. She is a homebody at heart, and no one loves her more dearly than her parents, and she reciprocates that love.

If you could name one characteristic you believe Emily inherited from you, what would that be?
I'm notoriously stubborn, which I think the whole family would agree that Emily definitely inherited my stubbornness.

Can you offer any advice to young or soon to be mothers/parents?
Becoming a mom is the most significant transformation in your lifetime. Embrace it with confidence. Motherhood is a blessing. Cherish it through the good and bad days. You'll end up being best friends for life (as Emily and I have).

Looking back, what would you say was the greatest gift you gave to your kids?
Looking back, the greatest gift we gave our kids was opportunity. The opportunity to explore and pursue their passion.

If you could tell the world one thing, what would it be?
Live your best life and live your life to its fullest. Make every second, moment and day count.

"I wanted all of them to know how much they were loved. Every one of them was different, but special in their own ways. I also felt it was important to teach them that being kind was as simple as sharing a smile. Faith and family were our foundation!"

Stephanie Gaitley
IG: @CoachGaitley

Martha Vanderslice is the mother of

Stephanie Gaitley, head coach of the Fordham University women's basketball team. Martha was raised in Norristown, PA, in a large, tight-knit family. Her father worked long hours in the steel industry, so it was her mother who stayed home and tended to the eight children. From enforcing mandatory family dinners every Sunday to instilling the values of kindness and individuality, Martha's mother had a major influence on her life. After graduating from Norristown High School, she earned an office clerk job in Philadelphia – biking 20 miles to and from work each day while getting paid $19 per week.

At 24 years-old, Martha met her husband Harry, who she married in 1951 and had eight children with. They started raising their family in Jeffersonville, PA, but moved to Ocean City, NJ, to give their family a better life. The Ocean City house was situated 50 yards from the beach on a large corner lot with a basketball court – the same court where Stephanie first learned how to dribble and shoot. Martha coached Stephanie's youth basketball teams and realized her daughter had a future in the sport when she was in eighth grade. After leading the Ocean City High School girls' basketball team that went 100-0 in league play from 1974-1978, Stephanie, along with her sister Courtney, played college basketball at Villanova. She was inducted into the Villanova and Philadelphia Big Five Halls of Fame following an All-American collegiate career.

Stephanie's historic coaching journey first started at the University of Richmond in 1985. She coached the Spiders for six seasons, leading them to the NCAA tournament in the final two. Then she coached at Saint Joseph's University for 10 years – totaling five 20-win seasons, five NCAA tournament berths and two Atlantic-10 championships. After successful coaching stints at LIU-Brooklyn and Monmouth, Stephanie was hired by Fordham in 2011 to rebuild a program that hadn't finished with a winning season in two decades. In the nine years since, she has become a household name in the Bronx – holding a 190-106 record at Fordham prior to the 2020-21 season with two Atlantic 10 championships and 654 total wins over her career. Her three sons are all involved with basketball – Dutch is an NBA assistant coach for the Charlotte Hornets, DC is an intern with the Miami Heat and Jordan plays at the University of Richmond.

In this chapter, we learn about Martha's approach to motherhood and the mark she left on Stephanie that helped foster her vast success on and off the court.

Did your mother inspire you in any way? What kind of values did you take from her and instill in your own life as a mother?

My mother had a huge influence on my life. She was a stay-at-home mom and my dad worked in the steel industry. We had a big family that shared a small space, but we were surrounded by love. My mom was the kindest person you would ever meet. It was rare to see her angry. She taught us how to care about each other as well as others. She believed in treating people the way you wanted to be treated.

She made sure we had dinner as a family every night. She also made it a point to make all eight of us feel very special as individuals. I really believe this carried over to how I raised my eight children. I taught the importance of honesty and kindness and caring about each other. There is no doubt it was the influence of my mother that helped me become the mother I am today!

When was the earliest indication that you thought Steph might have extraordinary talent?
I would probably go back to when she was in fourth grade. The fourth grade girls were split in half and played against each other. I coached one team and my friend and neighbor coached the other team. Stephanie was on the other team. We won 4-2. She cried all night and didn't speak to me for a while. That's when I knew she had a special competitiveness about her. Every summer she would go to work at the Cathy Rush basketball camp (after being a camper for a number of years), there was no doubt that basketball would be in her future!

Did you have to do anything to foster Steph's talent or was she always self-motivated?
Stephanie's dedication was second to none. I remember when she was in high school, she played in a Christmas tournament and missed a lot of foul shots in the first game. She came home that night and shoveled snow off the court to work on her foul shot.

Everyone faces self-doubt, did Steph ever want to give up on things, and if so, how did you go about handling that?
Failure really helps you grow. You can be angry and frustrated, but ultimately you have to learn and move on.

When Stephanie was an assistant for St. Joe's, she applied for every head coaching position that was open. She worked hard to get her master's degree which helped her get the job at the University of Richmond. Her season started off 0-6 and her dad and I came to visit for a week. We were supposed to leave but Harry and I wanted to hang around to watch her get her first win. Unfortunately, the next game came around and she lost again. Stephanie was so frustrated and angry, but it was through this experience that she learned from failure. She grew as a coach and now two of her sons are coaching and her youngest is playing at Richmond. Stephanie shares these experiences with her boys and teaches them that going through failure and losses will make you appreciate winning even more. One of Stephanie's favorite quotes is from Martin Luther King, "the ultimate measure of a man is not where he stands in moments of comfort and convenience, but where he stands at times of challenge and controversy."

Any stories of adversity?
A turning point for me was when my husband was hit by a drunk driver and was thrown through the windshield. Back then there were no seat belts. It was before Stephanie was born. We already had four children and I didn't work. Harry was bedridden for months. We said a lot of prayers for his recovery and for saving his life. This time in my life really made me look at things differently. We never had a lot of money, but we did have a lot of love. I had to take care of Harry but also four young children. It was getting through this tough time that made me appreciate everything we did have and put life in an even greater perspective for me. Harry fully recovered and we had four more children. Harry and I always felt we had the life of Camelot.

How did you handle Steph's accomplishments and keep things in perspective?

We had such a big family that we had to be in a lot of different places at different times. Most of our children were involved in sports or clubs. Harry and I were so proud of all our kids. Each one of them was special. Stephanie gained the most attention because of her success as a basketball player. She was very humble and we all kept her grounded. She believes her brothers and sisters were her role models to help her be successful. They were a terrific support system and she always made us feel like we were all a part of the awards she received. I let my kids know that as long as they did their best, they have not failed. They need to know failure will help them grow. You need to be okay with letting them find their way through these failures (hard to do, for sure), remind them that everyone's best is different and all you can ask is for them to do their best. Love them unconditionally. They will disappoint you at times but let them know you are there through the good and the bad.

If you were heavily involved, how did you make time for yourself?

We had such a busy household that I couldn't commit to much outside the home. I would get involved with activities involving my children. I didn't do much that didn't involve them. Harry and I would take an occasional vacation that he got with his job, but other than that, my commitments were all to the family.

What would you say were important qualities to possess to be the mother you were?

I knew I always wanted a big family. I also knew this is what I dreamed of. I feel loving each child "differently" but also the "same" was important. Loving them differently meant appreciating them for who they were and not trying to mold them into being someone different. They were unique and all had different goals and dreams. To "love them the same" meant being careful not to show favoritism and also being fair when it came to the rules of the house.

I also feel compassion was such a big part of being the mother I am. With so many children, you go down different paths with each of them. I wanted to be sure to celebrate their "highs" and also love them through their "lows."

Patience is another key virtue I needed to help me be the best mom I could be. There were times this was stretched a great deal but never broken.

Time management was critical in making sure each of the kids were organized. Especially in their early years. Everyone was going in eight different directions and with my husband working and me having the one car, we would really have to juggle schedules. It's interesting today because cell phones, computers, two family cars, Uber, etc. would have helped a great deal back then. I feel we had many more challenges because of limitations but we also had a great deal of love.

Unconditional love would be the number one quality I felt I possessed to be the mom I was and am today. I love my children, and at times, I had to raise them with tough love. Nowadays, I see my own children saying the hard things or setting tough rules. I think this had a lot to do with my success as a parent. We had discipline, but more importantly, we had (and have) love.

What is your relationship like now with Steph?
When Stephanie was younger, my role was to be her mother and teach her right from wrong. Like all of her brothers and sisters, she got a job at age 14 and learned to be responsible. My husband and I were very strict when it came to academics. We also went to church every Sunday as a family. Stephanie and I have always been very close. She is a great listener and makes me feel good about myself. She loves sharing her success and failures with me. She makes me laugh and I admire how she is so kind

to everyone and always makes them feel good about themselves. She still tells the story of when she was in the eighth grade and I found her crying in her room. I asked her why she was crying. She said, "time is going by so fast and I'm scared to grow up." She has never forgotten the advice I gave her when I said, "be the nicest person you can be every day and you will have a great life."

She calls me every day. Just to check in and tell me she loves me. She will also send me little packages with my favorite candy. I love going to her games. I love seeing her with her family and her team. She is a terrific mother and wife. She also cherishes her relationship with her brothers and sisters. Her dad was such an incredible role model with kids, and I see so much of him in her. She makes me incredibly proud.

As we have gotten older, we are more friends than mother and daughter. She still has the respect that a daughter would have of her mother, but she is always there to brighten up my day and tell me how much I mean to her! I get in trouble with my other children because sometimes I refer to her as my favorite.

If you could name one characteristic you believe Steph inherited from you, what would that be?
I would say kindness. Stephanie is sweet and caring. She puts other people's feelings before her own. We kid about her being "Switzerland" because she likes to see everyone's side. I love her strong faith and her ability to make others feel good about themselves

How did you respond to situations that made you feel overwhelmed?
Faith is a big part of my life and I rely on that.

Can you offer any advice to young or soon to be mothers/parents?
You are a parent first, not a friend. This is not always easy because you don't want them to be mad or to "hate you",

however boundaries need to be set. Teach them to be one for others. It is not just about them.

Time goes by so fast. You will feel overwhelmed at times and feel the cycle will never end. Savor every moment because one day those moments will be a special memory. Make time to know each of your children. Carve out time in your day for special time with each one of them.

Looking back, what would you say was the greatest gift you gave to your kids?
I think the greatest gift I gave my children is my unconditional love and my time. I also feel faith and family were established early in their childhood and that's why they all are so very close to this day!

If you could tell everyone in the world one thing, what would it be?
Cherish every moment, as many of them will become beautiful memories!

"One of our main concerns was not to project on Hugo our previous dreams and ambitions to become professional athletes. We knew that was something rather common for parents who had been frustrated athletes to do and we were super vigilant to not allow that to happen."

Hugo Calderano
IG: @HugoCalderano

Elisa Borges is the mother of Hugo

Calderano, a professional table tennis player and member of the Brazilian Olympic National Team. Elisa is a native of Rio de Janeiro, where she grew up in one of the city's middle-class neighborhoods with her parents and younger sister. She learned to speak English at a young age, which enabled her to work as a translator for international visitors and teach the language to refugees at 15 years old. Even though she had dreams of becoming an Olympic athlete, Elisa was always a strong student. She majored in Physical Education in college, and met her husband and Hugo's father, Marcos, during her undergraduate studies. They married following graduation, and both became teachers. Elisa eventually went back to school and earned a Master's in Applied Linguistics.

After that, Elisa began a distinguished career in education. She started teaching at one of the top language schools in Rio in 1994 and then became an Academic Coordinator in charge of teacher training and course design. In 2010, she was promoted to Academic

Superintendent, putting her in charge of 14 schools throughout Rio that held more than 12,000 students and 400 teachers. Elisa and Marcos have two children together – Hugo and Sofia.

As a son and grandson of educators, school was a major priority of Hugo's childhood. He is widely recognized for his high IQ (can complete a Rubix Cube in under nine seconds), but as his mother tells it, his advanced motor skills date back to when he was a toddler. Hugo taught himself to read, write and complete math calculations at age 4 – natural abilities that ultimately became the driving force behind his gift for table tennis. Hugo's pursuit for table tennis stardom took him all over the globe. At the age of 14, he left his hometown of Rio to live in São Caetano do Sul and practice with the Brazilian National Team. Then, when he was 16, he moved to France to train at the French National Training Center. In 2013, Hugo became the youngest player to ever win a leg of the ITTF World Tour and the first player to win a singles title on the ITTF Junior Circuit and on the ITTF World Tour in the same year. In 2014, he made history by winning the Bronze medal at the Youth Olympic Games in China - the first medal for Brazilian table tennis in an Olympic competition. In addition to being a 3x Latin American champion and the reigning Pan American champion, he has been an active member of the Ochsenhausen Table Tennis Club in the first division of the German Bundesliga.

This chapter explains the steps Elisa took in order to support her son's development as a mother at home and a fan from afar.

Did your mother inspire you in any way? What kind of values did you take from her and instill in your own life as a mother?

Our family has always been very close. I have always had

a good relationship with my mother, but growing up, my role model was my father. We have always had a strong connection that nowadays I can probably understand better. My younger sister was born when I was 6 and my father became in charge of me while my mother would tend to the baby. That was probably when we started bonding more deeply and sports were the glue that linked us together. We would watch sports on TV, go to stadiums, and that was when I started practicing different sports as well. He was always super supportive and made me feel very special.

My mother was a homemaker and from a very early age I knew that was something I didn't want to do. When I was young, it was sometimes hard for me to look past that and admire her for who she was beyond her lack of professional ambition. It took me some years and maturity to be able to appreciate her many qualities. She has a great sense of humor and is ready to make sacrifices for the benefit of her family. When Hugo was 14 and had to move from Rio de Janeiro to São Paulo (400 km away) to improve his game, we agreed my father would move with him since he was too young to be living alone. My mother was selfless enough to agree to that arrangement, although it meant that she would be living alone in Rio for most of the year. Every time Hugo's story is told, people mention his grandfather as the one who accompanied him to another city and made his development possible. He is a hero, for sure. But Hugo's grandmother, my mother, is the one who agreed to stay behind on her own so her husband of 43 years could live a little adventure with his beloved grandson. She did it out of love for Hugo, and, though nobody thinks much of it, she had an important role in breeding a champion.

When was the earliest indication that you thought Hugo might have extraordinary talent?
Being the child and grandchild of Physical Education professionals, Hugo has always had a lot of

encouragement to develop his motor skills. His father had also been an athlete in his younger years and, like my father and myself, he is obsessed with everything related to sports.

We found out, at a very early age, that Hugo's motor skills were more advanced than the average child his age. For example, at 1, he would hold, kick and throw a ball very easily. At age 2, he would show amazing arm/leg coordination when running. As he grew and experimented with other sports, he learned things very quickly and always performed well. When he was still a child, it was clear to us that he had a gift.

Around 14 years old is when we felt like we knew he could be a professional table tennis player. But in order to do that, he would have to leave Rio de Janeiro and start prioritizing practice over his formal education. We didn't put any pressure on him. It was all his choice. Despite the dilemma we faced as a family when we had to make the decision of allowing him to focus on sport over schooling, we realized we couldn't hold him back. That's when he moved to São Paulo and officially started a career in table tennis.

Did you have to do anything to foster Hugo's talent or was he always self-motivated?

We believed Hugo could be a professional athlete if he wanted to. We thought the best thing to do was to give him the chance to experiment with different sports and activities so he would develop various patterns of movement that would help him in whichever sport he chose to pursue. One of our main concerns, though, was not to project on Hugo our previous dreams and ambitions to become professional athletes. We knew that was something rather common for parents who had been "frustrated athletes" to do, and we were super vigilant not to allow that to happen.

Did you put any systems in place for Hugo to build the habits that led to his success?

We had several basic principles. School was first. If they had bad grades, they would not be able to travel for a competition, for example.

It's okay to lose, but it's not okay to have a bad attitude. We never really had to enforce that because Hugo was pretty cool most of the time. But we liked to talk about the importance of respecting the opponent and keeping a polite attitude all the time. His father taught him a lesson that Hugo still repeats to this day: "The game can never become more important than the person who is playing." I feel so proud when I see that he is able to play very aggressively and still show a gentle and respectful attitude towards his opponent. This is certainly a lesson we made sure he learned as he was growing up.

When he was older, already living away from home, I always made sure he was playing professionally because he wanted to. Too many kids continue in sports because they know it's their parents' dream and they don't know how to give up. So, every time he came home, when it was time for him to leave again, I would hold him and ask, "are you sure you don't want to stay? You can just give everything up and come back home and live a regular teenage life." He would just smile. It was obviously a joke, but I felt it helped reaffirm his commitment to go on and pursue a dream that was his own.

I guess the most important thing was that, as parents, we had something very clear. We weren't raising kids to be successful. We would do our best to make sure they had opportunities and choices and when the time came, they were equipped and prepared to choose well. But our ultimate goal was to help them grow up to be good people and to be happy.

How did you handle Hugo's accomplishments and keep things in perspective?

Hugo has always been very confident, but also very down

to earth. He likes to keep his cool and show his superiority only while playing. Something that helps illustrate his personality is the fact that he never cared about buying apparel from popular table tennis brands. This was something most young players did. They would show off their branded shirts during practice and Hugo would just wear whatever was more cost effective. He said, "I don't care what I wear if it's not what's going to make me win."

Any stories of adversity that Hugo faced?

We don't have many sad stories to tell. We have been very lucky in every aspect of our lives. If you consider the context of sports in general and table tennis in particular, the main adversity Hugo has faced was probably having been born in Brazil, and worse, in Rio. This is no criticism to the country or the city – both of which we love. But, for an aspiring table tennis professional, being born in Rio certainly meant a huge competitive disadvantage.

Of course, during his career so far, there have been difficult moments. This is one I remember well: Hugo was 16 when he moved to France to practice at the French National Training center. He was the only foreigner in the center and didn't feel very welcome. The first few weeks were very hard. He developed some kind of allergy that we thought could be caused by stress. He couldn't leave the dorm because he couldn't stop itching and he barely slept for several days. We would be texting during the night. He would sit under the shower to try and stop the itching while I tried to control my nerves and calm him down. I contacted his doctor in Brazil, who prescribed some medicine that required Hugo to leave the dorm to go get it. I remember that I was concerned he had developed some kind of panic disorder because he told me he felt anxious and weird about leaving his dorm. I guided him towards the pharmacy and he managed to get back to the dorm safely. After taking the medicine, he started to get better. I remember to this day how desperate I felt for not being able to help him more.

As a mother, what were you good at saying no to?
We always thought a lot before saying no. One of the principles we followed in bringing up our kids was that once we said no, we would have to keep our word. So, we did not say no to any little thing. If we said no to something, we wouldn't give in.

What would you say were important qualities to possess to be the mother you were?
I have always wanted to be a mother, but I don't believe this is a natural calling and it certainly shouldn't be imposed on women. I surely don't believe this is a one size fits all situation. But I think no matter what kind of parent you are, it is important to remember you are going to be a role model for your child and your actions are going to have an impact on them. It's not about being perfect. On the contrary, it's about being human. I usually felt bad about losing my temper or yelling at them, but then I learned to be more forgiving with myself. Everybody gets angry. Everybody makes mistakes. At the end of the day, what really matters is the example you give. I tried to make sure my dearest principles were part of what I did on a daily basis. For me, those have always been to be a good person, be honest and be fair.

What were things you think you may have handled differently?
There are always different possible ways to do things, including raising a child. I always put a lot of effort in my career, worked and studied very hard to achieve my professional goals and managed to accomplish everything I wanted to in my profession. When I retired, I was 100% satisfied with the path I had taken.

During the 22 years I had to juggle corporate work life and motherhood, I have certainly felt the occasional guilt for missing PTA meetings or not reading more for them. But I never dwelled on guilt. I knew I was doing my absolute best and I was convinced that I would be a good role model for them by having a fulfilled life.

As I got older, though, I realized there was one thing I should have done differently. I should have taken better care of my health. That is probably the one thing I would do differently if I could start over. Exercise more, do some yoga or meditation, prepare my body to enjoy my mature years. For the past two years, I have been trying to make up for the lost time. But if you can do it as a habit from early on, your body and mind will thank you.

If you could name one characteristic you believe Hugo inherited from you, what would that be?
In his own words, taken from an interview: "The way she goes after what she wants and always works hard. I think I get this from her." I agree.

Can you offer any advice to young or soon to be mothers/parents?
It's easier to talk about it after you have lived through the experiences. As Milan Kundera said, "There is no means of testing which decision is better, because there is no basis for comparison. The first rehearsal for life is life itself."

If I could give some advice to my 21-year-old self, I would say to follow your instincts, do things exactly as you think you should do, but remember there are 24 hours in a day. Take just one of those 24 hours every day to take care of your health and well-being. Your 50-year-old self will be forever thankful.

Looking back, what would you say was the greatest gift you gave to your kids?
I think I can say the greatest gift I have given my kids is the drive to do the right thing, to be honest and be fair.

If you could tell the world one thing, what would it be?

I would probably say, "Do unto others as you would have them do unto you." I am not a religious person, but I think if everyone lived by this golden rule, the world might be a better place.

"I think the most important thing is that one must have an open mind to first listen, then analyze and understand what their children are saying or going through before taking any action."

Laura Biondo
IG: @LauraBiondo

Maria Rosario Paladino is the

mother of Laura Biondo, an 11-time Guinness World Records title-holder and professional football freestyler. Maria was born and raised in Venezuela, growing up alongside her two brothers and sister in a mountainous area outside the Venezuelan city of Caracas. Her father ran one of the most prestigious shoe manufacturing companies in the country, which fostered a comfortable upbringing for Maria and her siblings. She was close with her mother and was a strong student all her life. With childhood dreams of becoming a doctor, Maria eventually earned a master's degree in the medical field. After graduating, she worked as a doctor in a Venezuelan children's hospital.

Maria had two children in Venezuela – Laura and her younger brother Pier. In 1999, they immigrated to the United States and settled in Weston, Florida. Laura was in middle school at the time and started playing soccer shortly after her arrival. As soccer, otherwise known as football outside the United States, became an integral part of her life, Laura made the decision to move to Italy at age 13 in order to play professionally. She earned a spot in the Italian Major League with football clubs like Foroni and Bardolino and then discovered the art of freestyle football – an alternative form of the sport made popular in the 1980s by Argentinian football legend Diego Maradona – that led her on a path to stardom.

After mastering the skill of freestyle, Laura became the first female freestyler to set a Guinness World Records in 2011. She then placed third in the 2014 Red Bull Street Style tournament and won the 2015 World Open Championship. In 2015, Laura's notoriety as a freestyler drew the attention of Cirque du Soleil. She joined the international contemporary circus company in the show called "Luzia" – performing nearly 10 Cirque du Soleil shows a week in front of thousands of spectators around the world for four years. To this day, Laura leads all Venezuelan's with 11 total Guinness World Records and is in charge of Women's Development for the World Freestyle Football Association. In addition to her accolades as a freestyler, Laura is also a certified personal trainer and a nutritionist. Her Instagram account, which plays home to her latest freestyle football videos, has over 120,000 followers.

In this chapter, Maria reflects on the inspiration behind her daughter's unique story and life lessons Laura taught her along the way.

Did your mother inspire you in any way? What kind of values did you take from her and instill in your own life as a mother?
We had a really beautiful relationship full of love, trust and comprehension. She taught me to be humble, loving, caring, forgiving and to respect others no matter their background or beliefs. In terms of being loving, for example, she loved to cook a lot, which I learned from her. Something that always caught my attention is that whenever she cooked, she thought not only about her kids but also feeding others. She would cook extra and

give to a neighbor or a family member. She was always taking care of others. This is something Laura also does that she took from her grandmother – she loves to cook like I do and is always making more to take to someone. In terms of being forgiving, she didn't hold any resentment to those who hurt her. She was strong and always respected herself, yet she also forgave. This taught me the true meaning of forgiving and today is something I feel also characterizes me and my daughter. In terms of being humble, when younger, she worked for Italian royalty and still never bragged about nor had any superior attitude because of what she did or who she was with. Again, this is a trait that has passed on generation to generation, in fact Laura and I at times don't even talk about our achievements. We just treat others the same way.

What kind of dreams and goals did you have when you were a kid? How much did they influence where you are today?

As a kid, I remember wanting medically inspired toys as I always dreamed of being a doctor, especially for those less fortunate. In fact, I worked in a charity hospital for children and still, to this day, my life revolves around medicine.

When was the earliest indication that you thought Laura might have extraordinary talent?

Since she was a baby, she was always very active, not even walking yet, she would hold on to the crib and jump constantly. She loved to play sports and always had to be doing something active. She also had fine motor development; she was a quick learner with anything she tried. This made me think she would be a very talented athlete.

How did you handle Laura's accomplishments and keep things in perspective?

As a kid, she won a lot in the sports she played. Of course, she didn't like to lose, who does? She always wanted to be among the best, yet she always remained humble. I would always tell her that no matter how successful she could be in the future, or how much she would have, to remember the example of her grandparents. There was no need to go around arrogantly showcasing success.

Any stories of adversity that Laura faced?

Moving to Italy is a big one. She moved to Italy to follow her soccer career. It was hard for her to leave her family, her friends, enter a new country and learn a new language. The decision to go to Italy came after we took Laura to an international women's soccer tournament. In this tournament, the head coach of the Italian national team told us she had potential to make it pro in Italy. She was 13 when she first went to Italy, at that age, with all the conflicts changing from a kid to a young adult, she had fears and worries about going to a place she knew nothing about. Even more because she always loved the U.S. since the time she first came here for vacation from Venezuela. She felt good here.

What would you say were important qualities to possess to be the mother you were?

Be loving and be able to explain why something is yes or something is no.

(Laura's answer) - "I think the same qualities my grandmother had which are the same my mother has and from what I have learned and always looked up to be. In all my interviews, I always talk about respect, honesty, transparency, dedication and acceptance. These are all values you learn from your family, especially a mother. My mom was understanding, she accepted me just how I am, respected my dreams and supported me in them, she also taught me to think if what I will do is something I would like or not like to be done to me, and she was always explaining things to better understand especially when making a decision that might affect others. I also learned self-love from them, and this is the base for all we do in our lives. If we love ourselves, we learn how to love and respect others."

What were things you think you may have handled differently?

I wish I was able to manage the divorce process with her father in a better fashion. In effort to not make my children suffer from seeing their parents divorced or not have a fatherly figure, I didn't make the decision when I had to and instead waited too long, and this affected the kids more. The relationship started to deteriorate when Laura was not even 2 years old and I was pregnant with my second child. At that moment, all I thought about was what could be done to save the relationship. I was willing to go to couples therapy as I didn't want my children to grow up without a father. If I would have made the decision to end it there, since they were so young, maybe they would have not suffered the problems we had later on as a family. In other words, I would have made the decision in the moment I saw that there was no change even after all the efforts and therapy instead of holding on to a false hope.

Can you offer any advice to young or soon to be mothers/parents?

I think the most important thing is that one must have an open mind to first listen, then analyze and understand what their children are saying or going through before taking any action. As young parents, we go towards the punishment to maintain authority and forget to educate and give an explanation to why things should be a certain way or why some things are being done wrong by the child. This punishing act is something that leads to the loss of a strong relationship between mother and child. A kid must be disciplined but there has to be reasons and examples that as parents we need to make sure our kids understand.

Also, never have negative affirmations towards your kids such as, "you are dumb" or "you are not good enough." This creates rejection, low self-esteem and fear in the child that will later in life affect them even as adults.

Looking back, what would you say was the greatest gift you gave to your kids?
Unconditional love. For me, unconditional love means to give the best of you to others. It's to respect and appreciate others without affecting your principles and values.

If you could tell everyone in the world one thing, what would it be?
Be more kind to each other.

Any closing thoughts?
As a kid, Laura was always very active and sports driven. She had a talent for sports, which ranged from swimming, karate, to track and field and more. She decided to stick to gymnastics as that was what she felt more passionate about.

As she always mentions in her interviews and in her bio, she only discovered soccer when she was 10. When she was a child, in Venezuela you would not see a woman play soccer, it was just the men. It was when we moved to the U.S. that she saw women playing soccer for the first time and she immediately said she wanted to play.

She looked up to Mia Hamm and always said she wanted to be a successful athlete just like her. Her determination to be the best led her step by step to play professional soccer and then transition to freestyle and become who she is today. Dating back to when she was a child, she was always motivated and driven to be the best and fight to make her dreams come true. It was hard for her to give up, she would just keep trying until she achieved what she set out to do.

"Relax and be patient. Don't be hard on yourself if you think you didn't do it quite right. We are all human and if you love them to death, they will survive and they will love you."

Dara Torres
IG: @SwimDara

Marylu Kauder is the mother of Dara

Torres, a five-time Olympic swimmer, author, speaker and entrepreneur. Marylu is a native of Van Nuys, California, where she was raised by both of her parents as an only child. Her father worked as a sound engineer for Paramount Studios while her mother was a homemaker. She enjoyed a comfortable upbringing and pursued becoming a professional model immediately after high school – eventually becoming a Miss Rheingold finalist during a successful modeling career in the 1950s and '60s.

Marylu's first husband, the late Eddie Torres, was a real estate mogul who owned several high-profile casinos and hotels along the Las Vegas strip. They had six children together – Mike, Kirk, Brad, Rick, Dara and Lara – and lived in a sprawling Beverly Hills estate, but divorced when Dara was 8 years-old. Two years later, she married prominent U.S. tennis player Edward Kauder, who played a role in Dara's evolution as an athlete during her adolescence. However, Dara also remained close with her biological father throughout her upbringing and adult life. He died in the early 2000s after a battle with colon cancer.

Following in the footsteps of her older brothers, Dara first started swimming when she was 8. At 14, she won the national open championship in the 50-yard freestyle. She attended the Westlake School for Girls from seventh grade to her sophomore year in high school while also a member of the basketball, volleyball and gymnastics teams. During her junior year, she left home to swim for the Mission Viejo Nadadores in Southern California while training for the 1984 Los Angeles Olympics in which she won a gold medal in the relay. Then, Dara joined the University of Florida swimming and diving team, winning nine SEC individual championship events over her four-year collegiate career as well as earning 28 All-American swimming honors. After Florida, she went on to compete in four more Olympic Games (1988, 1992, 2000, 2008) to become the first swimmer to represent the United States in five Olympics. In 2008, she became the oldest swimmer ever to earn a spot on the U.S. Olympic Team at age 41 before winning three silver medals in the 50-meter freestyle, 4x100-meter medley relay and 4x100-meter freestyle relay. She took home a combined 12 medals (four gold, four silver, four bronze) throughout her Olympic career.

Dara's trailblazing success extends far outside the pool. She's a two-time New York Times best-selling author and a dedicated mother of one. She was the first athlete model ever featured in the Sports Illustrated Swimsuit Issue and was an early contributor to CBS Sports' *We Need to Talk* – the first national all-female sports talk show. She has been a spokesperson for major companies like Toyota, Quaker Oats, Speedo, CaniBrands and Amlactin among others, and her philanthropy work includes involvement with several charities for drowning prevention.

This chapter includes Marylu's perspective on Dara's career with tips for how to help children navigate the ups and downs of life's journey.

Did your mother inspire you in any way? What kind of values did you take from her and instill in your own life as a mother?

My mother was always there for me. My parents were pretty distraught over my brother's early death. She certainly made sure I had everything I needed. Once in a while, my parents would take me away for a weekend trip. At about 17 though, I left and set out to do my own thing. The biggest thing I took from my mom was to do unto others as you would have them do unto you. Be respectful. And a weird but goodie - always write thank you notes.

When was the earliest indication that you thought Dara might have extraordinary talent?

I would say around 12 when she won her first U.S. Open title and then began to compete internationally. She was almost always a winner in her events from an early age, but you mentioned extraordinary, and I believe that it was around 12. It seemed to come easy to her from the beginning but when she really started to work hard is when she really succeeded.

When she was doing club swimming, I think some of her teammates resented her a little because she didn't seem to have to work as hard as they did and she still usually won her events. When she got the itch to capitalize on her natural talent and throw in the extra hard work is when she began to really make us think that she's a very special swimmer.

Did you put any systems in place for Dara to build the habits that lead to her success?

She was self-motivated. I was always there to drive her and encouraged her to reach her dreams. Swimming was always her choice. I never pushed her, just encouraged her.

How did you handle Dara's accomplishments and keep things in perspective?

She went to school and had many friends. We were all very excited for her when she swam well but I don't think we went overboard. Since she had so many siblings, we didn't want all the focus on Dara. I think she handled everything very well. She always encouraged her teammates and didn't brag.

If you were heavily involved, how did you make time for yourself?

It was great being a mom and I knew the day would come when I would have my own time, so I didn't fret too much over this.

Any stories of adversity that Dara faced?

Dara had an eating disorder. It was a very scary time for me as it was the time that Karen Carpenter died from her eating disorder. I realized that something had to be done. I called a doctor friend and got a referral to a doctor she could talk to. It was the answer as she got well. In my heart, I feel if I hadn't found help and had waited at all, we might have lost her. Thank the Lord.

What would you say were important qualities to possess to be the mother you were?

With so many kids, one quality was to be as fair as possible in raising and handling them. Also, a lot of patience and understanding. Me as being pretty much like an only child, I kind of learned as I went along. The first child is so scary, but you become more relaxed as each one comes along. Don't be hard on yourself. You are going to make mistakes along the way but it's okay.

What were things you think you may have handled differently?

I think you always look back and second guess yourself. With so many children you look back and say should I have done this or that. But they all turned out to be good adults. And they are all different so one way of raising them doesn't work. They are individuals and need individual ways of trying to raise them.

What is your relationship like now with Dara?
Dara calls me every single morning which means so much to me. She is a busy woman and always includes me on trips, shopping or just having me to lunch or dinner.

If you could name one characteristic you believe Dara inherited from you, what would that be?
I would like to think that it is being kind to others.

How did you respond to situations that made you feel overwhelmed?
Go hide in the closet with a jar of peanut butter and eat it with a spoon.

Can you offer any advice to young or soon to be mothers/parents?
Relax and be patient. Don't be hard on yourself if you think you didn't do it quite right. We are all human and if you love them to death, they will survive and they will love you.

Looking back, what would you say was the greatest gift you gave to your kids?
My TIME and unconditional love.

If you could tell the world one thing, what would it be?
Accept others as they are and don't be judgmental.

> **"If I preached anything to my kids it would be that they had to learn who they are apart from what they DO. You do a sport, but it isn't who you are."**

Haven Shepherd
IG: @HavenFaithShepherd

Shelly Shepherd is the adoptive mother of

Haven Shepherd, an 18-year-old Paralympic swimmer, CrossFit athlete, model, motivational speaker and brand ambassador. Shelly, the youngest of three children, was born in a small town in Missouri. Shelly grew up with middle class parents who were always trying to make ends meet. She had plenty of time to find independence early. Her parents moved her senior year and she moved in with her elderly grandmother which gave her a sense of freedom, but also a sense of abandonment. She was thrown into adulthood very quickly, she got married at 18 and began her path to motherhood.

When it comes to life aspirations, Shelly's dream was always to be a mom. In her words, she ended up "blessed to marry a man who let her do it seven times." Shelly and her husband, Rob, had six children while running a family flooring business in Carthage, MO. In 2004, they adopted Haven from Vietnam after she miraculously survived a murder-suicide attempt by her biological parents. Haven was 14 months-old when her father strapped himself and her mother with explosive devices and detonated them as they held her between them. The explosion killed both parents, but Haven, found 30 feet away from the burning hut, somehow survived it. However, in order to avoid infection, doctors needed to amputate both of her legs below the knee.

Shelly's children were between the ages of 7-21 when they brought Haven home. She was embraced by the family and enjoyed the benefits of growing up around four older sisters in a large, hectic household. Sports were an outlet for her. At 10, she began swimming, and two years later joined a competitive team that required her to train all year round. She posted back-to-back first-place finishes at the Paralympic Swimming World Series in 2018 and 2019 and is striving to represent Team USA at the 2021 Tokyo Paralympic Games.

From her experiences with Haven, Shelly has gained an unparalleled perspective on motherhood shared throughout the following chapter that can help guide parents who are raising their own children through trauma.

Did your mother inspire you in any way? What kind of values did you take from her and instill in your own life as a mother?

My mom tried her best with us. Me being the independent person I am, I parented myself most of the time from 12 years old and on. We had a lot of freedom growing up, but we also had been brought up in a very religious/spiritual environment. I think this kept me on the right track because I never got into partying or wild decisions. I was very strait-laced. I'm more laid back at 58 than I was at 18.

My mom did the best she could with the knowledge and experience she had growing up. I just knew that I wanted to be a different kind of mom. I decided when I became a parent, I would be very intentional and involved. My mom's dedication to raising us with a strong faith and having us make our own decisions is something I certainly took and passed down to my children.

When was the earliest indication that you thought Haven might have extraordinary talent?

The day we met her. Haven is a good swimmer, but her talent is being one of the happiest, most positive human beings I've ever met. She was 10 when we started competitive swimming. We realized quickly that she had some talent. We got an email from the USOPC (United States Olympic & Paralympic Committee) in the first six months as an identified future athlete. They told us we needed to join a USA swim club.

Did you have to do anything to foster Haven's talent or was she always self-motivated?

She has always been fairly self-disciplined although she was a child so, of course, there were days she was more excited to swim than others. We always told her it was up to her if she wanted to change her goal but if she said her goal was to go to the Paralympics then it was our job to keep her on track to help her reach her goals. There were some hard decisions. She didn't want to leave her YMCA team where she started swimming. I made a rookie mistake. I told her it was her decision. I explained to her why she needed to change teams and I really thought she would make the right decision, but she didn't. Then I had to go back on my word and say, "Sorry that's the wrong choice you have to move up." We had some tears and anger over that, but I knew that's what we needed to do. She got over it quickly though.

How did you handle Haven's accomplishments and keep things in perspective?

Haven has always been very outgoing and loved attention, until she was around 13 years old. She began to pull back and didn't want to do interviews or filming. It just didn't fit with who I knew her to be. We dealt with that for a couple of years. It was hard to navigate because I didn't ever want to be one of those crazy stage moms, but I knew in my heart she wasn't made to have a small life.

We were finally able to diagnose that she was dealing with fear. Everyone who would encourage her, tell her they were following her or cheering her on became just more pressure to her. She was finally able to voice the fear that the more people who knew what she was doing, the more people she would disappoint if she failed. We are strong minded in this family and do not give into fear, especially fear of failure. If I preached anything to my kids, it would be that they had to learn who they are apart from what they DO. You do a sport; it isn't who you are. It's a tough lesson but she had to know she would not have any less worth if she didn't make it to the Paralympics than if she did.

If you were heavily involved, how did you make time for yourself?
It was tough. I had been driving kids to practices for years but this was on a whole new level. It was also difficult because in 2012, we went through financial disaster. We lost our business, home, income and our whole way of life. I needed to get a job, but my husband was adamant that the eight dollars an hour I would bring home was not worth not being available to Haven to travel and take her to practice. I don't even know how we made it, but we did. There were always people who stepped up and supported Haven which was a huge relief and blessing to us.

Any stories of adversity that Haven faced?
We didn't have a great deal of adversity other than the obvious, but even then, Haven does not see it as adversity. She's so positive. She wasn't ever really bullied for her legs. One day in junior high some kid did say to her that she walked funny. She replied, "No crap, I don't have feet!" She had some mean girls who were jealous of some of the things she got to do, like going to a taping of Dancing with the Stars. Most of the time kids were very nice though.

As a mother, what were you good at saying no to?
I only had a few absolute no's: disobedience, disrespect
and mouthing off. I never let my kids treat me badly. I
always taught them to remember I am a human with
feelings too. My theory was to say yes as much as I could
so when I had to tell them no, they would respect it for a
good reason.

**What would you say were important qualities to
possess to be the mother you were?**
I dealt with my crap. I am a huge believer that you can't
give your children something you don't possess for
yourself. In my late 20's I found myself on the verge of
having an affair. I knew I wasn't being honest with the
brokenness I had inside. I had a need for attention,
especially from men. I wouldn't have done it for myself I
don't think, but when I looked at my girls, I knew I
wanted to pass on a strength and security I didn't possess
at that time. I worked hard to find who I was created to
be so I could pass it on to them. I was always very honest
with my kids about my journey.

What is your relationship like now with Haven?
Haven is 17 and still living at home. We are still extremely
close. She homeschools so we see each other a lot. We
just have a connection that happened in Vietnam and it
hasn't really changed. We love to travel together and can
always make each other laugh. I know she will spread her
wings and fly one day but I can't imagine there ever being
a time we aren't in contact with each other.

**If you could name one characteristic you believe
Haven inherited from you, what would that be?**
We talk a great deal about why she has the outlook on life
she has. I believe it was nature and then magnified by
nurture. I'm a very positive person so that magnifies her
natural personality.

Did any times of adversity set you up for later success?

We were a family who always took in extra children and people in need. Before we lost our big house, we had eight bedrooms and eight baths. We had many disappointments with the people we tried to help. We took in an 11-year-old boy who lived with us for seven years. He made a lot of bad choices and we found out after our daughter was older that he had molested her. We took in a 15-year-old runaway who we later found out was actually 25. I look back though and I never gave up on believing it was worth it to take a chance on people. If I had become so disappointed and jaded, I would never have opened my heart to take a chance on Haven. She was the completion of our family and we never took in any other children after that.

How did you respond to situations that made you feel overwhelmed?

There are many times as a parent you feel overwhelmed. My hardest times were when you knew your child was going to get hurt but you need to let them make their own mistakes. I would have my say and let it lay. It pays off in the end but there were times I thought it would break my heart.

Can you offer any advice to young or soon to be mothers/parents?

You won't do it all right. Kids are resilient. Don't believe these Pinterest moms and don't compare. Find your own voice. Give yourself some grace. You can do this!

I don't go along with a lot of books about parenting. I do not believe in allowing your children to be victims, even if your parents blew their legs off and killed themselves. I would be more than happy feeling sorry for them if I believed it ever did any good in the long run. I also believe you can't raise secure children by lying to them. They aren't stupid. Example: Ivy was 9, Chloe was

7. They needed a fill in player for Ivy's softball team. Chloe was good enough for them to ask her to stay on the team. One night as I tucked Ivy in, she started crying, "Chloe hits the ball better than I do." So often people will lie and say that's not true, but the child is smart. She can count. If you lie, it begins to erode trust and makes the situation worse. I said, "Yes, she does hit the ball better than you, but you run so fast. You are the fastest on the team (which was true)." Another example: my son had severe dyslexia and a very hard time reading. I can't tell him there's nothing to be ashamed of and then whisper behind his back that he can't read. I would say with confidence in front of him, "Sawyer has dyslexia, he struggles reading but he's a genius fixing the vacuum cleaner." Through the years, I feel as if some people felt this was hard or unkind but I'm lucky to get to see all seven of my adult children living as confident, responsible adults.

Looking back, what would you say was the greatest gift you gave to your kids?
I taught them to embrace truth, both positive and negative, about themselves which helped them find their strengths and be secure in their individuality. I believe that knowing who you are and being secure in that is one of the greatest gifts you can have.

If you could tell everyone in the world one thing, what would it be?
The grace and forgiveness you GIVE today, may be the grace and forgiveness you NEED tomorrow.

"At the dinner table, everyone had to say three things about the day that they're thankful for. It created a mindset of gratitude and fulfillment."

Zack Steffen
IG - @ZackSteffen_
TW - @ZackStef_23
voycenowfoundation.org

Stef Steffen is the mother of Zack Steffen, an international soccer star who currently plays goalkeeper for Manchester City in the English Premier League and the United States Men's National Team. Stef calls Downingtown, PA home, a southwestern suburb of Philadelphia where she's lived for the last 35 years. She moved to Downingtown as a teenager with her parents and two younger siblings, but the family suffered an insurmountable loss soon after in the death of her father. Stef was only 14 when her dad passed away, however it never deterred her from success. A self-described perfectionist, Stef assumed a larger role around the house to support her mother while still remaining focused on school, eventually graduating high school with a 4.3 GPA that led to an academic scholarship from Penn State.

Stef began motherhood in a small rented house in Downingtown, where she lived for six years as a single parent with three children all born 29 months apart. She always made sure Zack, Lexy and Katy, and later on Ben and Cole, were well provided for, well-educated and well acclimated to life outside of school. That's where sports came into the picture for Zack, and it was at 7 years-old that the family realized he might have a future in soccer. Fast forward to now, and you'll hear his name mentioned among some of the greatest players in the world.

Zack began his collegiate career in 2013 at the

University of Maryland, where as a freshman, he played every minute in goal during the Terrapins' 26-game schedule. His sophomore year was more of the same, posting nine shutouts with just 19 goals conceded as Maryland took home the Big 10 regular season title. He left college in 2014 to sign a professional contract with SC Freiburg in Germany and returned to the U.S. in 2016 and played with the Columbus Crew. After three years in the MLS, culminating in being named 2018 Goalkeeper of the Year, Zack finally reached soccer supremacy when Manchester City acquired him from the Crew for a fee that was reportedly "the largest ever received by an MLS club for a goalkeeper." In January 2021, he made his first career start for Manchester City and is expected to compete for the club's No.1 goalkeeper spot. On the U.S. national team, Zack has appeared in 19 games with nine wins and seven clean sheets. In 2020, Zack founded a non-profit called VoyceNow. The non-profit has a partnership with the Boys and Girls Clubs of America and features a group of over 100 professional athletes all working to use their platforms to help support kids in minority communities.

In this chapter, Stef expands on her relationship with Zack, detailing their journey from youth travel soccer to the sport's greatest stage. The path to get there wasn't always straight and narrow.

Did your mother inspire you in any way? What kind of values did you take from her and instill in your own life as a mother?
She certainly displayed extraordinary strength and courage raising the three of us on her own. We didn't have any family around to help. She scrimped and budgeted to make my dad's life insurance last for us. I know it was enormously stressful for her. I didn't realize until I became a parent how she poured her heart and soul into giving us as much normalcy as possible despite his death.

I believe I've poured every fiber of my being into parenthood largely because of her example.

What kind of dreams and goals did you have when you were a kid? How much did they influence where you are today?

After my dad died, we were all in survival mode. My mom was so overt about the grief, while I kind of went the opposite way and kept it all in. I was so caught up in helping out with my sister. My brother was dealing with the grief in his own ways, so I went into this parent mode as the oldest sibling. It just seemed like the right thing to do. My mindset was one foot in front of the other and I am going to help my mom with Lindsay and be there for my family. I still played sports. I was playing travel softball, so I was still doing some of my own things, just not as much as your average high school student. I knew I'd go to college. I didn't give much thought to what would come after.

Any stories of adversity?

I worked full time and the oldest three were in an awesome onsite daycare center. I visited every day to have lunch and read to them. I was trying to do everything I could to give these kids normalcy. They had some wonderful daycare teachers who showed them a lot of love. I was struggling to make ends meet. There were times I brought the kids home at night and my electricity wouldn't turn on because I couldn't pay the bill on time. I had a very deep bond with my oldest three kids because of those circumstances. I frequently invited their teachers over for pizza and beer on Fridays as I was so appreciative of the excellent care and attention they gave the kids. I guess it was kind of a bribe for them to continue the high level of care, too. The kids and I would have dance parties at night. They wrestled a lot, sometimes playfully with lots of giggling, sometimes not. We were a tight little unit of four.

When was the earliest indication that you thought Zack might have extraordinary talent?

I signed Zack up with a friend for a weekend soccer clinic. He was probably 7 or 8. One of the coaches approached us to see if he wanted to join a travel team. That was cool. But I'd say when things really clicked was when Zack was 13 and we got a letter from U.S. Soccer telling us to get his passport immediately. We knew he could be heading for something special then.

Did you have to do anything to foster Zack's talent or was he always self-motivated?

When Zack first started playing soccer at age 4 or 5, he cried before every game. He didn't want to get out of the car. I had to bribe him with treats to play the game. He overcame that eventually once he started enjoying the sport and the friendships it fostered for him, but it was dicey those first couple years. After that, he was always pretty self-motivated and disciplined. As he excelled and started playing at a higher level with greater pressure and expectations, I was just always very conscious of wanting it to stay fun for him.

He knew the sacrifices that would come along with chasing his dreams. Through middle and high school, when he was traveling all over the world, I know it was difficult for him. He just wanted to be a normal kid, hang with his friends. He flew to Turkey for the U20 World Cup the day after high school graduation instead of going to senior week with his buddies. He didn't want to get on that plane. But he knew it was what he had to do.

Did you put any systems in place for Zack to build the habits that lead to his success?

Hard work was always rewarded. We never had a ton of money, but if someone got a good grade or won a big game or achieved something great, we'd go out for pizza or ice cream, or they'd get to pick a special homemade dinner. I was always pretty unrelenting about the expectation being that the kids would exert 110% effort in anything they did – school, sports, work, everything.

Did you encourage Zack to take chances?
Yes, absolutely. Zack has been my hardest parenting job. I know getting on the plane to go to Freiburg at age 19, leaving the comfort and security and success he knew, was a huge chance. A part of him didn't want to go, but he knew it was the right thing to do.

Everyone faces self-doubt, did Zack ever want to give up on things, and if so, how did you go about handling that?
So, Zack graduated from high school in 2013. He could have gone pro right after but felt like it was best to experience college. He went to the University of Maryland for two years. He had a great two years there and decided to go pro after his second year. He chose to play in the Bundesliga league in Germany, one of the best leagues in the world. He took a chance and moved to Freiburg, Germany in 2015. He was there for 18 months and was miserable. He called me in July of 2017 and said he couldn't do it, he didn't know if he wanted to play soccer anymore. His agent, Dan Segal, the same agent Tim Howard (legendary U.S. Men's National Team Goalkeeper) used, always said, "If it's not good off the field, it's never going to be good on the field." Dan was able to get him out of his contract and Columbus Crew took a chance on him. They sent him to play for their minor league team in Pittsburgh at first.

Here is this kid who had this great college career where he was called, "THE NEXT TIM HOWARD" (as many liked to call him, he always hated comparisons, most pro athletes would probably agree). Then, here he's playing in the MLS minor league system for a team in Pittsburgh living in a dingy apartment with strangers. He did that for the last half of the season and was having fun again. He got called up to the Columbus team and then had an excellent two seasons there. There is something very unique about these lowly moments and times of struggle in not even just an athlete's life but anyone's life. It just goes to show you hard times can quite often lead to something great if you continue to persevere.

What changed in those two years at Columbus for him to be ready to try and go back to Germany again?

Those two years were tremendous for his growth. He was having fun again, he was playing extremely well, he wasn't far from home, he was gaining more and more confidence. When you're in that loop of being a professional athlete, he learned pretty quickly that most times you just don't have control. Focusing on what you can control was a very important lesson for Zack to understand. After his first full year with Columbus, he had offers to play overseas again, but he didn't want to go and insisted he wasn't ready. I tried to convey to him that these opportunities are not always going to be there, and he really insisted he just was not ready yet. So as a mother sometimes all you can do is say, "Okay, I trust you." Towards the middle of his second season, Manchester City started showing interest. That's a big name. That's when something clicked for him. It took months for an offer to come and I'm glad it took that long because it gave him the time needed to process everything and finish his year in Columbus. I remember he called me up one day and simply said, "I'm ready, this has been a great run here but I'm ready for what's next."

I totally believe in synchronicity; my family thinks I'm crazy. It was funny though. When Dan, his agent, called to tell him where in Germany he would be spending his first year, (it wouldn't be with Manchester City right away, they were going to loan him out so he could get his Visa and play in some games right away) Zack and his siblings were watching a Düsseldorf game on TV. And sure enough, Dan said, "You're going to go play for

Düsseldorf!" We knew it was meant to be.

How did you handle Zack's accomplishments and keep things in perspective?

I try hard not to add to the hype. I'm humble. He's very humble. He hates when I talk about what he is doing to others. He definitely wants to fly under the radar. To this day, he is extremely humble and grounded. He wears a black baseball cap in public so as not to be recognized. He's just a low-key guy. I'll get reprimanded if I even talk factually about what Zack is doing. We've always been a family that keeps things under the radar. I don't pay too much attention to what the media says about Zack. My husband and other family members send me articles about him sometimes. It is a kick to read an article about your kid on ESPN!

Last fall, we were talking about weekend plans at the preschool where I teach. I said we were traveling to New York for Zack's game. One of my colleagues googled Zack on her phone and her jaw dropped. She never realized his celebrity. I never talked about it or him any differently than my other kids.

If you were heavily involved, how did you make time for yourself?

There was not a lot of time to relax as Zack is the oldest of five. His sisters played several sports also, including travel and college. Then, when his little brothers came along, it was pretty crazy. I don't like too much down time, so it always worked pretty well. We dragged the little guys to lots of athletic fields through the years. They'd have a box of toys and lots of snacks. We made it fun.

As a mother, what were you good at saying no to?

I really like saying yes as a mom! I've always tried to pick my battles. Try to reserve saying no to the important things – issues of safety, health, respect, honesty – and not too many cookies for dessert!

I didn't raise spoiled kids; I think they're very grounded. I think I said no a good amount and I get better at saying no every day. My younger ones will tell you I say no more to them because I'm "older and cranky." With our tumultuous beginnings, I really just wanted Zach, Katy and Lexy to turn out well. I wanted them to be good people. I wanted them to be productive, normal-healthy functioning human beings. So, I said no and I did whatever I thought I had to do so they would grow into being good people. I must have said no more than I can remember. Zack and Lexy are very much people pleasers and they want to say yes to everything, so I talk to them a lot about how it's okay to say no. You don't have to give an excuse, just say, "No, it's not going to work for me." Take care of yourself. The energy you would give to that person you don't really care about – it doesn't work, you don't need to do that. There's so many people wanting Zack's time and attention and he's definitely getting better at saying no.

What would you say were important qualities to possess to be the mother you were?
Since it was just me with Zack and the girls for the first five to six years, I loved those kids so fiercely. They were my everything. I was kind of flying by the seat of my pants, but just wanted so badly to give them normalcy.

So, for me, important qualities to possess:
- Patience for when you hear "MOM!" for the 764th time in one hour.
- Creativity for when they're bored and driving you and each other crazy.
- Adaptability. Things never go the way you expect them to.
- Leadership and confidence.
- One of the most important qualities to possess is being able to laugh. I laugh at myself and my shortcomings. I want them to see and really understand how much fun I have with them and

how much joy they bring me whether we're
running errands or on vacation.

- Also, it is really important to say thank you and
role model thankfulness. For years at the dinner
table, everyone has had to say three things about
the day that they're thankful for as we're eating.
Doing that creates a mindset of gratitude and
fulfillment.

What were things you think you may have handled differently?

One of my favorite things to say, and I know my kids and
husband get sick of hearing it, is "We all make mistakes.
We learn from it and move forward, onward and better."
It's trite, but true. I have made all types of mistakes in my
parenting. I've been too strict. I've been too lax. I've been
over-protective and under-protective. I've tried to be a
friend when I should have been a parent and vice-versa.
I've made every mistake in the book. But I'm always
honest, always real, not afraid to have hard conversations,
not afraid to say I'm sorry. I've tried to be a role model to
the kids and show that it's okay to mess up, we're all
human, it's going to happen. But when you do, you own
it, you apologize, and you learn from it. I actually think
they're all pretty good about that. And looking back, I
don't really have any regrets. This is the journey I'm
meant to be on, warts and all. I'm stronger for the
adversity I've gone through and so are my kids.

Being a single parent of three small children gave me
a drive, work ethic and fierce independence. I believed
that I could handle anything by continuing to put one
foot in front of the other, find the good and keep going. I
think I've passed that on to my kids. I didn't necessarily
have an endgame or goal in mind, it was just one day at a
time. You look back on those ruts that you go through,
every day is not going to be great, you're going to go
through rough patches where things are going to suck,
but you keep going and you know it's going to turn up

eventually. Just fight through it and try to keep some perspective.

What is your relationship like now with Zack?
I love having adult children. We text daily and Facetime here and there. I still have one living at home, which I love, most of the time! The parenting never ends, so I still do that in a more selective, gentler way now. But now we can be friends, too. To see my big three grown, working hard, making good decisions, treating people with respect and kindness, making their lives happen – it's the biggest thrill and joy to me. It's tough when they're young. You want to impart so many lessons on top of just trying to get through the day-to-day grind as they're growing up. So having them as adults now, it's so nice to just be supportive like a cheerleader or a friend. I know I can talk honestly with my kids about anything, even the tough stuff. And if I do it in a loving, nurturing way, they'll be open to really hearing the conversation instead of tuning me out. But also giving them room to do their own thing, make their own decisions and mistakes. I wasn't very good at that initially, but I'm trying to be better there.

How did you respond to situations that made you feel overwhelmed?
I feel overwhelmed all the time! Parenting is the hardest, most important job there is. The pressure to make sure you give your kids everything that is good and right, to make sure they turn into responsible, kind, independent, awesome people is immense. Giving my energy to my five kids on a daily basis, supporting them and doing everything I can to encourage their physical, mental, emotional growth is a lot. Then you add on a marriage, two jobs, running a house and aging parents. It's a challenge! But like I said, you keep going. There's so much good and joy in my life and family. That makes being in the muck and dealing with the day-to-day grind and feeling overwhelmed sometimes, all worth it. Life is

good.

A reoccurring theme from talking with you is that you were very emphatic on having fun. Where do you think that comes from?

I never saw my mom have fun, particularly after my dad died. She was so busy just trying to hold things together and wore her grief on her sleeve so much that she was always sad. I loved her so much, so it was very hard to see. The holidays would come around, birthdays, graduations, etc. – but we never had family around. I don't recall too many joyous celebrations. The situation when my big three were little was very stressful – having no money and their dad was always in and out of our lives. I just came to the realization that I needed to have fun with these people, and they needed to see the joy in being alive. There's always going to be the muck of course, but every day I was and still am very conscious of my kids seeing me laugh and finding the good in life.

Can you offer any advice to young or soon to be mothers/parents?

One of my rules is to not give advice unless I'm asked, especially about parenting. No one really wants to hear it anyway. If a woman is smart and driven, she's going to be just fine as a mom. You really just have to figure out what works for you and your family. But what I will say is to keep going, keep putting one foot in front of the other, take the risk. If you make the mistake own it and say you're sorry and keep going. Be thankful and have fun. Life is supposed to be fun!

Looking back, what would you say was the greatest gift you gave to your kids?

Well, my kids are the greatest gifts I've ever received. But my gift to them? Parenting is a huge job. Is there really anything more important than the responsibility of raising, shaping, nurturing, empowering a child for 20 years so they can face the world with confidence, grace and courage? There are so many lessons to convey, values and character traits to instill, pitfalls to help them avoid. It's a colossal investment of time and energy to try to do it right. So that's my long-winded way of saying that I suppose that my time is the most important gift I've given my kids.

I've offered that "gift" in different ways through the years and I'm not sure the kids would agree that my time was always such a gift! Mom's "forced family time" is infamous in our house. Eyes often roll when I play that card, but we have created a lot of happy memories due to my insistence. Sometimes it's a hike, backyard wiffle-ball game, s'mores by the fire pit, movie night, midnight sledding in the backyard, Sunday family dinners, or a picnic at the lake. I know these experiences and interactions have enormously shaped their hearts and minds, and mine as well.

Though I think the real time is put in during the daily grind of life, those smaller, more mundane, sometimes considerably less fun moments – these are probably the most important times. The times where it's really vital to be present, have the conversations (the frivolous ones and the hard ones), engage, play, listen, guide, nudge, advise, pull, push and just know when to shut up sometimes (not one of my strengths).

So, I guess my hope is that in the course of the time I put in, my children learned some of those lessons, developed some of those values, figured out how to avoid making a few mistakes and that they felt loved, empowered and supported along the way. Hopefully, in all that time, the kids saw me demonstrate kindness, perseverance, hard work, compassion and empathy. Hopefully, they saw me do the best I could to keep going strong in the face of adversity, say please and thank you, volunteer at school, juggle a full-time job and motherhood and treat people with respect. And certainly, there were plenty of times they saw me make mistakes and hopefully learned that you say you're sorry when you screw up and move forward trying to be better. And now, when I see my children model these behaviors in their own lives, there isn't much else that makes me prouder. I think it has a little something to do with all that time we spent together.

If you could tell the world one thing, what would it be?
There are many things you can't control in life, but you can control your effort and your attitude.

"Love unconditionally and build up your children's self-esteem, always looking for the good and ignoring the bad. Do not live through your children's success – be a role model of hard work and good values. Have a lot of fun with them and maybe be a bit unorthodox crazy!"

Julia Mancuso
IG: @JuliaMancuso
TW: @JuliaMancuso

Andrea Mancuso Webber is the

mother of Julia Mancuso, a former professional alpine skier widely recognized as one of the most decorated female athletes in U.S. Olympic history. One of five daughters, Andrea grew up in a small town outside of Marin County, CA, where she attended public school while participating in soccer, dance, skiing and gymnastics. She eventually focused on high-level gymnastics throughout high school which earned her a varsity spot at the University of Nevada. It was there in Reno where Andrea met her now ex-husband, Ciro Mancuso. After school, the two moved to Squaw Valley, a world-renowned mountain resort in California just north of Lake Tahoe and had three daughters together.

When Julia was 5 years-old, Andrea became a single mother and continued to raise her children in Squaw Valley where all three were heavily involved in ski racing from an early age. Julia's passion-driven love for the slopes was evident. And so was her superior talent.

By the age of 13, Julia was already competing

internationally in Canada and Italy. Despite the challenges of being a single mother, Andrea remained right by Julia's side at every step along the way as she carved her path to skiing stardom. Julia made her skiing World Cup debut at 15, finished high school at 16 and immediately started her journey with the U.S. National Ski Team, spending the winters racing in Europe and summers training in Chile. She made her first Olympic appearance a year later at the 2002 Winter Olympics and earned her first gold medal at the 2006 Olympic games in Vancouver, Canada. Fast forward to today and Julia is best known for her storied 18-year career after hanging up her skis as one of the most successful big event American female athletes in Olympic history with a total of nine medals to her name. Julia's four medals won at the Sochi, Vancouver and Torino winter Olympic games are the most ever for an American female skier. She retired in January 2018 and now lives in Hawaii with her husband and 2-year-old son.

In this chapter, Andrea talks about the challenges of raising three daughters on the slopes of Squaw Valley as a single mother, where she learned firsthand the importance of unconditional love.

Did your mother inspire you in any way? What kind of values did you take from her and instill in your own life as a mother?

My mother is a very energetic, fun-loving woman. I was one of five daughters so there was always a lot going on in our household. My mother let us enroll in anything we wanted after school and I loved all sports, so I was very active doing soccer, dance, skiing and then gymnastics. We had a lot of fun with my mom. She went to Stanford University and education was very important in our home. We were always told we could do or be anything we wanted to be.

When was the earliest indication that you thought Julia might have extraordinary talent?

Julia started competing in ski racing when she was 7 or 8. She was on the Squaw Valley Ski team, spending many days chasing after her older sister, April, and her friends. By the time she was 10, she was at the top of her classes winning or placing in the top three. By the time she was 13, she was often beating the boys, and also at that age, she was part of the U.S. regional teams and was chosen to compete internationally in Italy and Canada. At those competitions, she was also in the top finishers against skiers from Europe.

Did you have to do anything to foster Julia's talent or was she always self-motivated?

Julia was very focused at a young age. She loved skiing, she loved the mountains and the freedom being on the mountains gave her. We were lucky to live in a community that supported ski racing and as early as third grade, she could leave school at noon and go to the mountain to train. She skied six days a week. She always wanted to be better than her older sister, who was also on the ski team. I remember one time we were in Mammoth, CA, she had just won a big race for her age and I was at the awards ceremony with all the other parents. When her name was called as the winner, no one could find her. She was outside on the ski hill playing around, practicing skiing on one ski.

During summers, she would go up to Mt. Hood for ski camp. One summer, before she made the U.S. Ski Team, she was at camp and wanted to stay another week, but I couldn't really afford it. She had some money in a college account and she wanted permission to access it, which I gave her. She was relentless.

Everyone faces self-doubt at one point or another, did Julia ever want to give up on things, and if so, how did you go about handling that?

Going into the 2010 Olympics in Vancouver, Julia was very discouraged. Her racing in the World Cup season that year was not very good. She was having a hard time with equipment and coaching. I remember she had called her sports agent and asked him what skiing would be like after her career at the World Cup.

Then as history shows, she won two silver medals at the Vancouver Olympics. She was in tears at the bottom of the course, so emotional to have won after doing so poorly all year. Julia is the best at the biggest events. She always rises to the top on the biggest stage.

Any stories of adversity that Julia faced?

Julia's father went to prison when she was in kindergarten and was gone for nine years. That event led to my divorce from her father and also to hardness inside her. She was very hurt and sad. I feel like it was a driving factor in her wanting to escape into the mountains and her drive to be a fierce competitor.

How did you handle Julia's accomplishments and keep things in perspective?

This is a great question, because she was so good at an early age that there was a point in her childhood when she became a bit arrogant. At that time, she had a wonderful coach that grounded her and explained to her how an arrogant attitude will not make you well liked. We also had many conversations about how humility is a good attribute to have.

As a mother, what were you good at saying no to?

Because I was a single mother of three girls, I had set good boundaries with my children. I had to keep our lives running smoothly. I am also a big advocate of tough love and natural consequences. An example of natural consequences would be forgetting their lunch for school or forgetting to put on a jacket before going somewhere in the cold. That's something I'd let them deal with on their own to learn from.

What would you say were important qualities to possess to be the mother you were?
I am very task oriented but also love to have fun. Our lives were very structured and well planned. I made sure the girls were always busy with some sort of sport or schoolwork. I was always planning fun places to go.

What were things you think you may have handled differently?
I think I would have been more involved in her career, although there is a lot of push back from the governing body of the U.S. Ski team to allow parental involvement. I feel like her career would have gone better if she would have had an advocate to help her with some of her decisions about coaching and equipment. You see this a lot nowadays with very successful young skiers like Mikaela Shiffrin.

What is your relationship like now with Julia?
I am really close to all my daughters. We love and respect each other unconditionally. We talk several times a week and I would love to see her and her family more except she lives in Fiji and Hawaii. I don't get to see her enough, especially during this pandemic, it has been incredibly hard. Our relationship has changed with her retirement and now having a child that we both can love together.

If you could name one characteristic you believe Julia inherited from you, what would that be?
Her unbounded love of adventure and life.

What is something you think the media or public has wrong about Julia?

There were rumors going around that Julia's success came naturally and she didn't have to work or train hard. This is untrue. When other skiers were in the locker room or hanging out, Julia would be the last one on the hill. She loved skiing, being in the snow and on the mountain. She was very disciplined and motivated to be the best in the world.

Did any times of adversity set you up for later success?

My marriage with Julia's father ending was a moment of adversity. It set me up later for success as a mother because I was able to focus all my attention on the girls and their interests.

I loved being the girl's mother, planning, organizing and directing their lives. I do remember one time I was scheduled to attend an event at Julia's school and missed it because of work. She was so incredibly disappointed that I didn't show up. I made a promise to myself to never disappoint any of my daughters that way again.

How did you respond to situations that made you feel overwhelmed?

I have a wonderful meditation practice I do every morning. I will do a reading from a spiritual book and then I will put on some meditation music. I will then meditate on whatever the reading was about. It's a morning routine that takes about 30-40 minutes and I've been doing it for years.

Can you offer any advice to young or soon to be mothers/parents?

Love unconditionally and build up your children's self-esteem, always looking for the good and ignoring the bad. Do not live through your children's success – be a role model of hard work and good values. Have a lot of fun with them and maybe be a bit unorthodox crazy!

Looking back, what would you say was the greatest gift you gave to your kids?
The greatest gift I gave my children when they were growing up is teaching them the principles of optimism, intention, expectation, gratitude, humility and forgiveness.

If you could tell everyone in the world one thing, what would it be?
The one thing I would tell everyone is, "love is always the answer."

"One of the lessons I've learned is not to give advice, so the best thing I can offer is the life-changing, one-size-fits-all set of core principles found in '*The Four Agreements*':

1. Be impeccable with your word.
2. Don't take anything personally.
3. Don't make assumptions.
4. Always do your best.

I've found that following this simple, yet challenging guidance leads to positive outcomes no matter what it relates to — and that's especially wonderful when it comes to being with children."

Elena Hight
IG: @ElenaHight

Myra Hight is the mother of Elena Hight, a world-renowned pro snowboarder and two-time Olympian widely known as one of the most influential female pioneers of the sport. Myra's story began in Southern California. The daughter of two local college professors, she grew up in a middle-class family in the southeastern suburbs of Los Angeles, but left home at 16 and started supporting herself through multiple part-time restaurant and house-cleaning jobs. Eventually, she met her husband, Mike, moved to Hawaii and had Elena in

1989 – her first and their combined third of four children.

Myra and Mike moved the family to Lake Tahoe when Elena was 6 years-old and it was around that time that her father, a renowned surfer in his own right, introduced her to snowboarding. From there, the rest was history. Elena fell in love with the slopes as snowboarding quickly turned into an enduring passion. By the time she was 13, Elena went pro and then became the first female to land a frontside 900 in competition (we highly recommend you check it out on YouTube). At the 2006 Winter Olympics, she was the youngest member of the U.S. Team as a 16-year-old, and in 2013, she landed the sport's first-ever double backside alley-oop rodeo in a halfpipe contest. The seven-time X Game medalist's decorated snowboarding resume includes two Olympic appearances (2006 and 2010) and a Burton U.S. Open championship (2012) among numerous other accomplishments. Outside of snowboarding, she is an advocate for health, wellness and environmental protection.

After nearly two decades of pro snowboarding success, Elena credits her mother's intentions to be among her most vital inspirations in life. This chapter delves into those intentions from Myra's perspective, showcasing the value of encouraging children to "be better than their parents."

Did your mother inspire you in any way? What kind of values did you take from her and instill in your own life as a mother?
My relationship with my mother was mostly good. I say that because we are both stubborn and fought because of that. She passed on many treasured qualities. She was dedicated to her work, thoughtful, an excellent hostess and she encouraged me to excel and to pursue my ambitions no matter what.

What kind of dreams and goals did you have when you were a kid? How much did they influence where you are today?

My grandmother taught me to sew when I was very young and I used to make doll clothes. I loved playing with fabrics and molding them into shape which led me to pursue a career in fashion. After 12 years in the business, I was burnt out and moved on to other things. The influence this trajectory had was an undying thirst for entrepreneurship.

When was the earliest indication that you thought Elena might have extraordinary talent?

Well, she did start walking at 7 months, she was tandem surfing with her dad at 9 months and at 2 years old she was trotting along fence tops (think balance beam) but that wasn't it. It was during a tumbling class at age 4; the instructor said to me that Elena had natural talent and that this should be nurtured. I knew she was coordinated but I just saw a child doing somersaults! So, deferring to the expert I figured okay, we can do that, and that's why we introduced her to different things, to let her develop what pleased her.

Did you have to do anything to foster Elena's talent or was she always self-motivated?

Elena has always been self-motivated. It was her always asking for another dance class or sport to try. I believe the biggest thing was her being asked to be on the Tahoe gymnastics team at age 7. She thrived on it. She trained four nights a week, three hours a night, doing a workout that not many people could handle, child or adult. This made her very strong, physically and mentally. Elena has a will power that I truly envy.

How did you handle Elena's accomplishments and keep things in perspective?

I did my best to teach her humility and good

sportsmanship. Never gloat, it's ugly. She also hated losing and so when she did, we'd go into the bathroom where she'd kick the trashcan 'really good' and walk out without a frown. Then she'd go hang and laugh with friends, probably with who had just won. I also did my best not to push her too hard; after all, this was her thing, and I was just there to support her. One example, at the end of the snow season she'd always be burnt out and want to quit, and I'd say, "well let's just finish these last couple weeks and if you don't want to come back next year that's A-OK." Every winter she was excited to get back on the mountain to train and compete.

Was Elena interested in dating in high school? How did you handle her romantic relationships if the person she was attracted to did not seem like a good fit based on your motherly instincts?
She was interested in dating/boys, but she put her sports first, boys second. I liked her choices on the surface but knowing that the surface doesn't always count, my goal was to teach her to recognize when intentions were not honorable. For instance, my key words of wisdom were, "If a boy is saying 'I love you' while their hands are wandering, don't believe the words and don't be afraid to say stop." My goal was to help her develop her own radar and healthy boundaries.

Any stories of adversity that Elena faced?
Many, this is life after all. She was 6 when her dad and I split up – that's always a bugger. Looking back, I would say most of her adversity came by the way of injuries (concussions mostly). I believe they've had a long-term effect on her.

What would you say were important qualities to possess to be the mother you were?
Perseverance, strength and faith in a loving universe. A conviction to encourage my children to discover and be

who they are by giving them the space and freedom to explore life.

What were things you think you may have handled differently?

Ah, the brutal self-reflection. I wish I could have added patience to the important qualities question. I had a hot temper that has really only quelled in the past decade. I wish I was as good a teacher as my dad. Mom was a tad dictatorial (hence the fights) and when I was doing things with the kids, I modeled giving directions rather than guiding the learning process. We often model that which needs healing. Those are my two biggest regrets. I also wish I would have played with my kids more. I did my best, but it never felt like enough.

If you could name one characteristic you believe Elena inherited from you, what would that be?

Stubbornness, which becomes perseverance when used positively.

Can you offer any advice to young or soon to be mothers/parents?

One of the lessons I've learned is not to give advice, so the best thing I can offer are the life-changing, "one-size-fits-all" set of core principles found in *The Four Agreements*:

1. Be impeccable with your word.
2. Don't take anything personally.
3. Don't make assumptions.
4. Always do your best.

I've found that following this simple, but not easy guidance, leads to positive outcomes no matter what it relates to and that it's especially wonderful when it comes to being with children.

Another wisdom I've espoused to my kids is to be better than their parents. If we all follow this then evolution will take care of the rest.

Looking back, what would you say was the greatest gift you gave to your kids?
The freedom and support to chase their dreams.

If you could tell everyone in the world one thing, what would it be?
Think, what is your true, innate desire? Truth, beauty, goodness, love? You need only to look within and live what you find the best you can. The rest will take care of itself.

Any closing thoughts?
Elena loved snowboarding from her first time out. She joined a snowboard team at 7 and because they went to weekend USASA competitions, she went too, competing in the (very cute) Ruggie division. Since she has a competitive nature, she loved the USASA events for the competition and the sheer fun of it. She always made it to Nationals where she was at the top of her class, winning more events than anyone across the board for years except for Shaun White, who she was nearly equal to. Okay, and who she later bested with her perfect, double-backside-alley-oop-rodeo. (Yes, moms are allowed to say that when it comes to Shaun!)

When we moved to Tahoe, her dad met Trevor Brown, an exceptional snowboard coach that headed the local mountain team, which her dad then signed her up for. Trevor was her teacher, mentor and protector for those crucial early years. I say protector because at a young age, her exceptional talent drew not-so-nice treatment from competitors, which he helped her through. So, I just want to express my gratitude and honor to Trevor and my heartfelt thanks to two other amazing coaches who were 100% there for her early on, Kyle P. Franklin and Ed McClain.

"Always focus on your child's well-being and pay no attention to other people's expectations; be respectful of the boundaries that as parents we should never trespass; respect your child's time and preferences; and allow them to be happy and enjoy what they are doing."

Maria Fassi
IG: @MariaFassi1

Fabiana Alvarez is the mother of Maria

Fassi, a professional golfer rising on the LPGA Tour. Fabiana is a native of Argentina. She grew up with her parents and two older brothers in a small, rural city within the Argentine province of Buenos Aires. Each year, the family would spend half the year living in the countryside and the other half of the year in the city. She held numerous jobs as an adolescent, ranging from babysitting and retail to teaching private swimming lessons in college.

Fabiana met her husband, Andres, and moved to Mexico to start her family. She had four children – Sebastian, Juan Pablo, Maria and Franco. All of them were raised in Pachuca, a city located in Hidalgo, Mexico. Their neighborhood resided on a golf course, which is where Maria was first introduced to the sport at 6 years old. For 12 years, Fabiana worked as a Physical Education teacher at the school her children attended but took a step back to focus on motherhood after her fourth child was born.

Maria was Fabiana's third child and only daughter.

She fell in love with golf at a young age. Her mom can remember the early mornings she'd spend out on the golf course determined to learn every intricacy of the game. After developing into a rising star throughout high school, highlighted by a first-place finish in the 2015 Mexican Amateur Tournament, Maria signed with the University of Arkansas in November 2015 to compete collegiately. She dominated the NCAA scene, ending her collegiate career as a two-time SEC Women's Golf Player of the Year, the SEC's 2019 Women's Athlete of the Year and the NCAA's 2019 Division I individual champion. Maria then made her professional debut at the 2019 U.S. Women's Open, where she earned a T12 finish. She finished the year with appearances in 11 events.

This chapter provides an inside look into Maria's success through her mother's eyes, highlighting the importance of encouraging children to chase their dreams no matter how difficult they are.

Did your mother inspire you in any way? What kind of values did you take from her and instill in your own life as a mother?
We had a good relationship. She would always support me in all my projects and was, without a doubt, my biggest supporter when I had my children. She was always there for us.

My mother introduced me to the world of sports and gave me the values that make me the person I am today. With time, I was able to realize the benefits behind the practice of sports. I, in turn, transmitted this to my children. I think this has made a big difference in their overall education. There are many values in sports that contribute to developing a well-rounded individual. Some of these include the value of hard work, perseverance, fair play, teamwork and dedication.

What kind of dreams and goals did you have when you were a kid? How much did they influence where you are today?

As a child, I always dreamed of dedicating my life to teaching and having a family. What I dreamt as a child no doubt marked my path throughout my life.

When was the earliest indication that you thought Maria might have extraordinary talent?

Ever since Maria started to play golf at age 6, people would approach me at tournaments to tell me how natural her swing looked. I never thought her swing was anything out of the ordinary. It is worth mentioning that I knew nothing about golf then. I actually thought their comments were more related to the fact that they liked her because she was very easy going and always in good spirits and this was a way to praise her.

As she grew up and developed her different strokes, we noticed that her drive was particularly strong so when Maria was 16, we went to San Diego, to TaylorMade, to test her swing. Then I understood what people were referring to. It was very moving to hear what people were saying about her and about her natural skill and the future they saw for her during that visit. I realized that what people had been telling me throughout the years was actually true. Since we have dedicated our lives to sports, we have always reminded her that her game was the fruit of hard work and not necessarily natural skill. We always reminded her to bring together personal effort and talent.

Did you have to do anything to foster Maria's talent or was she always self-motivated?

Maria fell in love with golf at a very young age and from the beginning, she was very focused and determined to learn the sport and do her best. We were able to support her fully from the outset. It wasn't necessary to motivate her. She would set her alarm clock to wake up early to play and practice every day. When we went on holidays, her golf bag was the first thing she packed.

From a very young age, we imprinted in her a sense of responsibility and commitment. If she was going to do it, she was going to do it to the best of her ability. The most important thing of all was that she played golf because she liked it; and if it ever came to a point that she didn't want to play anymore, she didn't have to and she knew that. As she grew older and got more serious about it, we realized we needed to incorporate a multidisciplinary working team for her to develop in an integral way. The team included a coach, a caddie, a physical trainer, a physical therapist and a sport psychologist. From there on, every decision was well thought through so that she would feel at ease while doing what she loved. She always participated in the planning of all activities and in the decisions made.

How did you handle Maria's accomplishments and keep things in perspective?

Maria exploded as a player in her adolescence. As a child, she was one more of the pack and every so often would have a win. When it happened, we would take it very naturally and didn't give it more importance than what it really had. We always made sure she was grounded in reality. We were new to the world of golf and understood very little of it. In hindsight, I think this helped us keep her successes in perspective. We have educated her with a sense of humility, always bearing in mind that the most important thing of all is to be a good person.

Any stories of adversity that Maria faced?

When Maria went back to college to start her sophomore year, she went through an existential crisis to the point that she seriously considered not playing golf anymore. She was depressed, missed her home and her family and couldn't find any motivation to get up in the morning. Luckily, her golf coach realized what was happening and gave her the support she needed to get through this very challenging time. My husband and I also realized early what was happening, so I started to travel to Fayetteville, AR once a month. I would rent a house for a week and her coach would allow Maria to stay with me. Those were very difficult times, but with everyone's support she came through. We often say, "What doesn't kill you makes you stronger." This was the case. She came out of this crisis stronger and with more clarity about many things in her life as well as with a strong determination with regards to what she wanted to do with her future.

Maria has adopted a phrase that pretty much sums up her attitude towards failure: "I never fail, I LEARN." I believe there lies the key to success, to learn from our mistakes and strive to be better.

If you were heavily involved, how did you make time for yourself?

Since Maria started playing golf, this became a very special activity we both were very happy and excited to share. It strengthened our mother-daughter bond greatly. We both enjoyed it and continue to enjoy it to this day. Luckily Maria's dad and older brothers supported our activities and helped by taking care of the younger member of the family. I would find time for myself during our trips with Maria, since they gave me time away from taking care of a large family. I have always enjoyed my role as a mother. When I was at home, I would get equally involved with the boys and be present in the family's daily activities. When there were things I wanted to do with my husband, we would always have a good friend or my mother who would come to the rescue and take care of the kids.

What would you say were important qualities to possess to be the mother you were?

The most important qualities I believe I have had in my journey as a mother are unlimited amounts of love, patience, dedication, knowing when to set limits and constant encouragement.

What were things you think you may have handled differently?

When Maria started to play golf, I didn't have the slightest idea what it entailed. However, I would find myself making comments and giving my opinion regarding this or that stroke Maria had made. I neither played golf nor had the patience to learn it. I think it is a very frustrating sport. Still, without knowing anything, I found myself speaking about it, often out of turn, giving advice or questioning what Maria was doing. I was fortunate to receive the advice of a great golfer who told me, kindly but forcefully, that the golf details Maria had to correct would be corrected with time. But if I didn't stop talking, it would be very difficult for her to do so. She added that the best thing parents can do is accompany their child and provide anything they think their child may need. From that moment on, I accompanied Maria to the golf course, brought with me snacks and water and enjoyed every bit of it. I regret not having done this sooner. It would have been healthier for both of us.

What is your relationship like now with Maria?

As time goes by our relationship is stronger. We continue to enjoy spending time together whenever we can. The difference is that now, I wait for her to invite me to come and spend time with her. Luckily, those invitations come often. With time, I learned to be by her side whenever she needs me and in the manner she needs me. I try to listen to her carefully, provide my advice whenever I can and support her fully when she makes her decisions. Now that she lives in the U.S., I travel to tournaments whenever I can and visit her at her home as often as possible. We stay in contact a lot and we miss each other when we don't see each other for a while.

If you could name one characteristic you believe Maria inherited from you, what would that be?

Maria inherited my perseverance as well as being a people person.

How did you respond to situations that made you feel overwhelmed?

When my children were young, there were times when it was very difficult to keep everything under control. My husband traveled a lot and I was alone with the kids a lot. At that time, I remember looking for all sorts of outdoor activities for the kids. This would allow me to go to the countryside, breathe fresh air and decompress. Soon things were back in place.

Can you offer any advice for young or soon to be mothers/parents?

I would tell her to always focus on her child's well-being and pay no attention to other people's expectations; to be respectful of the boundaries that as parents we should never trespass; to respect her child's time and preferences; and to allow them to be happy and enjoy what they are doing.

Looking back, what would you say was the greatest gift you gave to your kids?

I believe I gave my children a solid basis to stand on and face whatever life may bring them. I gave them all my time, my unwavering support and undivided love. I gave them values I believe are essential and I made them resilient. They are life warriors.

If you could tell everyone in the world one thing, what would it be?

I would tell them to not let anything stand between your children and their dreams. And I would share the family phrase that we adopted several years ago and has illuminated our paths: "Make everything worthwhile.

Make each day count."

Any closing thoughts?
Something I can't emphasize enough and that I would like to share with other mothers, is the importance of encouraging our children to enjoy whatever sport they practice. As parents, we should become their greatest fans. Kids should forget the concept of winners and losers. Sports educate well-rounded people. Time will tell what kind of future their kid may have in sport. Mothers should always feel proud of their children and their accomplishments. Winning or losing a competition doesn't define who their child is. Neither does it define how good of a parent we are.

"Self-belief is one big thing I believe in and discuss with my kids often. As a young mother it is great advice to have self-belief and optimism for a better life and to raise happy children."

Bronte Macaulay
IG: @BronteMacaulay
Lorraine Macaulay
IG: @LorraineMacaulay

Lorraine Macaulay is the mother of

Bronte Macaulay, a 27-year-old Australian second-generation professional surfer following in the footsteps of her father, Dave Macaulay, who was a world-renowned surfer in the 1980s and '90s. Before Lorraine met and later married Dave, she spent her adolescent years in Edinburgh, Scotland in a single-parent household. Her mother worked multiple jobs to provide for Lorraine and her two brothers; however, the family moved to Australia just before Lorraine reached high school in search of more financial stability. She's called it home ever since.

Lorraine had four children with Dave – Ellie, Laura, Bronte and Jack – all raised in Gracetown; a small surfing town in Western Australia's surf-abundant Margaret River region. Bronte was introduced to surfing by her father and older sisters at age 10 and began competing in the sport by the time she was 13. She turned pro in 2017 and made the World Surf League's Women's Championship Tour as a rookie, becoming the first surfer from the state of Western Australia to qualify since 2004. At the time of this writing, Bronte is 13th in the Women's Circuit World Rankings. She remains primed to continue her rise in 2021 and beyond.

Just like her relationship with her own mother, Lorraine remains extremely close with Bronte today. Lorraine's chapter provides an inside look into her life expanding on everything from her mom's influence, to Bronte's progression through the professional surfing waters.

Did your mother inspire you in any way? What kind of values did you take from her and instill in your own life as a mother?
I was and still am so close with my mum. She inspired me with everything I do and was the greatest mentor to me. She made so many sacrifices to give her children a better life. She is such a strong woman.

Any stories of adversity?
Being seen as a kid from a single parent home was tough. My mum worked hard to ensure we had food, shelter, clothing and an amazing birthday and Christmas every single year. My younger brother became quite sick when we were still settling into our new home in Australia and my mum navigated kidney transplants, dialysis, etc, to help my brother. She gave everything to her family and is the most selfless person I know.

When was the earliest indication that you thought Bronte might have extraordinary talent?
Bronte was always very athletic and strong with her choices. Growing up, she did gymnastics and there was an ex-Olympic gymnast who had a gymnastic club 40 minutes from where we lived and she wanted her to join her club so badly. Bronte was not interested.

We were on a road trip, as a family, driving across the country and we stopped so my husband could show the kids how to surf. That's when she was first introduced to the sport. She was a natural and it's been her biggest passion ever since.

Did you have to do anything to foster Bronte's talent or was she always self-motivated?
She was very self-motivated. Bronte has strong values and commitment. She could have done anything she wanted to.

How did you handle Bronte's accomplishments and keep things in perspective?
We kept things in perspective by focusing on values - live and speak your truth, have respect, be humble and follow your dreams. We had a very supportive family and low-key life with zero ego. I encouraged her to use social media wisely and only in a constructive way. Whatever you post is on there forever.

Any stories of adversity that Bronte faced?
Unsportsmanlike behavior was prevalent in a bunch of junior events in our state when Bronte was first competing in the early years. This had an effect on young female surfers at the time. This could have very easily discouraged her and been a reason for her to stop competing in surfing. She was so committed though, and never lost sight of the bigger picture.

What would you say were important qualities to possess to be the mother you were?
Being the best version of myself and supporting my family 100%. I always put family first. It's also important to understand that as mothers, we all make mistakes.

If you could name one characteristic you believe Bronte inherited from you, what would that be?
DETERMINATION. She also lets her actions speak louder than words. I like to think she learned that from me too.

How did you respond to situations that made you feel overwhelmed?
Walk it off, talk it off, bathe and sleep!

Can you offer any advice to young or soon to be mothers/parents?
Do not obsess about feeling guilty. Always try your best and understand that that is good enough. And sleep! You will always feel better after you sleep.

Looking back, what would you say was the greatest gift you gave to your kids?
Unconditional love at all times.

If you could tell everyone in the world one thing, what would it be?
Love and be loved with kindness and empathy every day.

"One failure of losing economically taught me that things come and go, and that the things money can't buy are truly priceless – joy, peace of mind, faith and unconditional love – and you do not understand until you lose them."

Ryan Garcia
IG: @KingRyanG
Lisa Garcia
IG: @KingRyMa2

Lisa Garcia is the mother of Ryan Garcia, a professional boxer widely considered as one of the sport's top lightweight fighters. Lisa grew up in Los Angeles in the 1960s with her parents and her sister and two brothers, Robert, Ronnie and Katherine. Lisa attended the L.A. public school system throughout high school. She was a good student through 10th grade, but school took a backseat due to the divorce of her parents followed by the sudden death of her father. It took Lisa several years to heal from the tragedy, but she persevered through it and attended junior college, transferred to the University of Southern California and graduated with a B.S. in Public Administration and Urban Planning.

Lisa and her husband, Henry, raised their family in San Bernardino County. They had three children together – Ryan, Sean and Kayla – who had six stepsiblings all born before their parents met (four were Henry's, two were Lisa's). As a mother, Lisa worked as a housing manager and a librarian. Her husband taught Ryan and Sean how to box inside a home-gym in the family garage. They were homeschooled as they competed nationally, which led to Ryan's stardom as an amateur boxer.

In his amateur career, Ryan won 15 national championships with a 215-15 record before turning pro at age 17. He signed to Golden Boy Promotions in November 2016 and was named ESPN's Prospect of the Year in 2017. He's undefeated in 21 professional matches, 16 of which were won by knockout. Now 22 years-old, Ryan has over 8.5 million Instagram followers and has become one of the sport's brightest rising stars. In January 2021, he earned the WBC interim lightweight title after defeating Olympic gold medalist Luke Campbell in the seventh round. Following the fight, he was ranked the world's fourth-best active lightweight fighter by ESPN.

It's not common for a young boxer to reach the pinnacle of the sport at such an early age. Lisa shares the formula to Ryan's success in the following chapter and explains how a parental focus on guidance helped him accomplish his dreams, but he's just getting started...

Did your mother inspire you in any way? What kind of values did you take from her and instill in your own life as a mother?
My relationship with my mother was loving. My mom was my nurturer and my rock. However, I was a lot like my father: silly, talkative and very athletic.

My mother is such a self-sacrificing person. She will absolutely give the shirt off her back for her children. My mom instilled in me that tradition and family are important.

What kind of dreams and goals did you have when you were a kid? How much did they influence where you are today?
As I look back at my dreams as a kid, I have been so blessed to have been given the desires of my heart. These desires were given to me at one point of my life or another because I was able to experience most of them. I loved writing and producing. I wrote a play and produced

a documentary. I dreamed of reporting news or hosting a show and I have done that. I dreamed of jet skiing and flying to Europe and I have done that. In my young adult life, I realized I needed higher education and I did that! All my professions, education, life experiences and lessons have set me up and prepared me for the greater things God had in store for me.

When was the earliest indication that you thought Ryan might have extraordinary talent?
There were two moments I knew Ryan was especially talented –

The first was when he was 8 or 9 years old, and his uncle and father took him to spar a young undefeated boxer. Normally children just starting out would spar three one-minute rounds. The other coaches took advantage of the fact that we were not aware of this rule and had Ryan fight three three-minute rounds instead. Ryan sparred all three rounds with an undefeated boxer and was not stopped as the coaches thought he would be. Ryan was exhausted but he did it!

The second moment was when he had his third amateur bout. He had lost his first two amateur fights and had already told us that if he could not win his third fight then boxing was not for him. His dad had promised he would not put him in a bout with a boxer that had more fights than him. The day came and the only challenger was a boxer who had a lot of experience. Ryan declined at first but two of his friends encouraged him to take the fight because they wanted to see him box. Ryan ended up taking the fight despite his fears and ended up winning the bout, the tournament trophy for most outstanding boxer and bout of the night!

Did you have to do anything to foster Ryan's talent or was he always self-motivated?
Henry and I went all out when I gave approval for Henry to start training the boys to box. We both learned the

amateur scene and became boxing officials for USA Boxing. We dedicated our family weekends to attending tournaments and boxing shows to help develop the boys. I would say we helped foster it in the beginning, but the boys had a natural athletic ability and a competitive inheritance both paternal and maternal that made them want to pursue a path in boxing. Ryan and Sean were very disciplined when it came to their schedules. We built a gym in our garage and started homeschooling when they both began competing nationally and stuck to a daily schedule. Their father's motto was, "business before pleasure."

How did you handle Ryan's accomplishments and keep things in perspective?
We would let him know and reassure him that he was still just "Ryan" to us and not the superstar boxer. But we respected his hard work and we all knew he earned the fruits of his labor.

Any stories of adversity that Ryan faced?
When Ryan was 17, he went to stay with his older sister Demi so that he could continue training. His father had to take a trucking job temporarily so legendary trainer Joe Goossen offered to help us and trained Ryan for several months. During this time, Ryan started having anxiety. He has learned ways to cope with it when it arises and he is quite vocal about it. He has overcome many challenges in regard to his anxiety such as feeling depressed and dealing with the extremely high stress that comes with his career. Being honest and open about his anxiety has inspired many other young people to be open about mental health. This is what makes Ryan so fearless when he has to overcome any type of adversity. I am so proud of him.

As a mother, what were you good at saying no to?
Foreseen train wrecks! But now that they are older, they

have learned when you go against that inner still voice or your mama's good advice, you pay the consequences (or find yourself saying but never admitting, "dang my mom was right again!").

What would you say were important qualities to possess to be the mother you were?
Leadership, discipline and unconditional love. These are important qualities for me as a mother because, in my opinion, children need parental leadership; they need to be corrected and they need to know that even through the trials and challenges they will experience in life, the two people placed in their lives to parent them will love them through it unconditionally.

What were things you think you may have handled differently?
I would have been calmer and more patient, but it was tough raising five, sometimes even seven kids and working a full-time job. It was very difficult, but I enjoyed my babies and I enjoy them now (the good, the bad and the ugly) and would not change it for the world because trials and errors are all part of life. Your kids have to know you will love them through it all! I would say I would stop worrying so much and live in the present! Have more faith. This will lead to more peace and with peace, you have more joy!

What is your relationship like now with Ryan?
The things that have changed over the years are that we both established boundaries for each other. That process and transition was not fun! The transition from teenager to adult for Ryan was challenging for both of us. Ryan was my first-born son after having two daughters, so you know he was our Little King from the start, thus naming him Ryan (which means little king).

When Ryan turned pro and his Instagram following began growing rapidly, we, as a family, did not know what hit us when the attention and money started coming in. As his mom, I felt like I was on a ship that had been hit by a hurricane and I was trying to re-group and throw out the negative influences, the people with bad intentions and the wolves in sheep's clothing. Ryan was no different from any other young man trying to assert his independence from his parents. I was terrified knowing he did not have enough life experience (a regular job, rent, girlfriends, core friendships) to discern people with bad intentions. His heart is BIG and he is very generous and trusting. Ryan had sudden fame, money, girls, frenemies and I was overprotective at times. My over-protection of Ryan also came from knowing my son struggles with anxiety. So, Ryan and I honestly had a few rounds with each other during this process of me letting go and letting God takeover. But I finally did it and I trust God and his will and purpose for Ryan's life. We live in separate homes on a three-acre lot, primarily because we all work for Ryan. I am his administrative assistant and his father is second lead on his training team.

If you could name one characteristic you believe Ryan inherited from you, what would that be?
Ryan is creative and likes people to have fun and be joyful. He inherited that from me. I love to see people enjoying themselves at something I planned or organized. We both like to entertain. Ryan is also a champion, whatever that may mean. He has something built inside of him that is not built in a gym.

Did any times of adversity set you up for later success?
All my failures and achievements in life prepared me for success as a mother. I like to think of my failures as lessons. I try to ask myself, "What did you learn?" But the one failure of losing economically taught me that things come and go, and that the things money can't buy are truly priceless – joy, peace of mind, faith and

unconditional love – and you do not understand until you lose them.

How did you respond to situations that made you feel overwhelmed?

I took a nap, honestly. Sometimes it's as simple as that to help you regroup. Something else I do for myself is invite my friends to my house and we chill and make dinner. Other times, my husband and I have brunch at Barona Casino in San Diego and play war or Texas Hold 'Em.

Can you offer any advice to young or soon to be mothers/parents?

Don't rush to get old. Don't rush into anything. Be real with life's choices when it comes to marriage, children and careers. Be ready emotionally, because if you do, you make life a whole lot easier on yourself and your future husband and children.

What I would say to young mothers is try not to control everything. Be protective but learn to let go and let God in. There were times I wished I had really known how to apply the serenity prayer when it came to my kids.

Looking back, what would you say was the greatest gift you gave to your kids?

My greatest gift was showing them the way they should go, because when they become older, they will not depart from it. They will remember the things I taught them about faith, love and forgiveness.

If you could tell everyone in the world one thing, what would it be?

Have faith in God, keep fighting and finish this race strong!

"Listen to your heart, allow your son or daughter to be who they are and enjoy the person they will become. Always be there with support and love. The world is constantly changing, so the importance of YOU knowing who you are will only help your children become who they are destined to be."

Paul Rabil
IG: @PaulRabil
PaulRabil.com
PaulRabilFoundation.org

Jean Anne Rabil is the mother of Paul

Rabil, an American professional lacrosse player, entrepreneur and co-founder of the Premier Lacrosse League. Jean Anne grew up in Winston-Salem, N.C. in a middle-class suburban neighborhood. Her mother maintained the household while her father worked as an electrical engineer, allowing both Jean Anne and her younger brother to enjoy a comfortable upbringing. She began working in high school at age 16 and then attended East Carolina University to pursue a degree in Art Design/Art Education. However, her college experience wasn't always easy. Jean Anne's mother was diagnosed with an aggressive form of cancer while she was at ECU, and after battling the illness for several years, passed away shortly after her daughter's wedding.

Jean Anne and her husband, Allan, raised their three children – Mike, Paul and Becca – in Gaithersburg, MD. For the last 37 years, she has been an art instructor for the Archdiocese of Washington Catholic Schools, working for the same K-8 catholic elementary school that her sons attended. She doubled as their mother and their art teacher and was always involved in orchestrating their extracurricular activities and getting them from one practice to the next.

Paul's first sports of choice were basketball, soccer and swimming, which he excelled in. But in the sixth grade, he decided to give lacrosse a try and eventually fell in love with the game. In high school, he made a 40-minute commute each way to attend DeMatha Catholic and play for the school's nationally recognized lacrosse team. His career took off at DeMatha, and by the time he graduated, he was a two time All-American and the Washington Post's Player of the Year in 2004. He then played collegiately at Johns Hopkins and became one of the NCAA's most decorated lacrosse players ever. Among his long list of accomplishments, Paul led the Blue Jays to two national championships and ended as the all-time leading point scorer in school history.

In 2008, Paul began his professional lacrosse career and quickly became the face of the sport. He was selected No. 1 overall in the Major Lacrosse League draft and No. 2 overall by the San Jose Stealth in the National Lacrosse League draft. Paul won championships in both leagues and also led Team USA to gold medals at the 2010 and 2018 FIL World Championships. Alongside his brother Mike, Paul co-founded the Premier Lacrosse League (PLL) in 2018, which has since become the hub for professional lacrosse with over 200 of the world's best players on seven teams across North America. He has been named a "Top 40 Most Entrepreneurial Athlete" by *Entrepreneur Magazine* and was a 2018 Bloomberg 50 honoree. In addition to the PLL, Paul also founded the Paul Rabil Foundation in 2011, a charitable organization that helps children with learning differences by creating programs and partnerships through sports and scholarships. Jean Anne, Allan and Michael all serve on the organization's executive board with him.

In this chapter, we learn about some of the driving forces behind Paul's success as Jean Anne explains the importance of instilling commitment in children from a young age.

Did your mother inspire you in any way? What kind of values did you take from her and instill in your own life as a mother?

I don't think my mom was as close with us as I am with my children. She was always there ready to listen, and I remember when I was in elementary school, she was there meeting us as we walked in with snacks.

My mother had cancer while I was in college and passed away shortly after I was married. I missed her being there for the moments with my children a lot. I think if she had lived, she would have been a wonderful confidant and an awesome grandmother. It is incredibly sad that my children never got to meet her and to have a connection.

What kind of dreams and goals did you have when you were a kid? How much did they influence where you are today?

My love of art was always there, although it evolved at college. Teaching was never something I thought I would do, but after 37 years, I cannot imagine a more fulfilling career. I often tell people, "I have the best job in the world! Who would not love teaching something they love so much and brings such joy to others!"

When was the earliest indication that you thought Paul might have extraordinary talent?

The first time was in art class. We all think of Paul as an athlete, but he also showed great promise in the arts at a young age. With lacrosse, it was in high school that he excelled.

Did you have to do anything to foster Paul's talent or was he always self-motivated?

Paul was born self-motivated; he has always enjoyed all activities. I remember his fourth grade teacher telling me that when Paul was out with the flu, the entire energy of the class was down. I remember thinking that is so true. He brings not only his own enthusiasm, but he enables all around him to be better at what they do.

We always stressed the importance of committing. Finish what you start. And I always told him to have fun at whatever it is you are doing. Enjoy the moments.

How did you handle Paul's accomplishments and keep things in perspective?

Paul was always well-grounded. He learned early that the word team does not have an I, and it was always important to be a team player. Even with swim teams, as much as that is an individual sport, he would always see the importance of the total team.

My husband and I both emphasized this, as being humble and part of the team was always important. My constant quote would have been to always have fun. It is a sport, but once it stops being fun, it turns into something else.

Any stories of adversity that Paul faced?

I remember the time Paul transferred from public high school to DeMatha Catholic High School. It was quite a transition with a long commute. He did not know anyone and the workload was very intense. This was difficult for Paul when he arrived home late with lots of work and not like his usual excited self. He applied himself, seeing what he wanted even when it was difficult. After several months, he adapted to the new environment, made friends, found a carpool and found his place. I saw him struggle but he didn't give up and then was able to see the fruit of what he had worked so hard for: an excellent education, several lacrosse championships and a pathway to Johns Hopkins University.

What would you say were important qualities to possess to be the mother you were?
Flexibility first, not everything is the way you imagined as a mother. Forgiveness is essential, with yourself and each other, and the ability to live in the moment. Time is fleeting; it goes by so fast.

What were things you think you may have handled differently?
I believe, as I stated above, the ability to live in the moment. Time is a quality in retrospect that I wish I had seen as the most important. That is the advantage of looking back. Hindsight is 20-20. We can see our mistakes and dreams, but regrettably, there is not a do-over button.

Also, to not stress over the little things. It's very important to have open conversations with your children. If this is garnered when they are younger, it will continue in the more challenging teenage years. With sports or any extracurricular activity, always make sure they are enjoying it. Too many parents push for the elusive college scholarship. It should be something the child wants.

What is your relationship like now with Paul?
I believe Paul and I are very close. I have always said that adult children are the BEST! Paul and I have grown as his life has changed. We work together with the Paul Rabil Foundation. This was a challenge at the beginning, working with your son, but we managed and grew with the job now going on 10 years. We Facetime and talk every week now that he is on the West Coast. Thankfully, we have the technology to support this. It has grown into not only a parent/child relationship, but into a very meaningful friendship.

If you could name one characteristic you believe Paul inherited from you, what would that be?

His creativity, which he has channeled in many ways. He uses that creativity to think out of the box and look at life's challenges in a different perspective. I think he also inherited my stubbornness, which I believe he has channeled effectively into a "never give up on your dreams and keep going" mindset.

Can you offer any advice to young or soon to be mothers/parents?

Most of all, listen to your heart, allow your son or daughter to be who they are and enjoy the person they will become. Always be there with support and love. The world is constantly changing, so the importance of YOU knowing who you are will only help your children become who they are destined to be. Lastly, try not to stress, though easier said than done.

The most important thing I have realized is life is short. In the blink of an eye, your child becomes an adult. Please enjoy the time and remember it only gets better :)

Could you try to summarize Paul's journey?

Paul began his lacrosse career in sixth grade after deciding he wanted to take a break from soccer. He played with the neighborhood team and with his brother. Lacrosse was a great experience, as well as a challenging one. He was a star in soccer and then had to rebuild this in lacrosse. At times, it was overwhelming for him, but he persevered and started to love the game.

After transferring to DeMatha, his career quickly took off and he was soon on to JHU. Many times I have been asked if we knew he would have the college and professional career he now enjoys. My response is – never. We were always there to support his dreams, but we never drove them. Paul was ALWAYS very self-motivated. We often say we are along for the ride.

After college, Paul was the first-round pick for the

Boston Cannons and it hasn't stopped since. Indoor Lacrosse, three USA teams and now the PLL. This is the stuff that dreams are made of. Paul, I believe, is unique in that he is responsible for all that has happened in his career. Extreme hard work, a can-do attitude and lots of creativity to go along with this recipe for success.

Looking back, what would you say was the greatest gift you gave to your kids?
My greatest gift would be the ability to listen and not judge. This I have learned over the years and was not something that I was able to do when the kids were younger. As I moved in my journey as a mother, I changed. The value was in understanding that the world around us changes rapidly and we can also change but there is the constant of being a mom, that does not change.

If you could tell everyone in the world one thing, what would it be?
Make time for yourself. When you are in a good place physically, mentally and spiritually, you will be better able to have an impact on those around you. Time moves so quickly, enjoy each moment with your children.

"Put them in a place to make the most of their God-given talent and let their personality and talent dictate a path by setting priorities for getting the most out of your current situation."

Rose Lavelle
IG: @LavelleRose

Janet Lavelle is the mother of Rose Lavelle, an

elite international soccer player and a key member of the 2019 World Cup-winning United States Women's National Team. Janet is from Cincinnati, OH, where she was one of 11 siblings within a tight-knit family. She attended Catholic school at Mount Notre Dame High School, the same school her three daughters attended, and worked a series of different jobs after graduating. Her first, though, was at her father's deli, a staple of her neighborhood where all 11 siblings worked at one point in time.

Janet graduated college at 27 and became a second-grade teacher before meeting her husband, Marty, whom she has been married to for 31 years. They have four kids together – John, Nora, Rose and Mary – who are seven years apart. In Rose's youth soccer days, Janet was a travel mom. She took her to tournaments every weekend and was the team's manager until the U14 level. The two remain super close today.

As a four-year varsity soccer player at Mount Notre Dame, Rose was named Cincinnati's Player of the Year by *The Cincinnati Enquirer* her senior season. The same year, she scored 15 goals and finished her high school career as the program's leading scorer with 57 goals. Rose was named NSCAA All-Region as a junior and senior and received first-team All-State honors both years. She played college soccer at the University of Wisconsin, where she made 19 appearances as a freshman en-route to receiving the Big Ten Conference Freshman of the Year award. She went on to earn consecutive Big Ten Midfielder of the Year honors in 2015 and 2016 and was also named a first-team All-American, representing Wisconsin's first All-America selection since 1991. After starting six games for the U.S. National Team in the 2019 World Cup, Rose inked a professional contract with Manchester City of the English Football Association's Women's Super League ahead of the 2020-21 season. In February 2021, Rose scored the game-winning goal in the 79th minute of Team USA's 1-0 victory over Canada in the SheBelieves Cup.

In the ensuing pages, Janet walks us through her journey into motherhood and based on her experiences with Rose, provides invaluable advice for all the "soccer moms" who are raising competitive athletes.

Did your mother inspire you in any way? What kind of values did you take from her and instill in your own life as a mother?
I was close to my mom growing up; not "best friends/confidante" close, I had plenty of sisters for that, but we were close and I always admired her. She is smart and a bit of a rebel, but the most loving and accepting person I know. By college, my sisters and I would go on weekend trips with my mom to the mountains to hang out and shop at outlet malls or meet for drinks.

My mom is/was an avid reader. She reads books nonstop. There could be chaos all around the house and she could tune it out and read her book. She is the person I admire most. As I always tell my own kids, "Grandma is one of the smartest people you'll ever know." And she is! She still can kick everybody's butt in word games, math challenges, etc.

What kind of dreams and goals did you have when you were a kid? How much did they influence where you are today?

As a child of the '60s and '70s, my goals were pretty common for a female: go to college and have a family. Today, I would say I am still proud of my college degree where I got good grades. As my husband always says, "No matter what, a college degree, they can't take that away from you." All of my siblings went to college for a little bit but only four of us earned a four-year degree.

When was the earliest indication that you thought Rose might have extraordinary talent?

By the time Rose could roll around, she was ahead physically compared to her two older siblings at the same age. But I would say by the time she was 2, you could tell she was doing things that most 2-year-olds don't have the gross motor skills or balance to do. She was a climber. It seemed I couldn't find anything she couldn't climb on. She was in a diaper and while I still needed to push her 5-year-old sister on the swing, Rose could pump and swing like her older brother. She just needed one nudge to get going (since her feet didn't touch the ground and she couldn't start by standing). Her pre-school teachers, without prompting, would share in amazement some advanced "athletic" feat she mastered that they had never seen a student her age complete without effort. Marty and I would refer to her enduringly as 'monkey girl'. We knew she was above the curve at a very young age.

Did you have to do anything to foster Rose's talent or was she always self-motivated?

Rose was definitely self-motivated, naturally competitive, liked to win and be the best. "Who's your favorite?" Every time one of my kids would ask me that my answer was, "You, but don't tell the others. I don't want them to feel bad." No one asked me that more than Rose. And a funny story regarding her competitiveness even at a young age – when she was 5, we took all the kids to Disney. Mary was 3 and weighed a few pounds less than 5-year-old Rose. Although we rented a double stroller for them to hop in and out of during the day, we often had to hoist them up to see parades. I was charged with Rose because there was no effort to pick her up and carry her. She climbed on up and clung to you like a monkey. Mary, on the other hand, was dead weight like a sack of potatoes. One night we were rushing out of the park to get back to our hotel in time to watch the fireworks. We returned the stroller and rushed through the crowd, Rose clinging to me, Mary being held by Marty and the other two sticking close behind. The trek to get out and weave through the crowd was 15 minutes or so. Rose clung to me the entire time effortlessly… so I thought. Years later, as a teenager, she still recalled that dash to the exit. She told me by the time I set her down, her thighs were burning with pain. I asked her why she wouldn't just tell me. Her response, "because I had a reputation to uphold, I wasn't going to give in." It kind of defines her determination and self-motivation when she focuses on something she wants.

How did you handle Rose's accomplishments and keep things in perspective?

I think trying to keep things in perspective, we had a general rule when you were part of a team (having two other daughters who played varsity sports who were low on the depth chart), you had to lead by example whether you were on the top of the totem pole or the bottom. If you're on the top, have a good attitude, follow all the rules and do all the extra work the people on the bottom have to do. If you're on the bottom, have a good attitude, work your butt off and show them why you should move up the totem pole.

During college recruiting, I was very adamant that no

matter what a coach promised Rose about playing time or 'building a team around you', that Rose still had to hold up her end of the bargain. Don't take anything for granted. Be prepared to work for your spot.

Was Rose interested in dating in high school? How did you handle her romantic relationships if the person she was attracted to did not seem like a good fit based on your motherly instincts?
Rose didn't date much beyond a few school dances freshman and sophomore year. Her social circle was her sisters, her cousin and her soccer teammates. She might go to a country music concert in the summer, but mostly she was content to stay at home with her sister and cousin. Her schedule often kept her up late doing homework and weekends committed to soccer. She stayed out of trouble besides the innocuous detention for laughing at mass or eating skittles in class.

What would you say were important qualities to possess to be the mother you were?
An important quality as a mother is to go with the flow! Know that you're human and won't always get it right. Know that your kids are human and that they ARE kids. Their feelings are valid no matter what or who they are. I always told them, "You can't help how you feel, but you can help how you behave."

As a mother, what were you good at saying no to?
I was good at saying no to a lot of things (ask the kids), but it was always hardest to say no to Rose. Ask anyone in our family or anyone who knows her. The squeaky wheel gets the oil. Since she was very young, she had a way of talking you into something you resisted, whether it was something she wanted, or some goofy gag or playful dance. Or even getting you to just do things she didn't feel like doing (going to the store alone, making a sandwich, ironing her shirt). It's kind of a gift, go figure.

What were things you think you may have handled differently?

This is going to sound lame, like I didn't make mistakes, but I wouldn't do anything differently. Decisions that were questioned and mulled over or seemed like it was wrong at the time, turned out to be the "right" wrong decision as the journey played out. Related to Rose's sports, I was never a team searcher looking for greener pastures. If she made a switch, it came from her. For one thing, you can't make Rose do anything she doesn't want to do. She is intuitive enough to know when you're trying to manipulate her into something. This was a decision I often questioned - whether I should push her to something more competitive than where she was or a team/club with a big reputation. But I consciously focused on her enjoying what she was doing. I knew that she had to love it for herself and not for me. As long as she was loving it, she wanted to be there and was constantly learning. As long as she was being challenged, she would move when she was ready. After eighth grade, she did just that by taking a separate path from the girls she had played with since fifth grade.

What is your relationship like now with Rose?

Probably the best person to ask about our relationship right now is her. In many ways it's very similar in that if I'm available, I'm making a meal, happy to have her company, helping her do something like set up her house. I will say, though, she doesn't ask for so much now unless her schedule doesn't allow her to do something, like waiting for a delivery. We do talk and text daily. Another thing about Rose, you can't bombard her with questions when you're seeking information. She has to offer information on her own time. Whether it's good news or bad. She is much more open to sharing things more quickly than when she was younger. Still turned off by a bombardment of questions, but willing to share when asked.

How did you respond to situations that made you feel overwhelmed?
Whenever I feel overwhelmed or lose focus, I try to focus on my own controllables, not what others can do for me. What can I change, what can I do?

Can you offer any advice to young or soon to be mothers/parents?
Main advice: encourage but don't push. It has to come from within them. They have to set goals for themselves, not goals to please you. Let them know you love them even in the midst of failure and success. If you believe they are an elite athlete, don't project too much into the future (you never really know how things will unfold).

Put them in a place to make the most of their God-given talent and let their personality and talent dictate a path by setting priorities for getting the most out of your current situation. Are they having fun (keeping her interested, youth sports shouldn't be their job), are they being challenged (keeping her growing/developing)? If the first two are not being met, re-evaluate. Enjoy the ride, it's their journey. Try to maintain some balance of family and other activities.

Looking back, what would you say was the greatest gift you gave to your kids?
The gift of each other.

If you could tell everyone in the world one thing, what would it be?
Don't judge. Everyone has a story.

Any closing thoughts?
I think the most important part of her journey has been the adversity. She never quit when she failed. I think something that has really served her well was not making teams. As an 8-year-old trying out for the local select team, they had an A and B team, but she made neither.

She wasn't deterred and didn't take a confidence hit; she just found a different team. And that team, because of that trainer/coach in her life, was the springboard to where she is now.

She didn't make the regional ODP (Olympic Development Program) team when she was first age eligible. Early fall registration, she always wanted to sign up for it. ODP sessions were in late fall when the weather was always miserable. It was cold and wet and you weren't with your friends. She would say, "I didn't want to do this; I don't want to go. You made me sign up." That attitude was also related to the fact that her club teammates, none of whom made it beyond districts, would roll their eyes and say "politics" or "waste of time" when she would join ODP during the fall. But if I paid the check, she made the commitment and wasn't allowed out of the commitment until it was complete. By the time regional camp rolled around in the spring, she was ready to go, she had new friends. She went to camp and it was fun. And she wanted to sign up again, of course, until fall season when it was time to report.

The first year she was eligible for the regional team was also the first year I had to talk her into signing up. I encouraged her to see where she stood. I told her if she just does it one more time, I would never request it again. And I meant it.

She reluctantly attended and then didn't make the regional pool. I thought for sure she was done and I was going to hold up my end of the promise. But it didn't take a six-hour bus ride home for her to tell me, "I'm going back next year!" I didn't know if she'd ever make the team, but somehow, she knew. I allowed her to attend and the next year she did. The hardest thing about seeing your kid in defeat is seeing the raw emotion and pain that comes with it.

It breaks my heart to see her defeated. I just want to hug her. Sometimes I wouldn't get a hug and that's okay. But the tightest and most genuine hugs I've ever gotten from Rose were in devastating defeat (especially if she felt personally responsible for letting the team down). The same goes for hugs after the most joyous victories. It's their journey, but parents are on the ride. It can be a roller coaster of emotion for both the athlete and the parents. You never truly know for certain where you're headed. But the elite athlete chooses it over and over and as a parent, I'm thrilled to be along for the ride.

"If I could re-do anything, it would have been to relax a bit more and have less self-doubt about letting the boys go. Also, not worry so much about what I felt other parents were thinking or feeling about my parenting choices."

Craig + Mark McMorris
IG: @MarkMcmorris
IG: @CraigMcmorris

Cindy McMorris is the mother of Craig

and Mark McMorris, a pair of professional snowboarders known for their work on the slopes and the screen. Cindy, a native of Canada, grew up in a small, rural town located within the southeast region of Saskatchewan. The value of hard work was instilled in Cindy at an early age by her parents. Her father was a farmer and her mother, the second youngest of 14 children, was a teacher. Cindy was the youngest of their three daughters, so she grew up fast. She held several jobs as a teenager, ranging from babysitting, cleaning houses and waitressing to giving figure skating and swimming lessons. She graduated from nursing school and became an R.N., spending the majority of her career as an Operating Room Nurse.

Cindy married her husband, Don, and had Craig and Mark, the couple's only children, in Regina, the capital city of Saskatchewan. The boys were born two years apart and, as one can imagine, spent the majority of their childhood competing with one another. Sports were among their first interests. Summers were spent at their grandparent's house on Echo Lake, which is where the brothers first developed their passion for board sports. The boys started snowboarding at ages 6 (Craig) and 4

(Mark) on a local ski hill called Mission Ridge, but hockey remained their top priority growing up. However, it progressively became apparent that snowboarding was turning into more than just a hobby.

Mark's snowboarding success came before his older brother's. He won a World Cup event in Calgary at age 15 and then earned back-to-back gold medals at the 2012 and 2013 Winter X Games two years later. Next, Mark qualified for the 2014 Sochi Winter Olympics, where he won a Bronze medal in the Slopestyle event and took home the Bronze again at the 2018 Winter Olympics in PyeongChang, South Korea. Craig, on the other hand, signed a snowboarding sponsorship with Red Bull at 18. He competed in Canada's Winter Games in 2007 and 2011 and made the Canadian National Snowboard Team in 2012. During the 2014 Olympics, Craig worked as an analyst for the Canadian Broadcast Company, which led to an on-air commentator opportunity with ESPN to cover the X Games. Both brothers starred in an MTV reality show "*McMorris & McMorris*" and have contributed to several other film projects. Today, Craig (28) and Mark (26) host the "Brothers McMorris", a YouTube series in partnership with Red Bull.

In the following chapter, Cindy sheds light on the importance of allowing your children to pursue their own passions. If she hadn't, the snowboarding world never would've met the McMorris brothers.

Did your mother inspire you in any way? What kind of values did you take from her and instill in your own life as a mother?

I had a good relationship with my mother. She always stressed that hard work paid off and that education was important. She also led by example and maintained the value of proper manners. My mom was the second youngest of 14 children so a lot of what she taught me was, "don't be selfish, share, always use good manners, it's not about material things and be appreciative of what you have." I think those were the core values I took from my mom and instilled in my boys.

When was the earliest indication that you thought Mark and Craig might have extraordinary talent?
My earliest indication that I thought Craig might have talent was when he was doing competitive gymnastics and was doing well at Provincial meets. For Mark, it was in elementary school winning cross country runs in the school city meets.

In their tweens, they began wakeboarding in the summers at our lake. There was a small group of riders who started competing provincially, nationally and eventually globally over about a five-year period where they had good results. I knew then that they were great with a board.

Did you have to do anything to foster their talent or were they always self-motivated?
They were both very self-motivated when it came to sports.

Did you put any systems in place for Mark and Craig to build the habits that led to their success?
The only systems we put in place to foster their success was encouragement, providing opportunities to play all sports, give it your best and good sportsmanship.

How did you handle their accomplishments and keep things in perspective?
As a mother, the hardest thing to handle about their accomplishments was letting go at such a young age. Mark was flying over to Europe by himself at age 15. There definitely was a lot of worry and self-doubting if we were doing the right thing.

Any stories of adversity that Mark or Craig faced?
Our adversity was the location of their sport. They were
eight hours from any mountain. Craig and Mark were
fortunate enough to have grandparents that lived on a
lake with a ski resort close by. This was the beginning of
both of their passion for board sports.

Both have had major injuries that they have had to
persevere and work hard through their rehabilitation to
get back to the sport they love. For Mark, his injury was
in the backcountry in Whistler on a Saturday afternoon.
The light wasn't great, so they were waiting for the sun to
come out. When it did, Mark said, "okay let's do this."
On one of his first runs down, he ended up hitting a tree.
They waited over two hours for the helicopter to get
there. He was losing consciousness. Craig built a bed and
they all took their clothes off to keep him warm. Craig
knew how to radio for help. We were very close to losing
Mark. He ended up with a broken humerus, fractured
pelvis and ruptured spleen. They had to do emergency
surgery in Vancouver for his spleen, but they were able to
get him stable. The big man was looking down on him
and us for sure. Both boys are still grateful to be making a
living in the industry they love.

**What were things you think you may have handled
differently?**
If I could re-do anything, it would have been to relax a bit
more and have less self-doubt about letting the boys go.
Also, not worry so much about what I felt other parents
were feeling about my parenting choices.

**If you could name one characteristic you believe
Craig and Mark inherited from you, what would that
be?**
I am proud that both Craig and Mark have great manners
and I am hopeful that came from me.

Can you offer any advice to young or soon to be mothers/parents?

Oh, I could go on forever about advice to young parents:

- Expose your children to as many activities as they are willing to try.
- Let them find their own passion.
- When they become teenagers, especially boys, if you want to communicate with them, don't ask too many questions at once, or you will only get one answer.
- Be supportive and encouraging, even if it is outside the norm.
- Ignore the gossip and chatter from others and be confident in your decisions.

Looking back, what would you say was the greatest gift you gave to your kids?

I would say opportunity. There's lots of very talented athletic people out there but not all of them are fortunate enough to be able to pursue some of their dreams.

If you could tell the world one thing, what would it be?

Respect other people and their property.

Any closing thoughts?

I am proud of the young men they have become. Mark and Craig launched the McMorris Foundation in 2012 with a vision of creating a more affordable, accessible and inclusive sport culture for the youth in Canada. Since the beginning, the McMorris Foundation has served one main goal: to help kids experience the joy and power of sports. I am proud that my boys are giving back to their community and sport.

Craig's passion for snowboarding has branched into announcing at major snowboarding events. The first time I heard Craig speak was at a local wakeboard competition. The announcer that was hired for the event took a break and Craig temporarily took over the mic (he was in his early teens). I was so impressed; he was funny and did an amazing job. Others were impressed at how comfortable he was at the mic.

As a mom, my dream is that Craig and Mark stay healthy and continue to be passionate about what they are doing. I would also like to be a grandma someday, but I am willing to be patient!

"Your child's life is your child's journey, and we are companions. When we try to make our children a project or fulfill our own dreams, we are setting up for harm and disappointment."

Colleen Quigley
IG: @Steeple_Squigs

Ann Quigley is the mother of Colleen

Quigley, a professional middle-distance runner, Olympian and Nike athlete. Ann grew up in a hard-working, middle-class family in Kirkwood, Missouri, a suburb of Saint Louis. Her father owned a family lumber/hardware business while her mother stayed home to take care of Ann and her three siblings. She attended Catholic school and started working in the ninth grade at her father's store as a cashier. He was an amputee (lost his left leg to cancer at 19), so she helped him take care of yard work and repairs around the house, maybe a little more than most kids would. As she got older, Ann followed her childhood aspiration to be a teacher. In 1982, she earned a degree in Education from Saint Joseph's College and began teaching high school math for the Indianapolis public school system.

After college, Ann got married and had three children – Dan, Colleen and Erin who were all raised in Saint Louis. She continued to teach and, in addition to homeschooling her own children, has served as owner and lead instructor of the Kumon Math and Reading Center of Kirkwood for the last 26 years and counting.

As her mom tells it, Colleen's love for track and field didn't come naturally. In order to get in shape for spring soccer tryouts, she joined Nerinx Hall High School's cross-country team in the fall of her freshman year. But by the time tryouts came, Colleen had already discovered a joy (and natural talent) for running. Soccer faded and track became her full priority. With her dad as her coach, Colleen went on to win the 2010-11 Missouri Girls Track and Field Gatorade Player of the Year award (for both track and cross country) after winning the state's 3200 and 1600-meter titles.

Colleen's high school accolades earned her a scholarship to run at Florida State University, which is where her success really took off. She was a nine-time All-American over the course of her collegiate career as an integral member of FSU's top-ranked cross country and track and field teams. In her final race for the Seminoles, she won the Outdoor 3000 Steeplechase title at the 2015 NCAA Outdoor Track and Field Championships with the third-fastest time (9:29.32) in collegiate history. Colleen signed a contract with Nike and became a member of the Bowerman Track Club that following summer and then finished third in the steeplechase at the 2015 USA Outdoor Track and Field Championships. A year later, she placed 8th in the 3000-meter steeplechase at the Rio Summer Olympics – the second-highest finish among Americans. Colleen also played an active role in student leadership and community service while studying diligently in the field of Dietetics at FSU, something that often goes unmentioned in the sports world. FSU recognized Colleen's contributions off the track her senior year, naming her their Woman of the Year in the NCAA – an award that acknowledges scholar athletes who demonstrated academic excellence, student leadership and gave back to their respective universities in additions to their athletic excellence.

This chapter portrays the story of Colleen's success from her mother's point of view, unveiling what it means to be a "fully present" parent.

Did your mother inspire you in any way? What kind of values did you take from her and instill in your own life as a mother?

Growing up, I didn't always get along with my mom, but as an adult, I have learned to appreciate her for the love and effort she gave us and how she matured on her journey. She worked hard around the house and volunteered a lot at our grade school and parish and I admired that. She loved us and wanted to give us all the opportunities our family could afford. As we all have our work to do as adults, I also worked to understand what I needed and did not always get that from her when I was young. I vowed I would do better by my kids, somehow. My mom shared her struggles growing up and as I matured, I came to appreciate her journey and I truly admire how even today she continues to grow and heal at the age of 88. I often share with my daughters that each generation stands on the shoulders of the previous generation and builds on what they did and experienced. Values I took from her were a great work ethic and to keep peace and harmony in marriage and family and a love of crafty creating.

What kind of dreams and goals did you have when you were a kid? How much did they influence where you are today?

I dreamt of being a teacher from the third grade and that has greatly influenced me today. I taught math in high school, math and reading in middle school and homeschooled my children. I have owned and directed a Kumon Math and Reading Center for 26 years supporting kids and their parents as well as giving many teenagers their first jobs.

I also wanted to be an athlete to honor my dad. He was a locally competitive bicyclist when he was a teenager before he lost his leg to cancer. Then he played wheelchair basketball on a traveling team after his amputation. There was a trophy case in our basement with lots of BIG trophies that dad never talked about, but I admired them and wanted to earn some of my own to make him proud. As a young adult runner experiencing much success locally, I aspired to reach the Olympic Trial in the marathon. I knew making the team would not be possible but making the trials would be a dream come true. I fell short in my last attempt, but by that point, I was married and we were starting a family so my priorities changed.

When was the earliest indication that you thought Colleen might have extraordinary talent?

Colleen was energetic and competitive with her brother at an incredibly early age. I knew her strong will was going to lead her to something big if I could be patient and if her dad and I could guide her well. Colleen was first very into dancing and soccer. She played soccer in the fall on a CYC team but year-round she danced. Dance was her passion. In the third grade, she started running each spring with the local Catholic school team her dad and I coached. She absolutely hated it at first because she wasn't winning! I always knew she had a driving, passionate personality and that she would do something big someday. I did not really entertain a thought about "extreme" talent until she was gaining success in college.

This is a small story most might not believe. Before she was even conceived, I woke up from a nap in a summer afternoon, hearing a voice saying, "I'm Colleen and I'm going to be your next child." I thought it was the craziest thing. It was almost like she was speaking to me before she was even born. I always wondered what that meant. I had this message in this subconscious state, and of course two years later the next child I had was a girl and we named her Colleen. How could we not? She had a strong personality all along. She was always trying to catch up with her brother who's four years older than her. She would want to get into everything and anything before she was even physically able or big enough. She was always trying to do more. That became a theme for her.

Did you put any systems in place for Colleen to build the habits that lead to her success?
I think every engaged parent does this in some fashion. We held her accountable for her responsibilities, helped her set goals and create a path to achieve the goals. We homeschooled all three children and had a collaborative philosophy about creating their learning year with them. I set some non-negotiables such as math and reading practices but history and science we collaborated on topics and materials. Our children took art and music classes of their choosing and always played a sport. They were limited to one sport at a time and never did we consider something like a soccer club that required daily practice or traveling. As teachers and a coach, Gaylerd and I saw too many athletes, especially girls, burnout in sports they loved when parents were over involved or let the child become too consumed in elementary or middle school with the sport. We valued balance and knew that a well-rounded physical, emotional, academic and spiritual experience would better prepare our children for life success, if we could figure out how to do that.

Gaylerd and I did not really expect any of our children would have such outstanding talent because we knew it was a rare combination of DNA, mindset and opportunity. I don't think we really tried to engineer that, we just knew to do our best to raise good human beings that liked themselves and could find a place in the world that made them happy while serving their community as well. We tried to build a mindset of confidence, willingness to work, habits of perseverance and grit that would set them up for success as they followed their own paths.

If you were heavily involved, how did you make time for yourself?

That is the motherhood long dilemma and a need I am learning to fulfill as my children are launched. Sometimes I stayed up really late reading a book or doing a creative project. This was not always a balanced way to deal with my time, but it filled some creative needs. I participated in arts and crafts with the kids, sewed clothes for the girls and their dolls and we made jewelry together that we sold at craft fairs. We also gardened, appreciating the abundance of the earth, appreciation for food and enjoyed cooking our crops. I guess I wove my interests into our homeschool and took my joy in exploring the creative activities that interested the kids and expanding them to science or history or cultural experiences. My female friendships were mostly through church and home school activities. We do not attend a church or homeschool currently, but these women are still the women I socialize with today.

Any stories of adversity that Colleen faced?

Mostly social adversity in high school. She is intense and has high expectations for herself. It can be a challenge in friendships. She does love deeply though and holds those close to her in great love and affection and shows it. Self-reflection and work with her mental coach as well as maturity are shifting these dynamics of her person.

Another adversity that is a nemesis of most high-level athletes is training edges. Colleen always trains at the edge of what her body is going to be able to tolerate. She has had to work hard to be aware of that thin line and not overstep it to avoid injury in training, which she has accidentally done in the past. This is a mind game as well to be attuned to your body as much as the workout plan and to be aware when your desire to be equal to or better than the other athletes in the workout or race is clouding better judgment. Balance is key. There are many metaphors here for us at every stage of our lives or any level of performance in the athletic realm.

As a mother, what were you good at saying no to?
That is a question for Colleen! There is one thing when she was very young that I did often say no to. She would want a boost up into the tree or on a jungle gym at the park that was too high for her. I knew she would scramble quickly above my reach and I could not protect her when she overstepped her ability. I would always say when she could get there herself, she could climb and I would stand below to catch her if she fell. I would not boost her up to a dangerous place before she was strong enough to do it herself. Her brother seemed to know and respect his current limits, but I don't think she saw any limits. This was a theme for her growing up though, we would not push her or put her in any situations she could not get herself into but Gaylerd and I were there to walk alongside her and prevent serious injury. Her life, her choices.

I was good at saying no to spending lots of money on something frivolous. I was also good at saying no to extended curfews or last-minute sleepovers negotiated at 10pm. I was good at saying no to things that were big in popular culture and did not fit our values. An example of this is when we were allowing her to explore a modeling career. Modeling was not in our value system, but she was presented the opportunity and wanted to explore it, so we walked the path with her. There were certain modeling companies that we did not like due to what they stood for so we would not let her work for them. We also said no to traveling alone as a teenager to a job. She always had a chaperone, mom or dad usually or a trusted adult. She also stayed in St. Louis at her hometown high school living a "normal" teenage life when she was not on a trip.

What would you say were important qualities to possess to be the mother you were?
Seeking and questioning. I knew I wanted to be a better

mother than my mother was and I had to learn how. My mother did not have the resources I did so I read many books, asked questions, took classes and went to therapy. I also was deeply interested in stages of child development and wanted to understand what was coming next for my kids so I could provide the resources and materials to help foster their growth physically, cognitively, emotionally and spiritually. I tried, and still work on, listening and questioning to guide the kids to good choices. I think this is something I developed as they grew and was not as successful as I wanted to be.

What were things you think you may have handled differently?
This is tricky because I believe everything that happened was for a reason. If I had done anything differently, Colleen would not be the same as she is today, nor I. I do wish I could have been more relaxed and trusting of the future. I know I was working through my own issues about being lovable even when I made mistakes and trusting the future will work out. I think I am constantly learning to live with less fear of what bad things could happen. I might have rolled with day-to-day things better when I was parenting had I not had the fear that if I didn't do it right and protect the kids, they would become bums or bad people.

What is your relationship like now with Colleen?
We speak one or two times a week, most weeks. She is really good at calling when she is in the car transitioning. Her schedule is so packed and with a two-hour time difference between Portland and St. Louis as well as all the responsibilities she has, it can be hard to be free at the same time. She will run her newsletter past me before she sends it out and often talks through the background feelings going on around what is happening in her work. We are much more friends. I think we have always had a strong thread of this in high school and college, even

though it was exhibited less often then. It has been steadily growing in the last couple of years as she finds her footing in the world on her terms and I am doing my own work on personal growth.

If you could name one characteristic you believe Colleen inherited from you, what would that be?
Seeking the better self and her creativity.

Did any times of adversity set you up for later success?
I failed to qualify for the Olympic Trials in the Marathon before I had children. I think I blame myself for my lack of self-discipline when training. This probably comes from my lack of self-confidence and a limiting belief I was not good enough or worthy and I did not understand these things back then. I had talent but needed a coach and more faith in myself. There may be a bit of perfectionism in there as well with the fear of failure, so I do give up easily if I sense I am failing. I think I wanted to give my kids more sense of self-worth and self-discipline so they would be empowered to achieve their goals as adults. Doing that without putting them on fragile pedestals or propping them up is a challenge. This would be interesting to talk with all three of them about. I am not sure how well I balanced judging versus supporting. I also wanted to stay aware that I was not going to project my unfulfilled dreams on my children. I am so proud of their journeys and celebrate their achievements as theirs.

How did you respond to situations that made you feel overwhelmed?
I cried, screamed, scooped up the kid or kids and hugged and cried with them, went for a long walk in the woods or planned a camping trip, it all just depends on the situation.

Can you offer any advice to young or soon to be mothers/parents?

WOW! Relax and let it unfold. Read all you can about growth and development and take it all with big grains of salt! Each human being unfolds in his/her own way. Books show us general trends, but we create the unique situation for the beings we are raising. We parents are here to protect from big harm (falling off a cliff when hiking) but not the little harms like skinned knees. Let your child struggle a bit. It builds strength and perseverance. Learn to step in gently before huge frustration, though. Observe lots. Hug and hold lots. Participate in life with your child. Lots of outdoor time getting messy and dirty. Lots of art and singing and building with blocks and knocking it down! As the child grows, listen and ask questions to know where your child is and guide from there. Your child's life is your child's journey and we are companions. When we try to make our children a project or to fulfill our own dreams, we are setting up for harm and disappointment. Do your work on you with friends and self-growth/spiritual development opportunities and be present for your children as they are. Seek out what might be needed educationally and make that a bigger priority than top athletic excellence at younger ages. Build balance into the day and week with your children and for you by nurturing the emotional, spiritual, physical and cognitive aspects of each child and yourself.

Looking back, what would you say was the greatest gift you gave to your kids?

I think the greatest gift I gave my kids was and still is being fully present to their joys, fears, needs, seeking, yearning and walking the path with them as best I could. It was more active and guiding when they were young to listen deeper and provide opportunities or resources they did not know they needed or existed. I strove to give them a framework to learn about the world and themselves and to explore both. Now it is more so cheerleading on the sidelines as well as sharing resources or time. I think Gaylerd and I gave them security in who they are and trust in the world that they are free to become whatever their hearts desire.

If you could tell the world one thing, what would it be?
Breathe deeply, slowly, often and hold all joys and sorrows, all challenges and gifts, all fears and triumphs, in a loving heart. A piano has 88 keys, as do we. Play them all and your life is a symphony of your creating.

Part II

Business
&
Culture

Behind every young child
who believes in themselves is
a parent who believed first.[2]

---

[2] Geckoandfly.com

"Trust your maternal instinct because it's usually right. Take time to breathe and exhale. Take breaks for yourself when you can. There's no such thing as too many kisses and hugs. Forgive yourself when you feel you've not parented well. Trust me – your children will remember the good and mostly forget your perceived shortcomings!"

Matt Pohlson
IG: @MattPohlson
IG: @Omaze

Teri Pohlson is the mother of Matt Pohlson,

co-founder and CEO of Omaze, an online fundraising company that auctions once-in-a-lifetime experiences and high-end merchandise in support of charitable causes. Teri grew up in Glendale, California with her parents and three siblings. She attended Arizona State University for two years before falling in love and getting married. She and her husband, Gary, started a family in the beautiful Orange County beach town of Laguna Niguel. They have three children, of whom Matthew is the oldest.

Teri and Matt always had a close bond during his upbringing, but a brief period of extreme uncertainty brought the pair closer than ever before. In June 2018, Matt flatlined due to a heart syndrome brought on by extreme physical stress. In Matt's case, the stress was induced by a bowel obstruction. Despite a successful surgery to remove the obstruction, the continued surge of stress chemicals caused his heart to stop. Teri was allowed in the hospital room as doctors and staff performed CPR to bring him back to life. She verbally pleaded to her son, who lied unresponsive without a pulse, to keep fighting. After four minutes, Matt miraculously returned to life.

Teri's actions during her son's near-death experience were just a microcosm of her role as a mother. For all three of her children, she relied on her maternal instinct to shape her parenting decisions. Under his mom's influence, Matt graduated from Stanford University with a degree in Economics/Political Science and later earned an M.B.A. from the University of Pennsylvania's Wharton Business School in 2011. Prior to Omaze, he worked as an executive producer for Fox Television and was a summer associate at McKinsey & Company while earning his Master's at Penn. Matt's business-savvy, entrepreneurial spirit was always the fuel to his fire, which eventually led to the founding of Omaze in 2012. Now, the company is unique to its kind, empowering nonprofits from around the world to bolster their fundraising through innovative business techniques. As of July 2020, Omaze grossed over $250 million for charity.

In this chapter, Teri details her steadfast approach to motherhood and how her son's near-death experience provided an entirely new perspective on life for the entire Pohlson family.

Did your mother inspire you in any way? What kind of values did you take from her and instill in your own life as a mother?

I was very close with my mom. I told her everything. She always listened and gave me advice that was easy to follow. She was a disciplinarian and I followed her strong but loving mothering. Evidently, I have a look I give if I'm displeased that all three children and my husband say, "scares the hell out of them." My mom had that look too! She was fair and gave me a sense of security that she was in control. I wanted my children to feel secure with me. She never said, "Wait until your father comes home!" I appreciated when I became a mom that she made us feel that she could handle whatever the situation was during her "watch."

I was inspired by her faith in her mothering style – Having the confidence in loving your children enough to discipline them when they're wrong so they can learn the right way. She said to me when I was young, "It's not my job to be your friend. You have a lot of friends. You need a mother. If I do my job right now, we'll be great friends later." She was right.

Any stories of adversity?
I was a fat kid growing up, so I was teased constantly. I credit that for developing my sense of humor that then enabled me to make friends. I credit those experiences with giving me the quality of having empathy for others. When you're the butt of a joke and the joke's not funny or a personal put-down, or you're bullied by someone, you don't forget what that feels like.

When was the earliest indication that you thought Matt might have extraordinary talent?
At age 3, he started asking questions I couldn't answer. I really could have used the internet/Google then! An example of this was when he was watching me blow dry my hair and asked me how the dryer worked. I answered simply that I plug it in, pointed to the wall socket, and that the wires behind the wall connect a thing called electricity that turns on the dryer when mommy presses the on button, and then it gives the dryer power to blow. Matt then wanted to know what the wires looked like, who put them there, what power was, who made the dryer, how did they make it – on and on. I finally said, "Because God made all of it!" and he just said, "Ohhh." You would have thought that from that day forward, I would start with that answer but being a slow learner, I continued to try to answer his questions. He was so inquisitive!

Did you have to do anything to foster Matt's talent or was he always self-motivated?

We always required that he get top grades because we told him that God had blessed him with a gifted mind. He always said that he got good grades because he loved playing sports, specifically basketball, and he believed us when we said if his grades faltered, sports would have to be put on hold. Other than that, he was very self-motivated.

How did you handle Matt's accomplishments and keep things in perspective?

We always praised him and acknowledged his hard work. We always told him he had been blessed with many talents and his gratitude would be shown in what he gave back.

Any stories of adversity that Matt faced?

I will never forget the family saga that began on Saturday, June 16, 2018 with Matt's admission into the hospital and then almost losing him less than 24 hours later. Matt was born with his stomach twisted in a knot and had surgery immediately to repair it. The scar tissue from that surgery narrowed a portion of his intestine that four years later caused another bowel obstruction. I still cry when I think, talk or write about that day. I was suspended in disbelief in his I.C.U. room watching an incredible medical team try to revive our son. Thoughts go racing and 4½ minutes seem like an eternity but, simultaneously, not enough time. Making my way through the people gathered outside and inside his room, seeing aggressive CPR, defibrillator paddles applied to his chest, his body lifting from the charge, yet no response to either, was terrifying. At first, I was emotional and said some of my favorite prayers out loud but caught myself for fear I was distracting the caregivers and might be asked to leave the room. I prayed for whatever God could give me to get through whatever the outcome was. I felt a sense of calm come over me. I'm not normally described as a calm person. Matt's dad was crying. I didn't know he'd overheard someone say, "I think they've lost him." At that point, Matt's younger brother Ross gently pushed him forward and said, "dad, you should be with mom." I turned to shush him for fear we'd be kicked out and at that moment I saw all of the people focusing on Matt, seeming to be sending prayer and positive energy toward him. To me, it was a juxtaposition of quiet care and concern, quiet as a chapel behind us, with fervor to save our son in front of us. I remember thinking how beautiful it was; the sea of faces caring for this young man and his family who were strangers to them. As I turned back around, Matt was still not responding. I remember asking God, "How did we get here? Are you really taking him now? Why? He's a light in the world and we need light more than ever right now." I then remembered being told that hearing is the last sense to go. I wanted to personalize Matt to those working so hard to save him. I started saying, "C'mon Matthew David Pohlson, you've got to fight! You've got all of these wonderful people working so hard to save you. They don't know you're a fighter, honey, c'mon Matt, you've got to show them what a fighter you are. Help them, fight Matt! I kept repeating, "C'mon Matthew David Pohlson, fight honey!"

I remember thinking maybe they'll keep going if I keep talking. Then standing on the precipice, waiting to hear him declared, the doctor said four words I'll never forget, "We've got a pulse." He was far from out of the woods, but at that moment we still had hope. I thanked God for bringing him back to us for however long and then Matt raised his left arm and gave us a thumb's up sign. Matt had been sedated since his early morning surgery. When I saw his hand gesture, I felt like neurologically he was intact, having made it through okay thus far. Again, many things happened after that but he's here still to tell the tale and continue his mission of helping others, spreading love and optimism and sharing his story with others.

I grieved afterward for my family and friends whose children did not survive sudden or prolonged illness or fatal accidents. We were almost there and I couldn't understand why Matt survived and their son or daughter didn't. That is something beyond human scope in my opinion. I have felt heartbroken for the families and spouses who couldn't be with their loved one's suffering and ultimately dying from COVID-19. I just can't imagine their pain.

What would you say were important qualities to possess to be the mother you were?

A loving, tactile but also fair disciplinarian. I know that I loved hugging and kissing my children and I tried to be fair to them when they disobeyed. I was more successful with the former and less consistent with the latter.

I find this and the other questions a challenge because I don't pretend to have the answers to what works for raising children. I've read or seen stories about moms who had far less financial or material comforts and/or more demands of their time comparatively who've raised outstanding humans.

On a scale of 1-10, 10 being the best, I'd score myself a 5. Not the best but not the worst. In the final analysis, all three of our children still speak to me and express their love, so I guess I didn't screw up too badly. I think children inherently want to love and be loved by their parents. So in that regard, I succeeded in conveying to them that they were and always will be loved no matter what. I also know that children are very forgiving. At least mine say they don't remember me as an impatient and stressed mom like the way I remember myself. I admire all moms and dads who try their very best. When that bar isn't met on a given day, keep trying.

What were things you think you may have handled differently?

I would've been more patient. I didn't manage stress too well. I prayed a lot, but I didn't implement meditation like Mother Teresa referenced. I lost patience and then beat myself up for being short tempered. If I could have a do-over, I would use a combination of prayer and meditation to start my day and then to help me to decompress and defuse it whenever I felt stress building. I'm still a work in progress when it comes to making these tools a habit.

That's why my wish for parents is finding what helps manage their stress and when they have a bad day to forgive themselves, try to avoid the same response and start again the next day. The pandemic brings stress to a whole new level. I don't know how parents are juggling all their obligations and staying sane.

If you could name one characteristic you believe Matt inherited from you, what would that be?

Humor and compassion for the human condition.

When did Matt come up with the idea for Omaze? What did he endure on the road leading up to its founding?

It was when he was in graduate school back East and his friend was attending school out here at UCLA. They wanted to do a venture together. He didn't share his idea with us right away. He waited until they put together their plans after graduation to launch. There was a lot of foundation and groundwork to complete before they were ready. As parents, we were excited and nervous at the same time. The concept of a start-up internet business was way out of our wheelhouse and hard for us to conceptualize at the time.

It was not a smooth road getting to that point though – before he went to grad school and he was struggling to make it as an actor, he was working nights as a waiter and auditioning during the day. There's so much rejection in that business and although he didn't talk about it much, we knew it wasn't an easy pursuit. During this time, he shared that he couldn't get his mind to stop racing. It was hard for him to get sleep. He was feeling exhausted. This was not a surprise to me. Remember all the questions about the blow dryer when he was 3? There was a saying back then that his dad used to apply to him: Inquisitive minds want to know _____ (fill in the blank). He was always thinking, always questioning and he didn't change as he grew older. Getting one's mind to quit on command is rarely accomplished. This is going to sound repetitive, but I had just come back from a girlfriend's weekend where meditation was taught and encouraged for centering your mind and soul. I told Matt that they swore it would change your life if you could practice it regularly. He started to try it and it helped. He enjoyed it and he hasn't stopped since.

Did any times of adversity set you up for later success?

Thanks to the adversity I have gone through, I became more open and able to acknowledge vulnerabilities. I apologize much more readily for my mistakes. I have strength in times of crisis I didn't know I possessed. I do believe my faith gets me through challenging times.

Can you offer any advice to young or soon to be mothers/parents?

Trust your maternal instinct because it's usually right. Take time to breathe and exhale. Take breaks for yourself when you can. There's no such thing as too many kisses and hugs. Forgive yourself when you feel you've not parented well. Trust me – your children will remember the good and mostly forget your perceived shortcomings!

Looking back, what would you say was the greatest gift you gave to your kids?

My unconditional love.

If you could tell everyone in the world one thing, what would it be?

I think the Golden Rule says it best: Do unto others as you would have them do unto you. (Bible verses Matthew 7:12 and Luke 6:31)

Any closing thoughts?

I don't know about advising anyone else, but I try to remember to think of at least one thing that I'm grateful for each day no matter the challenges of life at the time. Since Matt's health crisis, I do appreciate my family at a whole new level. I try to tell them often how much they mean to me/us and treasure our times together.

"For mothers – help your kids develop a sense of resiliency in the face of adversity and share good times with them. Exemplify being a beautiful person towards others."

Malika Favre
IG: @MalikaFavre
MalikaFavre.com

Ouiza Favre is the mother of Malika Favre, a French artist and illustrator based in London, England. Ouiza was born in France around the time of the Algerian War but spent a significant portion of her young life living in her father's native country of Algiers. After seven years, she returned to France at age 17 and started a career in sales.

Later on, Ouiza had two children – Lyes and Malika – who were both born and raised in the Parisian suburbs. As a young mother, her sales work included music commerce and organic products, with the latter being the main reason why the family ate strictly vegetarian. However, making art was also an integral part of her life. Ouiza was a free spirit who leveraged her creativity as a painter and illustrator. She taught her daughter how to draw at an early age and her influence was ultimately a key component to Malika's pursuit of an artistic life.

Art was a hobby for Malika when she was young, but it didn't become her actual career choice until realizations occurred in her late teens. Following high school, she attended a science prep school in hopes of becoming a quantum physicist. Though four months into her physics studies, Malika realized she had made a mistake. She changed course and enrolled in Oliver de Serres – a prestigious art school in Paris, where she focused on art advertising. After graduating, she moved to London and interned at a graphic design studio called Airside, which later turned into a full-time role. She worked there for four years and found herself as an artist.

Malika left Airside in 2011 and has flourished as an independent illustrator in the 10 years since. Now, she's one of the U.K.'s most popular artists whose work is often described as a mix of PopArt and OpArt that uses a striking combination of positive/negative space and color. Her work has been featured in *Vogue, The New York Times, The New Yorker, The Sunday Times* and *Vanity Fair*, while her unique graphics have been used by *Sephora, Le Bon Marche* and *Penguin Books*. The 38-year-old artist has over 411,000 followers on Instagram and a full-range online store.

From a house without television to a mandatory vegetarian diet, Malika's upbringing was unique to the common childhood today. This chapter tells that story through Ouiza's eyes, where she explains the reasoning behind her structure and methods.

Did your mother inspire you in any way? What kind of values did you take from her and instill in your own life as a mother?
My mother is Algerian, from the large Kabylie region. She arrived in France after her marriage in the 1950s. Not having been to school, she was illiterate and did not speak French. She came from a poor background and was orphaned at the age of 3. When I learned to read and write, I tried to teach her to read and write, but she never wanted to. She was too busy with her many pregnancies (11 children and I was the oldest girl). I remember she had fairy fingers for sewing, knitting and cooking, but little interest in culture.

She was a very sweet woman, but she had a

preference for her boys. I really liked school and especially literature. I devoured great authors. I remember my mother confiscating my books, considering I had to take care of my siblings as a priority. I was very thirsty to learn and a very good student, which she found unnecessary.

Unfortunately, my dreams of a "French" education were shattered shortly after I entered the Lycée Français in Algiers. Just after turning 11, the Algerian War ended and my father had decided to return to his home country, taking his whole family with him. Confronted with relationship problems with his father and several siblings, he had to quickly leave Algiers and go into exile in the countryside for survival. So, not speaking Arabic and refusing to adapt to local traditions and customs, I found myself immersed in another culture where girls and their education are ignored.

After very difficult years, living in isolation, destitution and wanting, where I prayed every day to return to France, we finally left. Seven long years had passed. I was 17. When we got back, my dad found me a job as a cleaner and, of course, took my salary every month. After two and a half years, I dared to break up with my family and worked in sales, which suited me better.

I learned perseverance and a taste for things done the right way from my mother. She was good with her hands; she sewed pretty dresses for me. She liked beautiful things. She did not know how to read and write but she knew how to manage. She was a discrete and kind woman. She was a woman in a patriarchal environment and discovered another culture, one that is more free. She allowed me to be freer even though I couldn't convince her to take literacy classes.

When was the earliest indication that you thought Malika might have extraordinary talent?
I understood that Malika had a real passion for drawing

when she was 8 years old, but I also pushed her towards musical training. She did five years of piano at the conservatory of our city. She was rather gifted and I observed an unusual force of concentration in her. I wanted her to have more self-confidence than I had. The piano and painting competitions helped her gain confidence. But her teachers pushed her towards mathematics and languages because she had an impressive memory.

Any stories of adversity that Malika faced?
It's always difficult to be a woman in a male environment, to be taken seriously and respected. She also had to deal with racism and people plagiarizing her drawings, which happened more frequently as her success grew.

After her Baccalaureate S, which she obtained with distinction, she was admitted to Math-Sup and received the physics vocation scholarship for girls. After a few months of boarding school, she had a realization that made her leave this elite path and decided to try the entrance examination to the Applied Arts of Olivier de Serres, a public school. A rather risky turn. We were a little worried, but it was her choice. I wanted more freedom for her than I had had as a girl subject to the Berber and Sharia Muslim tradition.

She was confronted early on with racism from some of her teachers and the stupidity of social reproduction. I remember one of her remarks when she was about 6 years old, "Mom, why don't I look like a barbie doll?" Fortunately, she was a very good student in all subjects and brilliant in drawing. I tried to give my children a lot of attention and confidence.

What would you say were important qualities to possess to be the mother you were?
An emotional intelligence based on empathy, an ability to work on oneself and to question one's own beliefs. This translates into more intimate conversations with others, a

confidence with oneself, and critical life experience. The first book that guided me in life was *Breaking Free from the Known* by Krishnamurti, an Indian sage and educator.

I expected revenge for my childhood, not just wanting to be a biological consequence of the reproductive instinct (we were 11 children!). I aspired to a higher ideal. I told myself that a family could be more fulfilled and richer inside than mine and that each person could fulfill their destiny, as in *The Alchemist* by Paolo Coelho.

If you could name one characteristic you believe Malika inherited from you, what would that be?
Concentration and curiosity for the world and humanity in its diversity. Perseverance in the work, an aesthetic sense and precision of the line. For the rest, it comes from her, from her own life path as well as from her intelligence.

Can you offer any advice to young or soon to be mothers/parents?
A child is the bearer of his or her own destiny. One part comes from heredity, another from education. Where we can perhaps help is in its orientation. For example, I wanted my children to learn music, dance and drawing, to have as open a career choice as possible. Creativity brings so much joy and strength in difficult times of life. I was convinced of it at 21 and I still am. Finally, there is a last part which belongs to them in their own right, which we can only accept even if we have to suffer from it. For example, cigarettes. I have suffered greatly from my inability to fight its ravages (for the health of my children). But as the poet Khalil Gibran says, "Your children are not your children but the call of life to itself, they belong to tomorrow, you are only the bow and they are the arrow." You do not control their destiny. You must accept having only a secondary role in their life, but always be there for them, love them unfailingly.

Looking back, what would you say was the greatest gift you gave to your kids?

Love, love and more love. True unconditional love. Also, self-confidence and acceptance of differences because of their mixed heritage. I tried to teach them how to make their difference a strength, develop a sense of the other and the capacity for resilience in the face of adversity.

If you could tell the world one thing, what would it be?

For me, it is, "Act in every situation according to the highest ideal that you carry within you."

"The best advice I can give to new mothers is to give your children a lot of love. It is the fertilizer for healthy growth. I hung a graphic in my studio that reads – Tell your children three times a day that you love them."

Carrie Hammer
IG: @CarrieHammer
Jean Wells
Wellsart.com

Jean Wells is the mother of Carrie Hammer, an innovative fashion designer, entrepreneur and early influencer of the "body positivity" movement in fashion and advertising. Jean grew up in Seattle, Washington in the 1950s surrounded by a large extended family full of artists. Her father worked as an illustrator in Applied Physics at the University of Washington while her mother maintained the household and watched over Jean and her brother, Tom. Jean was a strong student but wasn't entirely passionate about school until she attended the University of Washington. She earned a degree from UW in Fine Arts and then enrolled in Seattle's Burnley Art School to pursue graphic design.

Considered to be naturally career-driven with an entrepreneurial spirit, Jean dipped her hand in several different industries throughout her life. She created her own advertising agency, published two agricultural magazines, and served as VP of Marketing & Communications for an Orange County tech start-up founded by her and her husband, Steve Hamerslag, who is a prominent entrepreneur in the technology sector. Today, Jean is an internationally renowned contemporary artist known for her large-scaled and life-sized mosaic sculptures that blend postmodern pop culture iconography with autobiography. Her work has been shown in galleries and museums in 24 cities in the United States and 25 countries throughout the world since 2007.

Jean and Steve had two children together – Carrie and Blake – who were raised in a rural area outside San Diego. They enjoyed a comfortable upbringing with hobbies spanning from sports and hiking to sewing and art. Carrie's creative influence came from her mother, who noticed she was drawn to design as a child. She graduated from UCLA in 2007 with a double major in Economics and Sociology, with an emphasis in Women's Studies. However, after four years working in the media industry, she realized marketing wasn't her true passion and decided to switch paths into fashion design.

After studying Fashion Business and Marketing at the Parsons Paris New School of Art and Design, she launched her own company called CARRIE HAMMER in 2012 – an NYC-based clothing brand dedicated to professional women. Her debut fashion show, titled "Role Models, Not Runway Models" took place during New York Fashion Week in February 2014. The show replaced traditional fashion models with powerful women ranging from activists, executives and philanthropists who told their own personal stories and provided advice for women pursuing careers. Carrie has been featured by the *New York Times, Wall Street Journal, CNBC, Today Show, Fox Business News, Forbes and Good Morning America.* She was a *Forbes* 30 Under 30 honoree and listed as one of 2015's Top 15 Female Entrepreneurs to Watch by *Entrepreneur Magazine.*

This chapter contains insight from Jean on the parenting approach that helped foster her daughter's passion-driven desire to empower women through fashion.

Did your mother inspire you in any way? What kind of values did you take from her and instill in your own life as a mother?

We were opposites. I had a tremendous amount of energy and she was more reserved. I think it was difficult for her to raise me because I was so active. She was strict in a typical "mom" sense, looking out for us and keeping us out of trouble. My mom was very loving. Like most young people, I had ideas and dreams for my life that probably looked different than hers.

My mother taught me to be very loving. In my mind, the most important requirement for any mom is to let their children know how much they are loved every day. I think it gives the child a sense of security and confidence. I feel that role modeling is important, but secondary to showing love. The love has to be there to give any child a solid foundation. This value also came from my grandmother, who was empathetic, loving and one of the kindest people I've ever met. Kindness and love were values that have guided me in my experience as a mother.

What kind of dreams and goals did you have when you were a kid? How much did they influence where you are today?

My mother was resistant to my dreams. She came from an era where most women wanted to be housewives and she wanted that for me. I wanted to have a career. That being said, I think I'm living my dreams today and have throughout my working life. I wanted to do something challenging, impactful and independent. Working for someone else was never exciting to me. To create something on my own always appealed to me. I probably inherited that from my dad. Even though he worked at the Applied Physics Lab, he had his own business working nights and weekends. I was more excited by what he was doing outside of the university. It's a little like in the story of *The Three Little Pigs:* I wanted to be the one building the brick house, making something on my own that was unique and lasting.

When was the earliest indication that you thought Carrie might have extraordinary talent?

Observing Carrie in pre-school, it was obvious to me that she caught on quickly. She learned things easily at an early age. Her teachers recognized her gifts and gave her extra projects to help her reach her potential. You could see her work on puzzles and other problem-solving things very quickly. When Carrie was in middle school, she wanted me to teach her how to sew. I never learned that craft. Instead, I bought an instructional video, which she used to teach herself. She was an avid reader and always yearned to have books. As a result, she developed a large vocabulary. It was no surprise to me that when she was a bit older, she tested for Mensa (high IQ society) and became a member at a young age.

When she was applying to colleges, her guidance counselors told her she should apply to many colleges, even though she only wanted to go to UCLA. There was one college interview where they gave her a short "intelligence" test. The interviewer said later that in all his years of using this metric as part of their admissions process, he had never had anyone complete it so quickly and with such an exceptional outcome.

Did you have to do anything to foster Carrie's talent or was she always self-motivated?

Well, in raising my children, I would sometimes think more like a businesswoman than a mother. Hence, in grade school, I created a chore chart. Carrie received stars for doing certain tasks like emptying the dishwasher, feeding the animals or reading books. She was motivated to earn a lot of stars to make her meager allowance. It helped Carrie establish goals and enjoy the accomplishment of achieving those goals. It was important to me to teach both our kids what it meant to earn, save and contribute – 10% of their allowance had to go to charity.

How did you handle Carrie's accomplishments and keep things in perspective?

We required our kids to work summers and over holiday vacations to develop a work ethic and earn their own money to spend. Carrie had a job at Nordstrom, which she loved. Her boss saw how energized and driven she was and took to incentivizing her on the sales floor. She quickly became the top salesperson in her department.

If you were heavily involved, how did you make time for yourself?

I have always been involved in creative endeavors, so time for myself included learning to teach art projects in the classroom from time to time. When I was creating ceramic art sculptures, I would ask my children if they would like to join in.

What would you say were important qualities to possess to be the mother you were?

Energy and love. I think the most important quality for a mother is unconditional love and lots of it: love is the foundation of everything.

What were things you think you may have handled differently?

I would have taught delayed gratification. I think it's one of the building blocks for kids. I was a helicopter parent and always wanted to fix everything so that both kids wouldn't feel any pain. That's not realistic. They need to know how to skin their knees and soothe themselves.

What is your relationship like now with Carrie?

Carrie and I are very close. We have just spent the last three months in quarantine together 24/7. I feel very fortunate that I could have that time with her. She is inspiring, loving and very creative. It's very joyful and exciting to be around her. Before the pandemic, she was working in China for almost two years and that was hard for me. We did travel to see her and experienced one of her fashion shows in Shanghai. That was exciting. With the time difference, it was complicated to keep in touch. That being said, I'm not a mother who is dependent on my children for my own happiness. I am busy with my company (Wellsart) and sculpture career.

If you could name one characteristic you believe Carrie inherited from you, what would that be?
She inherited bravery, perseverance, creativity and a loving nature. I guess you could call it a bundled characteristic.

Did any times of adversity set you up for later success?
I'm not afraid of failure. I feel you can't succeed without failure. One cannot be challenged by it: keep moving forward or pivot in a new direction. I have always felt that failure is a part of success otherwise you're not taking the appropriate risks and stretching yourself.

Can you offer any advice to young or soon to be mothers/parents?
The best advice I can give to new mothers is to give your children a lot of love. It is the fertilizer for healthy growth. I have a graphic in my studio - "Tell your children three times a day that you love them."

Looking back, what would you say was the greatest gift you gave to your kids?
I believe my greatest gift to our children was to role model a healthy, productive lifestyle, and most importantly, demonstrate kindness to others.

If you could tell the world one thing, what would it be?
It is extremely important to be empathetic.

Are there any stories about Carrie and her journey that you would like to add?
Carrie loved her time working at Nordstrom's in high school when she was a teenager. Nordstrom's is a company with a long record of philanthropy. Around this same time, our family was dealing with my breast cancer diagnosis. Carrie decided that she was going to raise money for breast cancer through Nordstrom's. She decided to donate a percentage of her earnings to the cause. One of the Nordstrom brothers got wind of it and wanted to meet with Carrie. I remember Carrie telling me that her manager had remarked, "I've been working here for a long time and rarely see him in the store." Mr. Nordstrom complimented her and told her how much he admired what she was doing, but this was a big company and they had certain ways of handling these kinds of philanthropic initiatives. It was part of their corporate board's responsibility to choose the charity. Carrie listened respectfully and responded, "Well, why don't you make a donation?" He laughed and I think he did.

I read in the book by Bernie Siegel, *Love, Medicine, and Miracles* that one of the best things you can do when facing a critical diagnosis like I was with my breast cancer is to make art. I started ceramics. I made so many art pieces that there wasn't a surface in the house that didn't have a ceramic sculpture on it. Carrie said, "I'm going to sell your art and raise money for breast cancer." I asked her what her plan was and she said she was researching around at the Salk Institute (one of the premier medical research institutes in the country), and read up on a Dr. Inder Verma who, Carrie said, I think is going to be the one to find a cure for this cancer. She was so young she didn't even have her driver's license. I drove her to the Salk Institute and we met with someone in their development department. She told them about my cancer and her fundraising idea. And truthfully, I think they were a little amused and probably touched by this young person's audacity. There were five women in the meeting and Carrie spoke candidly about how my diagnosis impacted her emotionally and how it impacted the whole family. There was not a dry eye in the group. They told us that they typically would not do something like this because, like with Nordstrom's, they had practices and rules in place, but they were moved to make an exception for Carrie. Carrie ended up raising $86,000 for research. She helped set up a charity auction event. Dr. Verma spoke about Carrie and what an impressive young woman she was for doing this. Carrie spoke so well in front of a room full of adults. Because of the money she raised, Dr. Verma was able to hire two post-doc fellow researchers to further his work.

Giving back to the community has always been important to our entire family. Even when Carrie was a very young girl and earning a small allowance, she would take her money to the grocery store where there were "donate your change" collection boxes for various causes. Carrie contributed what she had set aside.

Carrie has always had a greater awareness of the community beyond herself. She has a "take action and do some good" attitude which later influenced her decision to start her *Role Models Not Runway Models* initiative, featuring one of the first wheelchair bound models to be on the runway during New York Fashion Week.

"MOM, Lil Uzi Vert wants to fly us to Atlanta for the weekend. Let's go!" "Matt, no."

Matt Ox
IG: @MattOx
TW: @MattOx__
Laurel Grau
IG: @Lalama_ox

Laurel Grau is the mother of Matt Ox, a highly popular teenage rap artist from Philadelphia, PA who is signed to Motown Records and released his debut studio album in 2018. Laurel, like her son, grew up in the Lawncrest neighborhood of Northeast Philadelphia. One of five siblings, she attended Catholic high school while working at a local recreation center with her mom. As a sophomore, she gave birth to Matt at age 15 and took on the challenges of being a teenage mom. Laurel's unexpected entrance into motherhood was an adverse situation in itself, but what would soon come next completely changed everything.

Matt's father died two weeks following Laurel's high school graduation, which placed the responsibility of raising and providing for her son directly on Laurel's shoulders. Her parents helped out, but it was on Laurel to uphold most of the parental responsibilities. She eventually graduated college and became a first grade teacher after working as a baker, bartender, exercise instructor, cashier and cleaner, doing whatever possible to make ends meet.

And now, based on her son's success, it's safe to say Laurel did just that and more. Matt was writing his own rhymes by the age of 5, influenced by the likes of Eminem, Michael Jackson and Ozzie Osbourne. In May 2017, Matt, as a 12-year-old, released a music video for his first viral single "Overwhelming" that immediately elevated him into a known commodity on the rap scene. Now four years later, the video has amassed more than 29 million views on YouTube. A few months after the release of his 2018 debut album titled *Ox*, Matt had already collaborated with mainstream rappers like XXXtentacion, Lil Uzi Vert, and PnB Rock. He currently averages 1.9 million monthly listeners on Spotify and has a number of future projects in the works.

This chapter highlights the life of Laurel Grau, touching on a variety of topics spanning from the challenges of her early days of motherhood, to her present-day relationship with Matt.

Did your mother inspire you in any way? What kind of values did you take from her and instill in your own life as a mother?

My mom and I got along very well, but it's hard not to get along with my mom. She's the best! She has five children and a close relationship with each of us. Our relationship changed drastically when I had Matt when I was 15 years old, a sophomore in high school.

My mom inspired me in every way! She was basically my parenting partner, especially after Matt's dad died when Matt was only 2 and I was 18 years old. My mom and I lived in the same house while I parented Matt, so she had a huge influence on me. She helped so much, but when it came down to it, I was Matt's mom. I made the decisions on everything with him. She gave me equal amounts of support and space. I think that's definitely something I took from her. I give Matt the space to learn, grow and be himself.

What kind of dreams and goals did you have when you were a kid? How much did they influence where you are today?

As a young child, I wasn't the type of kid who thought,

"This is what I am going to be!" However, I did always enjoy writing. I journaled a lot as a kid. I remember in third grade; I did a report on how I wanted to be an author when I grew up. But, because I had Matt so young, my focus during my teenage years wasn't trying to figure out who I was and what I enjoyed. It was about caring for Matt. That's what moms often have to do - put their dreams on hold because we have a huge and tiring responsibility. Now, as Matt gets older, I'm getting some personal freedom back and am beginning to tap in with what I really enjoy.

When was the earliest indication that you thought Matt might have extraordinary talent?

There was no specific moment that told me. Creativity and marching to the beat of his own drum was just embedded into who he was as a person. I'll give you a few examples:

- I know it sounds ridiculous, but when Matt was a baby, he would hear music and dance and he really had rhythm!
- We used to listen to one of my brother's Beatles albums. Matt was about 3 years old. One day, we got into the car, and a Beatles song was on the radio (it wasn't even a song that was on the album). We heard it and he instantly screamed "It's the Beatles!!" He did this with many artists. He was so attentive to specific sounds.
- When he was a toddler, he was able to listen to a song and tell me all the instruments he heard.
- As he got older, he loved to dance, put on shows for people and write stories. As early as first grade, he was writing raps. In grade school, his personality stood out compared to other kids. Oftentimes Matt was made fun of, but he did not care at all.
- The last indication was Matt constantly telling me he was going to be famous.

Did you have to do anything to foster Matt's talent or was he always self-motivated?

Matt was obsessed with creativity. I knew he was musically inclined, but the programming for something like that is pretty limiting (with the resources I had at that time). The way I helped foster Matt's talent was to completely let him be himself and express himself how he wanted to.

My brother is a drummer and was in a band. So, I think he did the best job at fostering Matt's musical talent. He would bring him to his studio and we used to go to his band's shows. Their favorite thing to do together would be when Uncle Chris would play a beat on the piano and Matthew would rap over top.

Matt was always so self-motivated. He taught himself so much on the computer. His earlier raps he made by himself in his bedroom.

Everyone faces self-doubt, did Matt ever want to give up, and if so, how did you go about handling that?

This question is tough. People, especially in the entertainment industry, work years and sacrifice so much to get an ounce of the success Matt has. Matt has been very lucky in his career. I mean, he was 12 and was receiving recognition from people all over the world. His success came quick. However, an important lesson we learned is after success comes, that doesn't mean everything is going to be perfect. After success is the time you have to work even harder. An important lesson is that fame or success doesn't mean you don't have struggle anymore, which is a great lesson to learn at a young age.

How did you handle Matt's accomplishments and keep things in perspective?

I am so proud of Matt. I am so glad he found something he loves to do and that he can make a career and a living out of it. But becoming famous is not easy, especially when you're a kid. And especially for that kid's parents.

My biggest fear when Matt first became big was that he might think he's better than everyone else just because of his notoriety. I try my best to make him think of other people. When people tell me their kids are fans of Matt, I get Matt to write a letter, send a shirt or give them a call. I try to make him connect with his fans and see how powerful "Matt OX" is and the good he can put out in the world. I hope as his success grows, so does his heart and he continues to do good for others. Keeping him around our family has helped keep him grounded as well.

Is Matt interested in dating? How do you think you would handle his romantic relationships if the person he was attracted to did not seem like a good fit based on your motherly instincts?
He's 15. He is girl crazy. The likely scenario is that I will have to warn the girl about Matt, not Matt about the girl!

Was there a time Matt ever got in big trouble with you or at school?
Matt's whole sixth grade year was a nightmare. That year, he learned everyone has a different opinion and not everyone will see things how you do.

As a mother, what were you good at saying no to?
Impulse decisions. I hate them. Rappers love impulse decisions. It drives me nuts. There are times when Matt will run into my room and say something like - "MOM, Lil Uzi Vert wants to fly us to Atlanta for the weekend. Let's go!" I say no to things like that!

What would you say were important qualities to possess to be the mother you were?
Not being judgmental, the need to be calm, understanding and patient. I've struggled with being a mother, especially the past couple years. Why was I chosen to lead him? I was a 15-year-old when I had him.

I'm not wise enough, not good enough. But then I think of the flip side: What other mom would be able to do this? A 40-year-old who's married with three other kids to look after? Kudos to those momagers who are able to do that, but I don't have other children. Matt is my main responsibility. I'm young, so I'm kinda hip to what's out there – both the good and bad. I try to be non-judgmental and laid back. I'm recognizing 15 years into motherhood that I bring great value. I don't know if I ever truly saw that before in myself.

What were things you think you may have handled differently?

Me raising Matt wasn't in the traditional sense at all. I was a single mom, sharing a room with him, in my family's home, I was so young. Oftentimes, I learned as Matt learned. We grew up together. I made a million mistakes. One that I think about often is I wish I was in the moment more. More present with Matt. I think I subconsciously struggled as a single mom. I worked a lot, I was in school, trying to do everything "right." But when I got one on one time with Matt, I'd be so tired and drained. I feel like I didn't fully enjoy moments because I was too worn out.

But my life has paid me back in many ways. I'm able to see the mistakes I made and look at life differently. Now, I get to be with Matt all the time! Although, at times it's hard, I know how lucky I am that I get to do this with him. I never got to be a stay-at-home mom. Now I am. And it's at a time that Matt is as busy as he's ever been, and I get to be there for every single moment.

What is your relationship like now with Matt?

We go everywhere together! We work from home together, we homeschool together, we travel together. We're super close.

It's funny how life works out. Being a single teen mom, I was so restricted. I didn't go on a senior week or have a summer shore house or even a weekend getaway like the rest of my friends. Between finances and finding a babysitter, traveling was out of the question. Now, it's like he's paying me back or something (not that he owes me anything) with the way everything has worked out. We get to travel the world together. We went to Paris and London in 2019!

If you could name one characteristic you believe Matt inherited from you, what would that be?
His compassion for others! Also, his face!

What is something you think the media or public has wrong about Matt?
That he doesn't wash his hair! I caught him using my $30 Olaplex shampoo on his mop head because there was none of the $4 Herbal Essence left. He is dedicated to washing. He just doesn't brush!

Any stories of adversity that Matt faced?
His sixth grade year was so hard. Teachers didn't like him. The kids didn't like him. He got beat up in the bathroom that year, almost got expelled, fights on the bus, fights outside of school. He was really unhappy.

At the end of that year, his song, *"Overwhelming"* came out. That taught both of us so much. Now when we reflect back on that year, Matt associates hard times with making amazing art and it feels balanced. He recognizes that people have to go through hard times and when you come out on the other end, you're a better and stronger person.

How did you respond to situations that made you feel overwhelmed?
Matt and I spend a lot of time together so naturally we get into arguments here and there. When we're ready to lose it on each other, I try to stop what I'm doing. I breathe and I step away. I'll tell Matt I need a few

minutes. During that time, I'll do something to distract me (a chore, take the dog for a walk, eat something, cry). Then when I come back, I can communicate better. Those days I'm prouder of myself. But the days I scream and yell, I try to talk to Matt afterwards. I think showing your kids that it's okay to lose it but communicating with them afterwards is important. Parents are human and make mistakes. Own your mistakes and try better next time.

Can you offer any advice to young or soon to be mothers/parents?
I find it hard to give or take parenting advice because everyone's situation is different. The best advice I received was from my mom: "When you become a parent, it's a choice YOU make. It is your responsibility. Don't ever make your kids feel like a burden."

My other piece of advice is to ignore any parenting critics! (They're everywhere!) The only people you need to prove anything to are your children. They're the only ones who matter.

Looking back, what would you say was the greatest gift you gave to your kid?
I provided an environment where Matt could always be himself with no judgement (the best that I could) and I encouraged exploration and creativity.

If you could tell everyone in the world one thing, what would it be?
The only way out is through.

"Don't think that because you're small that your problems are smaller than mine, your problems are as big as mine."

Bob Menery
IG: @BobMenery
TW: @BobMenery
Podcasts – Ripper
Magoos, Zapped

Patty Oakes Menery is the mother of

Bob Menery. Bob is a comedian, actor, podcast host and social media personality most notable for his "golden voice" of sportscaster impressions. Born and raised in North Andover, Massachusetts, Patty was 15 when her father died, leaving her mother widowed at 39 years-old with six children to raise ranging from ages 2 to 18. Despite the immense challenges in front of her, Patty's mother instilled a life of faith and resilience into her children, and because of that, Patty developed a deep-rooted desire to one day become a mom herself. She went on to have three children – Heather, Mark and Bobby.

The Menery children spent their early years in Lawrence, Massachusetts before the family moved back to North Andover when they were in grade school. Patty played an integral role in their lives, spending 15 years as a stay-at-home mom while her husband, Mark, worked at Northwestern Mutual to provide for the family. She later became a preschool teacher as her kids grew older and the need to be at home diminished.

As Patty tells it, Bob was *always* theatrical; whether it was getting in trouble in school or when she overheard him reciting mock play-by-play routines and sportscaster impersonations from the basement. His first passion was basketball, but comedy eventually became his top priority in high school. He took classes at the New York Film Academy and moved to Los Angeles in an attempt to begin an acting career. However, he struggled to gain traction in Hollywood and returned home four years later with little to show for it. Although in reality, his story was just beginning.

In 2017, one of Bob's faux sports broadcasting bits went viral, quickly sling-shotting him into internet fame. Since then, he has taken social media by storm with his unprecedented play-by-play calls over some of the most iconic moments in sports history. As of August 2020, the 32-year-old now has 2.8 million followers on Instagram, 1 million Facebook subscribers and an estimated net worth of $5 million.

For an inside look into the ups and downs of her life, Patty reflects back on her early childhood influences, discusses how the sudden death of her father affected the family and gives her opinion on Bob's unique meteoric rise to social media stardom.

Did your mother inspire you in any way? What kind of values did you take from her and instill in your own life as a mother?

My mother was one with a true Irish Catholic outlook on life. She was widowed at 39 with six children. I admired her so much for her perseverance under the circumstances. She had a good deal of faith and I felt that helped me to instill it in my children.

When was the earliest indication that you thought Bob might have extraordinary talent?

At every teacher conference that we attended, it was always the same comments, "I don't know what Bobby is going to end up doing, but, I know it's going to be something big!" Yet, they would always say it with a chuckle! I always thought of Bobby as this real-life Ferris

Bueller. An interesting thought looking back – Bobby was always very theatrical and when he was about 12, he would have these sessions in the basement with a neighbor, David. They would mimic a popular McDonald's commercial that Hank Azaria (of Simpson's fame) was the voice for, and they would go on for hours with that skit entertaining each other. And, what's interesting about that is, Bobby is partnering up with Hank Azaria now with a social media project 20 years later!

Any stories of adversity that Bob faced?
After his first stint in Hollywood, Bobby came home out of the blue, totally surprising us. It wasn't until then that I had learned he was living out of his car there for the last three months. I was heartbroken and felt saddened I didn't know of it until now. I know he didn't tell me because he didn't want me to worry. Those were tough times for him, he came home feeling like a failure. But, when he came home, he found a new spirit and had ideas of using social media as a way to get attention. So, one night, he did one of his typical announcing rants and he posted it. The next day it blew up and went viral. It was suddenly, "who is this guy with the golden voice and why isn't he in the broadcast booth with Joe Buck?"

What would you say were important qualities to possess to be the mother you were?
Sense of humor (especially with Bobby), faith, love and compassion are the real qualities that I believe were most important.

What were things you think you may have handled differently?
I feel like I held him back a bit because I tended to be extra cautious. I would have felt easier about letting them take more risks. That's what I would change.

What is your relationship like now with Bob?
Our relationship is wonderful as it is with his dad also!
Bobby and I speak four or five times a week. Bobby is
great with his brother and sister, brother-in-law, sister-in-
law and his niece and four nephews. My grandchildren
love him like a big brother!

**If you could name one characteristic you believe Bob
inherited from you, what would that be?**
The quality I think he most definitely got from me is his
sensitivity. But, if I may add another, it would be my
sense of humor! Bobby is a very kind person with a great
soul. I think sometimes he may come across more brash
at times, but it's just part of his schtick.

How has Bob grown from the adversity he has faced?
Bobby wasn't the best listener – he had his mind made up
to do things his way. It caused him setbacks at times, but,
in the end, was part of the secret to his current success.
Interestingly, Bobby didn't listen to anyone about some
of the chances he took as a social media personality. He
was doing things on the cutting edge and using language
that was never allowed in our household growing up! So
when Bobby started to do his schtick, which centered
around profane language that sportscaster's would love to
say but can't – with my upbringing, I was taken aback
some at first, but slowly realized that this was his path for
now and he seemed to be getting great feedback from all
of the important people in the industry.

**Can you offer any advice to young or soon to be
mothers/parents?**
The advice I would give to other mothers – just love your
kids unconditionally, you can't lose, they will feel secure,
and the rest will happen naturally. Give them room to be
who they are! If I could go back, I would tell myself to
worry less and relax more because it's all good.
 One last thing I always tried to convey to my kids was

a lesson I took from my father when he told me that don't think because you're small that your problems are smaller than mine, your problems are as big as mine. That always made me feel like I could talk to him and I always tried to relay that same message to my kids.

Looking back, what would you say was the greatest gift you gave to your kids?
The greatest gift I gave to my kids is the essence of family values: laughter, loyalty and love!

If you could tell everyone in the world one thing, what would it be?
There is good in everyone, you just need to look for it sometimes!

"There were many times parenting was only one of the things I was doing in my life. In retrospect, it is the most important thing – my practice could go, my finances could fail, I could even recover from the loss of my long happy marriage. But if my children did not become to a large extent, functioning, fairly happy adults with relationships, interests and interactions with the world outside of themselves, I believe that would be torture for me to live with."

Emmalee Bierly
IG: @WCtherapygroup
Podcast: @ShrinkChicks

Elin Bierly is the mother of Emmalee Bierly

L.M.F.T, a licensed marriage and family therapist who specializes in increasing intimacy within couples, fostering female self-esteem and self-worth and helping clients cope with life-stage transitions. Elin was raised on the Upper West Side of New York City. Both of her parents worked so Elin grew up fast holding various jobs by the time she was 13 and graduating high school early at age 16. After a brief stint at a Connecticut college, Elin moved across the country to Tempe, Arizona, where she co-owned and operated a clothing store for a few years before enrolling at Arizona State University. She graduated from ASU in the early 1970s and then earned a

M.A. in Psychology from U.S. International University in San Diego, CA while training to become a meditation teacher.

For Elin, motherhood began back on the East Coast. After marrying Emmalee's father in California, the couple moved to the Philadelphia area (where he was from) and started a family. Both of their children – Emmalee and Jake – were born in West Chester, Pennsylvania, a suburban town 45 minutes west of the city and were raised in nearby Malvern.

Like her mother, Emmalee used education to build the foundation for a career in psychology. She graduated from Penn State in 2012 and got her Master's in Marriage Family Therapy from Thomas Jefferson University in 2014. Soon after, she co-founded The West Chester Therapy Group, a practice of independently practicing therapists dedicated to helping clients work through life's challenges and develop a greater quality of life. They help clients foster better connections with themselves and those in their lives by providing individual, family and relationship therapy and are committed to helping them gain greater insight into themselves and their relationship patterns. Emmalee also co-hosts a podcast called Shrink Chicks, which strives to help "find the balance in all the bullshit by offering relatable therapeutic topics and leaving tiresome psychobabble behind." With over 35 episodes to date, the show has a 5-star average rating on Apple Podcasts from hundreds of reviews.

This chapter offers Elin's perspective on the importance of being a model of authenticity for your children to help them discover who they are and who they want to be.

Did your mother inspire you in any way? What kind of values did you take from her and instill in your own life as a mother?
I had a very contentious relationship with my own

mother and early on I felt like we had no love shared. I strongly leaned on my father and his sweet disposition for security, while my mother was more mercurial and even emotionally volatile. What I could not understand, until much later, was that my mother had not really been mothered and in fact, as a child, she was called to take on adult responsibilities. When my father died in 1975, I was 28 and my mother was 58 and still teaching full time. We lived on different coasts and I did not have much sympathy for what I saw as self-pity, neediness and insecurity. I was very involved in my own life, had moved 3,000 miles away and had no intention of moving back. Later, I came to really admire how she rebuilt her life, returning to college at 40, working a full 25-year teaching career and remarrying at age 65. I think she thoroughly enjoyed the freedom and financial security of her retirement years, traveling, moving outside of New York City and when widowed again at age 88, she was comfortable with her life and who she had become.

My mother showed me nothing but approval and admiration for my own choices. She was thrilled I finally settled down (at age 36) and was crazy about my husband and his family and our children and that we too had come back to the East Coast. She lived to be nearly 96 years old and even in her last years, with dementia, made many good choices, empowering me to make decisions for her that I thought she would want. After she died, I found a paper on the table of her living room in her assisted living apartment, where she had spent her last year. It said, "Thank you, thank you, thank you."

I was inspired by my mother to be a lifelong learner and to keep an interest in enjoying life. She participated in every activity offered to her and after returning from a concert, I asked her how she enjoyed it. She said, "I can't remember a thing about it, but I'm sure I loved it because I always do."

When was the earliest indication that you thought Emmalee might have extraordinary talent?

Emmalee's extraordinary talent was that she could fit into any situation or occasion and make it her own. She was attractive and engaging and showed highly developed emotional intelligence from her earliest childhood. She loved to interact with both children and adults. Before she was 2 and could not yet speak, she set herself in a child's chair in the middle of a group, at an unfamiliar relatives' home, and proceeded with a doll as a prop, to act out a scene, talking to her doll in gibberish baby English and taking it around and sitting back down but making sure that every adult was involved and watching her. We all just looked at each other thinking, "What is she doing?" The world was her stage. There was no situation where she could make herself uncomfortable.

Did you have to do anything to foster Emmalee's talent or was she always self-motivated?

Emmalee was interested in everything. She wanted to try every sport or extracurricular activity but wasn't really keen on any one thing or practicing for that matter. She was more interested in the performance. She was social. Before age 7, she said she knew the name of every child in her school. This would only have been just over one hundred people and I never really tested it out, but I can believe it. She had one hundred friends by first grade. Knowing Emmalee today, I think it is true. She liked everyone and they liked her. I tried to find some balance in allowing her to participate in anything she wanted but I think I kept my eye on the prize that academic achievement was a necessity. I was concerned at times that she could fall through the cracks by not getting enough help in school because she wasn't needy enough. I defended her weakness in elementary school French by saying "She can't even hear the different sounds in English, how is she supposed to "hear" French? She needs to be taught." I would say that "needing to be taught" was a feature of Emmalee's learning style. She did not learn intuitively, she understood people intuitively. Academically, she really had to be taught what to listen for, what to look for, how to break assignments into parts. However, her retention of this learning was incredible and she could generalize it as well. Her natural abilities are in comprehension, she can connect ideas and facts like nobody else I know.

How did you handle Emmalee's accomplishments and keep things in perspective?
It was not hard to do. Emmalee has always shown compassion and sensitivity towards others. When she was young, she asked to stop and buy flowers to put at a statue of Jesus (she called him, "cheese-us") in a cemetery we passed on the way to school. She noticed that many of the graves had Christmas wreaths and adornments, but his statue had none. When we had a burial ceremony for our cat who had been hit by a car, she thanked the cat for coming home to die because otherwise we wouldn't have known what happened and that would have made all of us sad forever instead of sad for just a while. We had a period when our family made and served lunch once a month at a homeless shelter and Emmalee was the most involved server in our family and the most comfortable with seeing the person beyond the difference. She was always interested in any service project but never missed an opportunity to put on a costume and be center stage.

Any stories of adversity that Emmalee faced?
Emmalee had every kind of academic challenge. She didn't talk until after 3 and had to go to speech therapy for the first few years of school. She couldn't really discriminate sounds, which made reading difficult. She had to have optical training to align her eyes for reading. She was a dreamer and a thinker. In kindergarten, there was a song she made up that she would sing on the way home. It was called, "Why is right right and left left?" I

remember the line, "They both have houses, they both have trees so why is right right and left left?" I thought this was brilliant – everyone was acting as if there really was a difference between right and left and this 5-year-old had to come to terms with the fact that their names were arbitrary designations.

As a mother, what were you good at saying no to?

I was never very good at saying "no" to Emmalee. She could take away my power both through her sweetness and sometimes through her sadness, but her anger always turned me off. I couldn't get in touch with the pain she was in under the anger (when it was coming toward me) until she finally told me. I'm sorry about that now because it was not necessarily personal toward me in those high school years, but it sure felt personal. I retreated into spirituality and used prayer when I couldn't find ways to communicate my hopes and fears.

What would you say were important qualities to possess to be the mother you were?

I think the most important qualities to possess are perseverance and authenticity. Perseverance really is just realizing that there is no end point and relationships have to evolve – even parent/daughter relationships, continuously. Authenticity is crucial, you can't play being a mother (though sometimes that will get you over a difficult patch). You can say, "I am your parent and as a parent it is my responsibility to feed and clothe you and make sure you do your homework and get to sleep. But, as a person, I feel for you. I understand that it is a stupid assignment and you are never going to use that chemistry class or whatever." The authentic part is admitting that you do not have all the answers, that you can't always fix things, that your child is a separate person. This is very hard and heart-breaking at times.

What were things you think you may have handled differently?
This is so hard. I think I would have prevented harm coming to her in situations that were unsupervised, if I could have. I didn't imagine some of the things that could happen. But if I had been able to prevent that harm, would Emmalee have become who she is or will be? Probably not. So, I would just say to a reader – do the best you can but accept your limitations. Our children are and are supposed to be separate. Her stories are her stories, not mine.

What is your relationship like now with Emmalee?
I think Emmalee and I have an excellent relationship. I'm pretty much as in love with her now as I was when she was born. But I now know that others are too. Somewhere in the college years (I think) Emmalee decided she really wanted to have a close relationship with me and her dad (I think the dad-daughter dynamic was always easier if not closer). She has included us in her life and often expresses gratitude and personal admiration toward us. Being a role model really makes you want to live up to that standard, even if you know all the reasons you don't deserve it. Her choices have been her own and I often hear about things after she makes decisions.

If you could name one characteristic you believe Emmalee inherited from you, what would that be?
I think the answer to this is the compassion piece of her heart. She's a good therapist because she can empathize. She didn't learn that. One morning when she was in high school, she asked if I would still be in practice when she graduated from college because she had dreamed we had adjacent offices. I guess the imprint of becoming a therapist was already there (though she started college as a Special Ed major).

Did any times of adversity set you up for later success?

I think an early failure of mine that set me up for greater success later (as a parent) was the sincere regret that I wasn't always there to "save" her. During her childhood, I was building my own practice. I was also parenting her brother – a very different person. I was trying to maintain a relationship with my husband by getting a little time alone. I was managing the house, paying bills, etc. There were many times parenting was only one of the things I was doing in my life. In retrospect, it is the most important thing – my practice could go, my finances could fail, I could even recover from the loss of my long happy marriage. But, if my children did not become to a large extent, functioning, fairly happy adults with relationships, interests and interactions with the world outside of themselves, I believe that would be torture for me to live with. I wanted to be, as a parent, what I thought I didn't have. So maybe I wanted Emmalee to feel like she mattered, like she was an adult who made her own decisions (like I feel I am) but one who was loved and approved of in those choices. As a parent of adults now, I find I don't really care so much what choices they make – even ones that aren't the best and you have to learn from. What I care about is who they are as humans and I want more than anything for them to experience the joy of loving their children.

Can you offer any advice to young or soon to be mothers/parents?

This would be my advice to younger mothers – your children are people. Tiny humans are born with the seed of becoming something. As parents, we are called to help them become themselves. That is terrifically hard, however, since we don't know what that is. It's the idea of the acorn and the oak. An acorn doesn't have to do anything else to succeed except become an oak. The child is a gift even in their acorn-ness. We know they are humans, that's all we really know, and it is the most important thing so if we have some idea of what people need to be fully human, we can parent. And if we don't know, we need to be working on ourselves and asking that question so our children can figure it out. I think the emphasis on achievement is reprehensible but very difficult to avoid.

Looking back, what would you say was the greatest gift you gave to your kids?

I think I showed them a model of authenticity. In an age-appropriate way, I tried to let my children know me, know my limits and my ability to change and grow. As they grew into adulthood, we could understand each other better and the fact that parenting only goes so far. It is more important to be true to yourself than it is to do the right thing. There are always consequences for decisions but if our motivation is clearer, those consequences are easier to accept. There are no simple solutions to life's challenges.

If you could tell everyone in the world one thing, what would it be?

Be yourself. Trying to be anyone else is exhausting and ultimately unsuccessful. Play life to your strengths. It's good to keep improving on the weak side of your personality or skills but don't spend too much time on them. Hint: Who you are has to do with your gifts.

"Show your children love and respect, encourage them on their goals but have rules and stay firm. Most importantly - instill faith."

Vincent Vargas
IG: @Vincent.Rocco.Vargas
VinnyRoc Podcast

Alicia Vargas is the mother of Vincent "Rocco" Vargas, a prominent film producer, actor, writer and U.S. Army veteran. Alicia grew up as the second oldest of eight siblings in the suburbs of El Paso, Texas. Her father worked for the City of El Paso Parks and Recreation Department while her mother stayed home to look after their eight children. She started working at a very young age, spending summers picking cotton and onions in the 90-degree Texas heat to contribute money for the family. Alicia moved to Los Angeles a few days after her 18th birthday with dreams of becoming a model or actress. However, after her Hollywood pursuit fizzled out, she worked numerous jobs in order to make ends meet.

Alicia met her husband, Carlos, while in Los Angeles. They had four kids together – Junior, Genise, Vincent and Vanessa – and raised them in the San Fernando Valley area. At first, money was scarce, but their situation drastically improved after Carlos got accepted into the Los Angeles Fire Department. He served as a firefighter for 32 years in addition to maintaining his role as a high-profile boxing cutman. Sports were always a central figure of the Vargas household. Vince had dreams of becoming a professional baseball player and even earned a scholarship to play at Brescia University in Kentucky.

However, he struggled in college which made him academically ineligible for his scholarship. He couldn't afford to stay without it, so he joined the United States Army.

Vince's time in the Army changed his life and helped shape the man he is today. He served three combat deployments to Iraq and Afghanistan in 2003 with the U.S. Army's 2nd Ranger Battalion, 75th Ranger Regiment. Upon leaving active duty in 2007, he joined the U.S. Army Reserves and then worked for Arizona Corrections and the U.S. Border Patrol. In 2013, Vince changed paths and pursued a career as an entertainer. In the eight years since, he has built a brand as an actor, writer, producer, blogger, podcaster, business entrepreneur and social media influencer. He was an original member of the *Drinkin' Bros* podcast, appeared in the 2017 zombie apocalypse comedy *Range 15* and has a recurring role on the FX series *Mayans M.C.* But his most notable accomplishment may be the positive impact he's made on fellow veterans who struggle with the challenges of post-combat life. Through his work, Vince has shed light on his own personal struggles with depression, alcoholism, and PTSD to provide advice on how to overcome them and live a meaningful life. He encourages veterans to become "Beterans" – a phrase he ultimately turned into a clothing company that sells apparel to raise money for veteran transition centers across the country.

In this chapter, Alicia shares her own personal stories from Vince's upbringing and details how he became the husband and father he is today.

Did your mother inspire you in any way? What kind of values did you take from her and instill in your own life as a mother?
We had a close relationship. I felt comfortable sharing with her my feelings and my dreams. She was supportive and encouraging and never was judgmental of my dreams.

For example, when I told her I wanted to move to LA, I was 17 then, she said, "first finish high school and then you can move but be careful and make wise decisions." When I moved to LA, I still made sure I called her weekly to stay connected.

My mother inspired me by being a great example of a hard worker with a positive outlook and always thinking of other people's feelings first. These important qualities, along with being honest and humble, were values she instilled in me that in return I did my best to carry onto my children.

Did you have to do anything to foster Vince's talent or was he always self-motivated?

He was self-motivated. I always told him hard work pays off but remember to always stay humble and that you catch more bees with honey.

How did you handle Vince's accomplishments and keep things in perspective?

I was proud of him because he reminded me of me. He wasn't afraid to take chances which I encouraged him to do.

Any stories of adversity that Vince faced?

He was dyslexic and I felt bad because not one teacher ever told me. I do remember one of his high school teachers mentioning to me that Vince never took his backpack off his back in class but would always raise his hand to answer all the questions. When I asked Vince about it, he said he was embarrassed because he couldn't read or spell at his grade level.

I feel these challenges only helped strengthen who he is because he had to work harder than other kids. I remember him calling me when he was taking any test in college, the army, or border patrol to tell me how he was struggling to pass tests. I would always reinforce him and say, "you can do it." And now to see that he writes books is amazing. I feel he is a role model for children that suffer from the same disability. He didn't give up.

If you were heavily involved, how did you make time for yourself?
I would go for a jog or exercise and bring the kids along while I ran around the track, they would play on the football field. I joke because people always ask me how did you do it with two kids and twins? I would say I ignored them, but in reality it was tough because my husband was a firefighter and was at work most days.

What would you say were important qualities to possess to be the mother you were?
I tried to role model having respect for others, responsibility, hard work and honesty.

What were things you think you may have handled differently?
I wish I would have known Vince was dyslexic and gotten him the proper help he needed. He struggled so much on test taking. However, I'm very proud of him that it didn't stop him from going after his dreams.

If you could name one characteristic you believe Vince inherited from you, what would that be?
Determination!

Can you offer any advice to young or soon to be mothers/parents?
Show your children love and respect, encourage them on their goals but have rules and stay firm. Most importantly, instill faith.

Looking back, what would you say was the greatest gift you gave to your kids?
My unconditional love and support, although I may have not always agreed with all of their choices, they will

always have my support.

If you could tell everyone in the world, one thing, what would it be?
Believe in yourself because anything is possible.

> **"When he says I am driving him mad my response is, there's only one thing worse than loving someone too much, not loving them at all."**

James Harris
IG: @Jamesbondst
TW: @Jamesbondst
Bondstreetpartners.com

Dawn Deyong is the mother of James

Harris, a high-profile California real estate agent who stars on Bravo Network's hit television series *Million Dollar Listing Los Angeles*. Dawn is originally from London where she was born into a Jewish family and had one sister, Gail, who she is best friends with to this day. Their parents owned and operated a fashion company that sold exclusive clothing brands to celebrities and royals, igniting a passion for fashion design that Dawn still carries out today. Her upbringing was far from normal. At age 12, Dawn was diagnosed with Crohn's Disease which caused her to be hospitalized for several months at a time. She didn't have the best relationship with her mother, who struggled from bipolar disorder and never held a meaningful role in her life.

In need of a change, Dawn left home when she was 17 and got her first job at Gucci on Old Bond Street, a famous road through the West End of London widely known as the city's home for prestigious fashion outlets. She got married at age 22 and had James, her only child, a year later, but divorced his father by the time James was in preschool and raised him on her own. In the early 1980s, she became a buyer for the elite designers Joseph and Kenzo and later transitioned into a personal stylist. Today, she runs her own interior design/lifestyle consulting company called Dawn Deyong Lifestyle. As of the writing of this book, Dawn was battling serious health concerns, having had emergency stoma surgery in November 2020.

James began his career in real estate at 16 years old. After working as a residential investment agent in the United Kingdom, he moved to Los Angeles with his childhood friend and business partner, David Parnes. Today, they are the co-founders of Bond Street Partners, a California realty company that specializes in high-end residential real estate and investment properties in Beverly Hills, Bel Air, Holmby Hills, Sunset Strip, Hollywood Hills, Brentwood, Pacific Palisades, Malibu and the greater Los Angeles region. Bond Street Partners has eclipsed more than $1 billion in property sales since 2016, earning James awards and recognition from the likes of *Variety, Hollywood Reporter, Los Angeles Business Journal and Wall Street Journal.* He has starred on *Million Dollar Los Angeles* since 2014.

Dawn and James maintain a very close mother-son connection today although both faced a fair share of obstacles in life such as Dawn's constant battle with Crohn's disease and James' severe ADHD. This chapter unpacks the real stories behind their challenges and successes.

Did your mother inspire you in any way? What kind of values did you take from her and instill in your own life as a mother?
I did not have the greatest relationship with my mother. My sister and I felt very alone. We didn't know anyone else who wasn't close with their mum. There is a story that sticks out to me from my childhood that I think sums up how my mum was. When I was in the hospital getting ready for another operation, my friends came to visit and one of them had on a leather jacket. My mother asked her where she got the jacket and my friend told her.

So she said, "Come on, we're going." And she left. I went into surgery and I remember waking up and seeing that jacket on my mum. She went to the store right then and there just to get the jacket. It's memories like these that helped me make sure I was very warm with James when I had him and was raising him.

My grandmother on the other hand, was a very lively and warm person. My mother was nothing like that. My grandmother was terribly sad about my relationship with her daughter (my mum). My mother did not know the meaning of the word love.

When was the earliest indication that you thought James might have extraordinary talent?

James was special, not in the most apparent ways though. My boy was asked to leave nursery school at the age of 3. What child gets asked to leave nursery at 3!? James did! Apparently, he didn't fit in and from then on, every school he attended said the same! This happened nine times until he left school altogether. After every exam he took, he would tell me that it was easy and that's why he finished early. He actually never passed an exam until his driving test at 17.

James entered a special needs school when he was 14. It really helped him. They had kids with Asperger's, Tourette Syndrome, ADHD, etc. Their philosophy was, "There's always someone who has it worse than you." James had a job to look after a child there who had been abused. This child did not speak. I swear that this was the making of James. Within weeks James and his charm had this boy talking and actually going outside of his room. Everyone who worked there was astonished. James was at this school for two years and then he left and started to look for work.

How did you handle James' accomplishments and keep things in perspective?

I always believed in looking at the positive side of things

and encouraging him for his effort. I remember when he finished in eighth place in the egg and spoon race, I made him feel like a superstar. You'd think he just earned a scholarship or something! What else can you do other than make someone feel loved, whoever they are?

Any stories of adversity that James faced?
Yes, a few weeks after getting his first job in real estate at the age of 16, James got a DUI and lost his driver's license. As an agent, you need a car to be able to do showings. He wouldn't leave his room; he was so ashamed. So, I called up his boss and told him what happened. He said he was coming over to the house. When he came over, he told James he was going to buy him a bicycle and that he would have to use it for showings. He wouldn't even ride it. We used to drive by and see him pushing his bike all over town. It was hysterical.

What would you say were important qualities to possess to be the mother you were?
Resilience, patience, unconditional love and humor. You have to be able to laugh.

If you could name one characteristic you believe James inherited from you, what would that be?
His salesmanship. I always believed I could sell ice to an eskimo but I've never seen anything like what he has. His outgoing personality and charisma are truly special.

How has James grown from the adversity he has faced?
For James, I think there were two turning points in his life. The first was when he was kicked out of all of those schools and attended the special needs school. The second was when he went to Alcoholics Anonymous to get away from alcohol and marijuana. Everyone is affected differently by these things, but it's tough to have

ADHD and quit them. He got the help he needed. He has remained clean ever since and has been ultra-successful. James has an addictive personality, so once he was able to channel that and put it towards work, that was perfect for him.

Can you offer any advice to young or soon to be mothers/parents?

It's the same thing I always say – once you become a mother you are a mother for life. Your kids are your responsibility forever, at any age. It's a full-time job and it's worth every second. To have and love a child is such a blessing. Don't have one unless you are prepared to make sacrifices. When I look at my son, I am very proud and I feel like I do play a part, a huge part, and all mothers do – even when it feels like you don't. We all play an integral part and we have tremendous value.

Looking back, what would you say was the greatest gift you gave to your kids?

The greatest gift you can give anyone is your time.

If you could tell the world one thing, what would it be?

Actions speak louder than words, every time.

"Sometimes, as a parent, you are unpopular, annoying, or too hard on your kids, but you do it out of love. Children need to always know you believe in them and will be their advocate in challenging times and for the long haul. It is easy to be proud of your children's successes, but kids need to know you will be there for them when they experience heartache or disappointments along the way."

Field Yates
IG: @FieldYates
TW: @FieldYates

Paige Yates is the mother of Field Yates, a former NFL scout who now works as an on-air host and NFL Insider for ESPN. Paige grew up just outside of Columbus, Ohio as one of four siblings. Her father owned an insurance agency and her mother was a stay-at-home mom who volunteered heavily in their local community until she opened her own interior design company. Paige spent 13 years in private school at the Columbus School for Girls. After a brief stint playing three varsity sports for an all-women's college, Colby, she transferred to Wheelock College (Massachusetts) and graduated with a B.S. in Education in 1975.

Paige stayed in Massachusetts for three years teaching and then moved back to her hometown of Columbus, OH. She returned to Boston once she married and had three children – Field, Taylor and Charlotte. She worked part time at the Carroll School, a school for dyslexic kids before getting her real estate license in 1989. She has now been an active agent for more than 30 years. As a Premier Associate of Coldwell Banker, she has been a consistent top producer in the Boston area and recognized as a Top Real Estate Agent by the Wall Street Journal (2011). She's a member of the prestigious Coldwell Banker International President's Elite, a Relocation Specialist and a Previews Specialist for Luxury Homes.

From Paige's perspective, Field was a sports-invested "numbers guy" from an early age, two qualities that comprise his professional success. He graduated from Wesleyan University, where he spent four summers interning with the New England Patriots, IMG and Octagon before earning his Bachelor of Arts degree in psychology. Following his graduation, Field took an unpaid summer internship with the Kansas City Chiefs, which turned into a full-time role on the team's scouting and coaching staffs once the season began. After two years with the Chiefs, Field returned home to Boston and later joined ESPN in 2012. He started with the network as a writer for ESPN Boston while co-hosting a pair of radio shows - Operational Football and Football Friendzy. He also served as an NFL Insider on Fantasy Football Now for five seasons (2015-2019) before becoming the show's host in 2020.

In his current role, Field is an NFL Insider who provides analysis, news and fantasy football insight year-round across ESPN's multimedia platforms. He co-hosts the popular *Fantasy Focus Football* podcast, as well as ESPN Radio's weekly *Primetime* show. In addition to being a regular contributor to *NFL Live, SportsCenter, The Fantasy Show with Matthew Berry* on ESPN+ and more, Field also takes part in ESPN's annual NFL Draft and Fantasy Football Marathon coverage.

For this chapter, Paige provides her tips on motherhood while detailing Field's unconventional path to becoming a mainstay at the world's premier sports media company.

Did your mother inspire you in any way? What kind of values did you take from her and instill in your own life as a mother?

My relationship with my mother was complicated. My mother was not easily satisfied. She was competitive by nature, compared her children to friend's children and never took a moment to enjoy her children's athletic, academic and social achievements. My mother never believed our individual successes were enough. Because my mother was never satisfied with her children's accomplishments, we all struggled to believe in ourselves and to have confidence. Without confidence, the path to success is long and hard. I learned that children need to find both individual successes, pursue their unique passions and be given enough latitude to meet challenges head on and enough time to wallow in their achievements.

My mother's style of parenting made me understand there is a fine line between a parent encouraging their child, nurturing their potential, accepting who they are, and acknowledging how their individual skill set will be valued as they become an adult. I worked hard to encourage my children to pursue their own interests, experiment with life's opportunities, make wrong choices, enjoy moments of success, find their inner confidence and be the best.

My mother was determined. I used that value to help my children conquer setbacks along the way and open doors that provided them with opportunities to succeed. My dad was the one whose values I most admired though. He was hard-working, loved life and did not know a stranger. The only thing he asked of his kids was that they try their hardest and always do their best.

When was the earliest indication that you thought Field might have extraordinary talent?

I don't think there was an exact moment that a light bulb went off and I thought Field had a talent that was going to land him in a successful career. His interests from a very young age and his early passion to play and watch sports were always encouraged. He was consistently a self-starter, highly disciplined, tenacious and observant. He was determined to always stay ahead of what was being asked of him and eager to please people (teachers, colleagues, coaches).

Until the summer after fourth grade, Field was a good student but a very quiet classmate. He always got his work done and completed everything on time, but he was not the standout class leader or the vivacious kid that raised his hand and answered all the questions. He was shy.

During that summer of 1996, the local community theater in Siasconset produced a children's play. The play they chose that summer was *Fantastic Mr. Fox* by Roald Dahl, which was one of Field's favorite authors. He came to me and told me he was going to be the lead, Fantastic Mr. Fox. (You must understand these plays were casual, made up of kids ranging in age from 6 to 12, rehearsed and performed in three weeks.) I pointed out to Field that in order to be Fantastic Mr. Fox, he would be on stage performing in front of hundreds of people. He had never wanted to be the center of attention, so as his mother, I worried he didn't understand what would be expected of him or the pressure of being the center of attention. He actually turned to me and said, "Mom, I know I have to be on stage. Mr. Fox has 86 lines and I have already memorized the entire play." He was selected to be Fantastic Mr. Fox and a star was born.

How did you handle Field's accomplishments and keep things in perspective?

We were always excited to celebrate accomplishments with our children at a young age. We were fortunate to be able to watch many of their games. We enjoyed post game events, end of year celebrations and titles. Field chose to participate in sports that were team sports. He was never the fastest kid or the top scorer, but he always knew his position, knew what the coaches wanted him to do and worked every day in practice to his fullest potential. To keep success in perspective, we encouraged team spirit, cooperation, discipline and to learn from the losses.

Did you have to do anything to foster Field's talent or was he always self-motivated?
Field naturally had good habits whether they were being used in sports, school, summer activities, internships or as a young adult in his career. He is incredibly organized, never misses a deadline, doesn't do things last minute, utterly prepared, respectful of everyone he comes in contact with, thoughtful and hardworking, polite to people who have helped him, self-motivated and incredibly loyal to his friends, co-workers and family.

Any stories of adversity that Field faced?
I think Field had two serious moments of self-doubt. After college, he was scheduled to be part of a professional coaching staff, but days before the opportunity was set to begin, it fell through. It left him stunned, distressed, hurt and hard pressed to find a job with another NFL team. As you may know, coaches and staff are hired in February before the draft. A few calls were made on his behalf to other teams, like the Washington Football Team and Eagles. They basically said they had no jobs, but if he was in the area, he should call and they would meet with him. I suggested Field drive down to D.C. to visit his brother and reach out to both organizations and meet with them. Sadly, he was told there were no opportunities for him to join their organizations at this late of a date. Devastated and at a loss of what to do, I suggested that Field reach out to

Scott Pioli who was the new General Manager of the Kansas City Chiefs. Scott knew Field from the Patriots but also didn't necessarily have a job for him. I suggested to Field that he offer to work as an intern at the Chiefs' training camp at no pay and then see if perhaps Scott might find a place in his organization for him after training camp ended. Thankfully, after training camp, Field was offered a job to work for the Chiefs as a scout. We were all incredibly grateful and thankful to Scott for giving him a chance. Field, like so many young people, had hoped to become part of an NFL coaching staff and one day be a head coach.

The second serious moment of self-doubt in Field's career path was when he left the Chiefs. He came back to Boston with no idea of what he was going to do next, but was still in love with football. He was 24 years old, passionate about football and facing his own internal question of, "What next? What opportunities are out there that use my football passion and knowledge?" Field's experience in the sports world had included summer internships at both IMG and Octagon. A consideration for him was to be involved in his passion for sports by joining a sports marketing agency. Field's passion for sports, their statistics, his knowledge of players and teams was so vast and such a part of him, he didn't see himself in the world of marketing.

With no obvious career direction, Field decided to write a blog called *"Thoughts from the Field."* He had moved home, was not getting paid to write the blog and had no obvious career direction in the making. With incredible determination, he diligently studied and wrote on the subject of football. His first break came when SB Nation asked him to write for them. He was assigned shifts like 8-11 p.m. on a Saturday night (not the most desirable time slot) to report on sports, which he always agreed to cover in his eagerness to get experience.

What would you say were important qualities to possess to be the mother you were?
Belief and encouragement. I tried to always believe in my kids and treat them as individuals. Life is a journey, not a race. I have always encouraged my kids to go for their dreams. If they wanted to attend a certain school, travel to a new country, take a job faraway, or try something new, together we would figure out a way to accomplish this goal. I believed in working hard, doing the best you can and not giving up on your goals.

What were things you think you may have handled differently?
I don't think there are things I would've handled differently because so much of motherhood is about being in the moment. I am not sure, as a parent, you can ever know the perfect thing to say or do in those crisis moments. I think you react to the situation, hoping your advice, hug or words of wisdom will soften the current disappointment and help them with future challenges. As a parent, I recognized early on that each of my children had a different personality and coping style. I tried to honor their styles and not put each of them into the same box.

My real estate job certainly cut into my family obligations and there were times we had eggs and bacon for dinner. My days were long and often times chaotic. I missed some sporting events but managed to attend about 90% of my kid's games. My job helped my kids understand that the best-laid plans can sometimes change on a dime. Flexibility in life is important.

If you could name one characteristic you believe Field inherited from you, what would that be?
I think both Field and I are tenacious. We believe in being kind and respectful to all people we work with. Our personalities have lots of similarities. He and I are both very social and have lots of friends. Both of our jobs

involve networking, guiding people with different objectives, knowledge of professional facts, organizational skills and time sensitive material. We seem to attack our daily schedules in the same fashion.

Did any times of adversity set you up for later success?

I don't think motherhood can be measured by failures or successes. I think there are life situations we are faced with that make us come out of future challenges successfully. Because we didn't get on the honor roll, got sidelined by an injury, or left a job, it doesn't mean they are failures. They are life's stumbling blocks and challenges. It is how we redirect ourselves by learning and improving from these situations that speak to our future success and how we create a road map to reach our personal life goals.

Can you offer any advice to young or soon to be mothers/parents?

- Encourage them, do not push them.
- Don't pick their passion for them.
- Provide your child the opportunities to succeed. Know their personality and style. Some kids need prodding, others need constant supervision, and some put too much pressure on themselves already, so you need to learn to back off a bit.
- Find opportunities that improve their skill set – believe in coaches, mentors, and take lessons from professionals.
- Educate yourself on opportunities your child should be exposed to before choosing his/her career.
- Being an athlete is not the only career choice if your child is passionate about a sport. Look at marketing, coaching, agents and media opportunities.

- Teach them to be kind and respectful of all people and to give back.

Suggestions for helping to find your child's passion –
- Many people focus on one advisor to help them navigate the path their child should take to succeed. Be confident in knowing your child and do not be afraid to seek out advice from more than one coach or teacher.
- Treat children as individuals – just because they are in the same household does not mean that their styles and personalities are the same.
- Don't be afraid to take your child off a team when the coach is not good. A bad coach can hurt a child's passion and determination.

Looking back, what would you say was the greatest gift you gave to your kids?
I think the greatest gift I gave my children is the trait of never giving up. I believed that if you want something badly enough, we could figure out a way to get there. I never gave up on their dreams or goals. If my kids couldn't accomplish what they wanted when they wanted, I encouraged them to try again. I told them that setbacks were not failures, but rather just stumbling blocks to overcome.

I always believed in my kids pursuing their passions (in sometimes unconventional ways). There were choices they made that I knew were going to be unsatisfying or keep them from moving forward in developing their lifelong talents. Sometimes kids need to stray from their path to redirect their focus. I believe in giving something a try, even if you are a bit afraid or unsure of its long-term value. The modern world is moving at a very, very fast pace and asking our youth to specialize at a very early age. Making a decision for a child's interest at the age of 6 or 8 is way too early. Choosing a specialty for your child at an early age can diminish their passion later on, burn them out in their teens, or silence some of their other talents. Exploring life and trying new things, whether it is a sport, a job or even an internship, builds character and creates opportunities you might not have expected.

When my children were young, I heard Carl Yastrzemski (MLB Hall of Famer) speak on a panel to a group of young boys. He was asked how he ended up playing baseball. He actually said that he grew up on Long Island and attended a small school called Bridgehampton. He played basketball in high school and at Notre Dame in college and only joined the high school baseball team because one of his friends said they were short on players. Thankfully for Red Sox Nation and the baseball world, Carl was not solely a basketball player, but in fact a great athlete with a skill set that transferred to another sport.

If you could tell everyone in the world one thing, what would it be?

Life is a journey, not a race! Allow your kids to explore, challenge themselves and live life on their own terms, even if the road seems to take a few detours.

"Take a deep breath. It's going to be okay. Most of the horrible things you worry about where your children are concerned will never come to pass. They will run wild and build forts and do silly, stupid kid things – and survive."

Nick Koumalatsos
IG: @NickKoumalatsos
River Jordan
IG: @RiverJordanInk

River Jordan is the mother of Nick

Koumalatsos, a 12-year Special Operations Marines Corps veteran, CEO, multi-business owner, philanthropist, YouTube series host and social media influencer. River was born in Florida and spent most of her upbringing there. After her family's house burned down, River lived in Germany for three years (her father was stationed there with the U.S. Army, but she still calls the "deep south" home). She can still remember the day her sixth grade teacher recognized her writing ability. And from that point on, writing was the only career River could see herself pursuing. She began her writing career as a playwright and spent more than 10 years writing and directing. Today, River is the author of four novels and three spiritual memoirs, with her work mentioned among the company of famous writers like Flannery O'Conner, William Faulkner and Harper Lee.

River has two children – Nick was born in Hollywood, Florida, and Chris, his younger brother, was born in Panama City, Florida. Rivers' work endeavors caused her to move around a lot as a young mother. She was divorced and raising her two sons as a single mom, living in five different states by the time Nick was 12. After a rough set of teenage years that put him in a juvenile detention center, Nick enlisted into the Marine Corps at 17 in what was ultimately a decision that changed the direction of his life for the better. He served 12 years with the Marine Reconnaissance and Marine Special Operations Command, where he trained foreign police, military and militia during seven total deployments – five of which were to Iraq and Afghanistan.

In his post-combat life, Nick has embodied the meaning of reaching one's full potential. He's the founder and CEO of Alexander Industries, a holding company that manages the numerous businesses co-owned by him and his wife, Alison. Then, there's his YouTube channel, home to a variety of adventure and informational videos and vlogs, that holds over 225,000 subscribers. There's also The Raider Project, his program that aims to connect with MARSOC and other USMC combat veterans to help them transition smoothly, peacefully and successfully into the private sector. And on top of it all, Nick is a two-time self-published Amazon author and co-authored three fitness training books.

This chapter tells Nick's story through the eyes of his mother, River, who watched her son grow from a once-troubled teenager into a beacon of light that spreads purpose and positivity to the people who need it most.

Did your mother inspire you in any way? What kind of values did you take from her and instill in your own life as a mother?
Our relationship was pretty cool when I was little. She had a big, white convertible when I was a little girl. I had a little white convertible push pedal car that matched hers. We'd go down the highway with the music on and her wearing big sunglasses and a scarf and lipstick and she looked like a movie star. When I hit about 15 or 16,

things got a little rocky. We both had very stubborn, independent streaks and didn't always see eye to eye. But she had a wicked sense of humor and was funny, so that helped. She lived with me for her final years. I was her caretaker. She turned 88 in November 2020 but unfortunately passed away the following month in December.

She absolutely inspired me. She was a go get it kind of girl and I didn't see her waiting for someone else to make a decision or tell her what to believe. My sister and I are both very independent. We are the type to get in the car and drive solo across the country and I later realized that not all women our age would do that. That kind of determination and independence we get from her. She was also always fighting or taking up for the underdog. That stuck with us. We'll both stand up for people who are outnumbered or being picked on.

Any stories of adversity?
Well, many. But two that stand out is my mother almost died from a bleeding ulcer when I was 7 years old. That was a very serious time. The helicopter had to pick her up that night to rush her to a hospital. She was there for three months and I felt very responsible for my baby sister who was just a newborn. Then, when I was 15, my mother had a car accident that wasn't her fault but almost killed her. That was a dark, shifting time in the family. It was years of recovery.

What kind of dreams and goals did you have when you were a kid? How much did they influence where you are today?
My sixth grade teacher discovered that I was a writer. From that moment on, I never wanted to be anything else. It's what I've always done, aspired to and what I do today. It's been the greatest influence.

When was the earliest indication that you thought Nick might have extraordinary talent?

I've always thought that he was talented and smart but when I was co-owner of a movie theatre, he learned how to operate the projector system to run movies and to work in the kitchen cooking at a very early age. He was a natural for things related to film and sound.

Did you have to do anything to foster Nick's talent or was he always self-motivated?

I was always willing to support his talents, but he really was self-motivated. He told me when he was 12, that I didn't need to do his laundry anymore because he could do a better job washing it himself.

How did you handle Nick's accomplishments and keep things in perspective?

I was always a hang in there, you can do it kind of mom. I felt like the world would knock you down fast enough. My job was to stay in his corner.

Any stories of adversity that Nick faced?

He got involved with gangs which is one of a mother's worst nightmares. It was a very rough time. I can honestly say every adversity that I have witnessed Nick endure has only served to make him more determined to achieve the next thing or to do something bigger and better than before. Also, I'm amazed at the way that he seems to have no limits in his mind. He can dream larger, bigger, better than anyone I know. Just because he has one thing doesn't mean he sees himself as having achieved all there is to reach for. For him, it's just the beginning.

What would you say were important qualities to possess to be the mother you were?

Unconditional love.

If you could name one characteristic you believe Nick inherited from you, what would that be?

Well, for one, his absolute love of all thing's movie. That's a common thread. His appreciation for a warm climate, sunshine and saltwater. That might be from me. And also, this little thing called the belief that one person can make a huge difference and change the world. And when seeing a wrong that should be righted, possessing a kind of absolute bravery and confidence in charging into the fray.

What is your relationship like now with Nick?

I would say it's great. We both really appreciate, respect and applaud one another's accomplishments. I feel like he is a thousand percent in my corner, and he knows I'm in his. That's all you can do. I wish he lived closer. He is extremely busy and so am I, but I know that he knows I love him and am thinking about him always. I just don't call him constantly. So sometimes we talk every week and sometimes weeks pass by before we speak or Facetime. It depends on the schedule.

Now that he is no longer in active-duty military, I worry just a little less. That takes some pressure off the conversation so that I am not constantly saying, "Are you okay? Are you sure you are okay? Do you need anything?" Like I did when he was deployed over and over again.

What would you have handled differently?

Oh my, I was such a young mother. I would have paid closer attention to the earliest signs of anything gang related. I was innocent at that point and just didn't see it coming or expect it from Nick who had always been such a good kid and in no trouble. But this was a tough time for him. I had remarried and he had trouble with his stepfather. That relationship ended in divorce, but it caused damage in the process. Looking back, I wouldn't have married that person. But hindsight is always twenty-

twenty, and we all make mistakes. I moved away from that neighborhood as quickly as I could to minimize Nick's contact with these people and changed the school he was in. I did what I could as a mother. It was all trial and error which added up to me being a great Zaza (grandmother), as Nick's oldest started calling me. I look back from the place I am now and the age I am now, and I would have done it all differently – one house instead of moving around, joining little league baseball and having more structure. But I can't hit the rewind button now.

How has Nick grown from the adversity he has faced?

He had an injury in basic training where he fractured his wrist and actually had to start basic training over again on Parris Island. My goodness. That was a tremendous change and a long, long time. But he ended up being a company honor grad out of that experience. It made him go the extra mile instead of giving up.

How did you respond to situations that made you feel overwhelmed?

Prayed. And I don't say that lightly. I mean – I prayed.

Can you offer any advice to young or soon to be mothers/parents?

Take a deep breath. It's going to be okay. Most of the horrible things you worry about where your children are concerned will never come to pass. They will run wild and build forts and do silly, stupid kid things – and survive.

Advice to ignore - Anything that goes against that still, small voice inside of them that knows what is best for their child. Again - BREATHE. Oh yeah, and don't move so much. Sign your son up for little league.

Looking back, what would you say was the greatest gift you gave to your kids?

I allowed them to be individuals. I enjoyed watching them

grow up and celebrating all their gifts and talents but I never put my imprint on who I thought they should be or forced them to be like me.

If you could tell everyone in the world one thing, what would it be?

I'd have to quote Mother Teresa on that one – "If we have no peace, it is because we have forgotten we belong to each other." The only way we get through it all is by being human and holding each other up along the way.

Any closing thoughts?

My son never stops amazing me. He flew the whole family to Nashville just to celebrate his Nana's 85th birthday and take everyone out to dinner to celebrate in style at a local Italian restaurant. The photos from that night really capture that moment. Wherever he goes, he brings a life and energy to the place that makes everyone want to be around him. I just stand back in awe, not only of what he has achieved, but as the amazing father and husband he is. I'm just in wonder at this supremely cool human being that I had the blessing of bringing into the world. It's like a miracle after all of it and all of these years. It truly is. I am exceedingly thankful to be his mother.

"Learn every word of this song – Humble and Kind by Tim McGraw. Then use those words to model parenting behavior for your children. It's really pretty simple; kids learn what they see."

Adam Glick
IG: @ChefAdamGlick

Cathy Glick is the mother of Adam Glick, a professional chef and TV personality. Cathy's childhood in the 1960s was unique. Her family moved every two years because of their father's oil company job, so during her upbringing, Cathy and her two sisters lived all across the United States along with Japan. After attending three different high schools, she enrolled in college. After a year, however, she left college and got a job in Houston where she met and married Adam's father, now her husband of over 40 years. Cathy eventually went back to college and earned a degree in Psychology as well as a teaching certification after having Adam, her second of two children, and pursued her career in education. She taught elementary and middle school grades before becoming a school principal.

Cathy's journey as a mother was a lot like her childhood, as her husband's career required the family to frequently switch locations. Though Cathy and her husband spent many years living overseas as expats, they were fortunate enough to spend 10 years in one place in California. When Adam was in high school, they were transferred to the Middle East. Two years later, they were evacuated because of the second Gulf War, which allowed Adam to finish high school back in California.

In his second year of college at Cal State, Adam dropped out of school to pursue his childhood passion of cooking. He moved to Southern California and attended the Art Institute of California in San Diego, where he earned a bachelor's degree in Culinary Management. While living in San Diego, Adam cooked and served in popular San Diego restaurants like the University Club in Symphony Towers, La Valencia Hotel and Bertrand at Mr. A's. Over the next 10 years, he rose to prominence as a private yacht chef, traveling over 75,000 miles at sea and docking in 30 countries while cooking for high-end clients and their crews. In 2013, he began his film career by starring in the Food Network's *Cutthroat Kitchen*. He went on to secure a role on Bravo's hit series *Below Deck Mediterranean* and *Below Deck Sailing* that showcases the lives of an everyday luxury yacht crew. Now, Adam classifies as an "outdoor adventure chef" and hosts his own cooking show, *Stoked*, on Outside TV and has partnered with Messermeister Knives to create a set of Adventure Chef knives.

Adam's culinary gift is the driving force behind his extensive success, but he couldn't have reached where he is today without remaining confident in his own abilities. That strong sense of self-confidence came directly from Cathy. In this chapter, she provided her perspective on the importance of empowerment through encouragement that can help parents instill confidence in their children.

Did your mother inspire you in any way? What kind of values did you take from her and instill in your own life as a mother?
My mom was a typical 1960s mom. All the decisions were deferred to my dad, none of the finances were in her name and all the housework and child rearing was done by her (even though she had a full-time teaching job); very June Cleaver-ish. That was really normal during that

time and she did the best she knew how to do. But I knew that when I got married and had children, I wanted more of a partnership. So, when I married and had children, we made sure that both kids knew we were equal partners.

In a sense, though, she inspired my love of learning. My mom was a teacher while I was growing up and I always knew she loved what she did for a living. It was always more than a job for her, it was her passion. I found the same thing in the classroom and loved teaching. More than that, though, was the love of learning that I have taken from her. Education has always been important in our household and has been an expectation from when the kids were little. We never told either child what they needed to do for a living – it never really mattered – but rather, love what you are doing and work hard at it. I think we've done a good job at instilling that value in both our children.

When was the earliest indication that you thought Adam might have extraordinary talent?
Adam was always interested in cooking, but really, he's been very creative and artistic for as long as I can remember. I think that cooking is an outlet for his art. Adam was always adventurous when it came to food. He would always try new and exotic foods in whatever location we happened to be visiting or living. He'd ask permission to go into the kitchen at a restaurant and ask questions or just watch them cook. I have this great picture of him in the street market in Beijing eating a scorpion.

When he went away to college, he and his sister lived in the same house. He would do all the cooking. In his second year, he was struggling to enjoy his coursework and was considering changing majors (he was studying graphic design). The problem was he just didn't know what he wanted to do but he knew he didn't want to sit in an office at a computer all day. When talking with his sister about what to do, she told him, "You should be a chef. It's what you really enjoy doing." At the end of that year Adam called me and said he wanted to leave college and study to be a chef. He decided he wanted to move down to San Diego and get his degree in Culinary Management from the Art Institute. He was finally in his element. We supported his decision 100% and could easily see it was the right move for him.

Adam is also an unbelievable photographer. I suggest checking out his Instagram. He enjoys the arrangement and visualization involved in setting up a photograph, which is very much like the arrangement of a plated dinner.

Did you have to do anything to foster Adam's talent or was he always self-motivated?

Adam was always self-motivated. My instinct has been to try and hold Adam back because he tends to want to just jump in and go 200% forward. I tend to want to look around corners and know solutions to obstacles first, whereas Adam jumps in with both feet. He's a doer and is a really hard worker.

Did you put any systems in place for Adam to build the habits that led to his success?

The biggest "system" we put in place was the idea that if you start something, you finish it. You might fail, but you'll learn something valuable.

Any stories of adversity that Adam faced?

Adam had to go to three different high schools and that was hard for him. Ironically, I also went to three different high schools and vowed to never do that to my child. He was involved in sports so that was a saving grace for him. Adam played football in high school, but mostly golf. He is a terrific golfer and played on two different high school teams. He doesn't play much these days but plays occasionally with his father and me.

He also made good friends – lifelong friends – in each place, so that was beneficial. He enjoyed traveling so when we moved to the Middle East, he had amazing experiences that have influenced who he has now become.

As a mother, what were you good at saying no to?
I, unfortunately for Adam, was very good at saying no. I probably said no to many more things than I should have. I was particularly good at saying no to "I'm just going to go hang out with my friends." Or "We're just going to be at so and so's house." Bad decisions are made frequently when a bunch of boys are just "hanging out."

What would you say were important qualities to possess to be the mother you were?
Patience, which I didn't always have but certainly tried to show. Patience was important because we were often living in an unusual place under unusual circumstances. I wasn't raising my kids under normal circumstances. But I think no matter where you are parenting and under whatever circumstances you are in, a parent needs patience. Kids will try and try to test you to find out where those limits are. It's *how* they learn that there are limits that's critical. Getting angry because a child is doing what is normal for a child to do will only frustrate the parent, not the child.

What were things you think you may have handled differently?
I think I tried to keep Adam from "falling down" too often. I'm the kind of person that wants to look at a challenge from all sides and anticipate problems in advance. I would tell him all the problems with an idea he had first, rather than encouraging the potential in the idea first. I think I just wanted to have him benefit from my life experiences and save him the hurt. It wasn't the best way to parent but fortunately for Adam, his dad leads

with encouragement and has shown me that I just need to stop worrying so much about Adam falling down.

If you could name one characteristic you believe Adam inherited from you, what would that be?

Perseverance. I'm so proud that Adam is the kind of person that does what he says he's going to do and works hard to achieve his successes. Not fame, success. When Adam was young, he joined Cub Scouts. After many years of hard work, he achieved the rank of Eagle Scout. I really think his perseverance through that program has had a huge impact on his life.

Did any times of adversity set you up for later success?

Being a mother is a lifelong learning experience. It doesn't stop after the kids have moved out. I'm still failing as a mother. I speak up and give my opinion when I should just listen but I'm learning to listen more these days.

How has Adam grown from the adversity he has faced?

Not seeing them as failures but rather looking at them as opportunities to grow, Adam has learned to be humble and to take ownership of mistakes. Being on a reality show for several years presents a unique opportunity to see yourself through the eyes of other people (even if it is heavily edited). Every mistake you make is on display for millions to see and comment on through social media. Through that, he's been able to face challenges head on and own the things he says and actions he takes.

Can you offer any advice to young or soon to be mothers/parents?

Listen more – give opinions less. Let your child fall down and learn from the experience. Be there with a hand extended to help them up when they need it.

Also, learn every word of this song - *Humble and Kind*

by Tim McGraw. Then use those words to model parenting behavior for your children. It's really pretty simple; kids learn what they see.

Looking back, what would you say was the greatest gift you gave to your kids?
Perhaps, self-confidence. I've always tried to make sure they knew to be confident in whatever they are doing – even if they didn't really feel it. Show it. Fake it if you have to but exude self-confidence. Sarah has grown into her self-confidence. Adam on the other hand, has had to learn the fine line between self-confidence and cockiness. He's now demonstrating that self-confidence is empowering and leads to personal growth. He now understands that self-confidence doesn't mean that you know everything and are an expert on everything. Self-confidence means you are comfortable saying I don't know but I'd like to learn more. It means that you believe in your ability to accomplish tasks. I hope I gave that to both kids.

If you could tell everyone in the world one thing, what would it be?
Treat others how you want to be treated. Speak to others how you want to be spoken to.

Are there any special stories about your son and his journey that you would like to share?
When Adam was about 2 years old, he decided to climb out of his crib and explore the house early in the morning before anyone else in the house was up. As I opened my eyes and saw Adam standing next to my bed, I noticed that something was off and he just didn't look right. As my eyes focused more, I could see that he had black markings all over his arms, legs and face. Apparently, Adam found a black Sharpie marker and used it while on a walkabout before anyone else was awake. He removed the cap from the marker and walked all over the house

drawing on everything. The computer keys were colored black. The front of the tv was scribbled on. The hallway had black lines all the way down the hall. Every kitchen cabinet and appliance was scribbled on. His sister's dolls in her room – all scribbled on as well. He had been up, apparently, for a long time. This event pretty much set the tone for Adam's life. He just wanted to explore and check things out, not bother anyone, to just enjoy the exploration that comes from freedom.

What is your dream for Adam and his future from here?
The only thing I want for Adam is that he's happy and healthy, but I sincerely hope he finds someone to share his life with (beside Tex the wonder dog). Adam's dad and I have been married for 40 years and I know how special it is to have someone always by your side – through good and bad – sharing in life's experiences.

Any closing thoughts?
Only that I don't think Adam knows just how proud I am of him. To me, being a hard worker, being a good person and treating others with respect is the measure of success. Not fame or money. Adam is all of those things and shows it through his lifelong friendships and through the perseverance of his career goals. I'm unbelievably proud of how he's grown in the past five years and look forward to where this adventure takes him next.

"Communication was a big thing for us. We can't help or give advice if we don't know what's going on. I never wanted our kids to be afraid to talk to us. If we weren't there for them, then who would be?"

Joey Mulinaro
IG - @JoeyMulinaro
TW - @JoeyMulinaro

Lori Mulinaro is the mother of Joey

Mulinaro, a comedian, podcast host and social media personality who currently works with Barstool Sports. Lori grew up on the southside of Indianapolis with her parents and younger sister before eventually attending Ball State University. Instead of going the career route after school, Lori got married and started a family. Motherhood became her full-time job. She eventually began to work part-time in accounting and bookkeeping while having three children – Joey, Maddie and Emily – all of whom were raised in the suburbs of Indianapolis.

Lori was the glue of their household, embodying all of the qualities that resemble an exemplary mom. Her and Joey, like all of her kids, were always close. Baseball was his first love, so it was Lori who made sure he was around the sport at an early age. From weekends on the road at travel baseball tournaments, to summer nights at Wrigley Field watching the Cubs, baseball was something the two bonded over. Though for all the home runs he hit back in the day, Joey's greatest talent didn't have anything to do with a bat in his hands. His natural ability to make people laugh is what ultimately shaped his future.

Joey studied media/communications at the University

of Indianapolis but struggled to gain traction in journalism during his first couple years out of college. He started in radio, eventually earning a full-time producer role at Indianapolis's 1070 The Fan sports radio station. Meanwhile, he hosted a podcast and made videos of comedy skits with his friends as side hustles, which is where he rose to internet fame with impersonations of college football coaches and sports media personalities. His impression of LSU head coach Ed Orgeron made him a favorite of ESPN 104.5 in Baton Rouge and he also regularly posted videos impersonating Alabama head coach Nick Saban and FS1's Colin Cowherd. This drew the attention of Barstool's *Pardon My Take* podcast, who shot a video segment with him live from the NFL Combine. Soon after, Joey was invited to New York to meet with Barstool founder Dave Portnoy and CEO Erika Nardini. He officially joined the company in March 2020.

In this chapter, Lori discusses her experiences raising a baseball-crazed son in Joey while expanding on the highs and lows of her son's unconventional path to becoming one of Barstool's brightest (and funniest) rising stars.

Did your mother inspire you in any way? What kind of values did you take from her and instill in your own life as a mother?
I really didn't have a good relationship with my mother. I always felt like she didn't like me very much and she was always unhappy when she got home from work. She loved her job and would have much rather been there than at home. She and I didn't see eye to eye on a lot of things. I could never talk to her about anything going on in my life. She grew up with four brothers so I'm not sure she knew how to talk about personal things. I wanted to go to college, but she didn't want me to. It seemed like she didn't want anything good for me and I always

thought that parents were supposed to want their kids to have a life better than they did.

The way she inspired me was that I learned that I wanted to be the kind of mother that was close to her kids, that cared about what was going on in their lives and would be there when they needed help. I knew that I wanted them to be my top priority. My mother did attend all of the school events that I participated in, so I did take that from her. Whatever my kids were participating in, whether it was a choir concert, sporting event or awards ceremony, I was there. I have always and will continue to always be there for them.

When was the earliest indication that you thought Joey might have extraordinary talent?

To be honest, I always felt Joey's talent was in baseball. He was a natural at it and was excellent from the first day he started playing. When he was 7 years old, he hit a homerun in his first game, and from then on, he just excelled at baseball.

As far as comedy goes, his second grade teacher would write in his planner at the end of the week and give him a conduct grade. There were multiple times that she would write "Joey feels it is his job to make the kids laugh", or "Joey is always talking and laughing." He would do impressions of his middle school teachers, cafeteria workers and his coaches, which were always funny, so I guess that was an indication that he had some kind of a comedic bone in him.

Did you have to do anything to foster Joey's talent or was he always self-motivated?

I think he was always self-motivated when it came to entertaining. He may have just had encouragement from his friends because I was just trying to make sure he did well in school and didn't end up in the principal's office.

Did you put any systems in place for Joey to build the habits that lead to his success?
The only systems that we put in place to build his success was that we always expected his best, no matter what it was. We expected that our rules be followed, and our expectations met, or there would be consequences. Communication was also a big thing for us. We can't help or give advice if we don't know what's going on. I never wanted our kids to be afraid to talk to us. If we weren't there for them, then who would be?

Everyone faces self-doubt, did Joey ever want to give up on things, and if so, how did you go about handling that?
When Joey graduated from college, he had some bouts with self-doubt and where he was going with his life. He had been very successful in college in the media/communications department and his college professor had said that he was the most ready for a job in radio or television that he had seen in a while, yet he struggled to find a full-time job. He had applied in states outside of Louisiana but did not receive much interest from anywhere. He took a job delivering snack foods so that he could earn a steady salary. That job made him realize he was going to have to do something special or different to be noticed.

After that, he did a morning drive host for the college classical music station from 5am-8am, then he would work part time at 1070 The Fan and also work weekends. It took him two years to be able to be a full-time employee at 1070 The Fan, and while working full time, he decided to go the extra mile. He and his friend from high school, Ben, started making funny videos, ranging from Mother's Day and Father's Day bits, to creating characters and making fun of everyday things. Their videos grew and they started a podcast, then his success kind of grew from there.

How did you handle Joey's accomplishments and keep things in perspective?

I've always tried to teach our kids to be humble and not to brag when they had accomplishments. I always wanted them to be thankful for their gifts. I didn't want him to be the "all about me kid." When he was a young boy on his all-star baseball team, he had hit many home runs, usually one or two each game. His coach was giving a speech on being a good teammate and a team player. He asked Joey how many home runs he had hit. Joey answered, "I don't know." The coach said that he was a great example of a team player because a selfish player keeps track of his home runs. I've always told him to appreciate having talent and to use it as best as he could. I knew then that he wouldn't have any trouble in this area.

Was there a time Joey ever got in trouble with you or at school?

Joey was never a troubled kid, but once in high school he got suspended for two days because he had filmed a video in school and a clip of it got put on *Tosh.O* and the school was not happy about how it made them look. It was all over our local news stations and he got interviewed at our home about it. I'm not sure it changed him, but it made him think to consider all the outcomes before he puts a video out there and that even though he thinks it's okay, someone else might not.

As a mother, what were you good at saying no to?

As a mother I was good at saying no to a lot of things. If I didn't believe in it or think it was a good idea, I was not afraid to say no. I was not afraid to be the enemy when it came to what I thought was right.

What would you say were important qualities to possess to be the mother you were?

I would say that the qualities I possess to be the mother I am are unselfishness, unconditional love, understanding, encouragement and a strong will.

What were things you think you may have handled differently?

I think if I could go back and handle anything different, it would be the amount of time that we spent at travel baseball tournaments when Joey was younger and a teen. We spent a lot of time away from family and friends to do what we thought was good for our child and his chances at furthering his baseball career. I'm very competitive so that competition could easily get to me and I wanted it more than Joey did. There's nothing wrong with competitive sports at all, it's just that kids need to be kids too, and that got lost a little with us, especially because Joey is our oldest, so we lived and learned with him.

What is your relationship like now with Joey?

Joey and I have always been close and still are. He is a "mama's boy" for sure. We talk or text almost every day and he and Riley, his wife, come over at least once a week or we go to their place or go out for dinner. In the summer, they may come over more to hang at our pool and in the fall, they come over for football Sunday. We gather as a family and watch our favorite team – the Pittsburgh Steelers – play and spend the day watching games.

If you could name one characteristic you believe Joey inherited from you, what would that be?

Most people would say he got his athletic ability from me, (my husband also likes to take credit for that) but I would say his strong will and comfort with who he is would be what he got from me. No one is going to tell us that we can't do something because we will prove them wrong. Some might say that is stubbornness and it may be, but if we put our mind to it, we will do it. I've always told Joey to just be himself and not to worry what others think about him. God made him who he is and he should not be afraid to just be himself in all that he does. It's easy to see other people's personalities or the way they live and think that you should be more like them. It's always good to learn from people but I think your life will be easier and you will be more successful if you are good with who you are.

Did any times of adversity set you up for later success?

A failure that sticks out to me, which may not seem like a failure, but it is to me, is when Joey quit baseball his senior year of high school. I was not happy with his decision. We've always told our kids not to quit, that if they started something, they were to finish it. He had such an awful season the year before and he did not want to go through that again. I felt like he was letting his team down and that I had failed as a mother for letting him quit. I could not change his mind, but he had a plan to work on his start in broadcasting that would help him with his future. He was so unhappy and seeing how much he disliked it and how he had been successful in broadcasting helped me to realize that it was his life and his happiness was what was more important. It helped me later to put things in perspective when situations like that came up again, which they did with our other kids.

How has Joey grown from the adversity he has faced?

For Joey, his failures have been just the struggles of trying to break through and his opportunities not always becoming what he had hoped. One that sticks out to me was when he was an intern for Barstool with Pat McAfee. It was not run well and at that time it amounted to nothing, but it was just another steppingstone because here he is now as an employee of Barstool, doing comedy for a living. He also met his wife, Riley, while at that internship, so it was not a total failure!

Can you offer any advice to young or soon to be mothers/parents?

My advice to young mothers is to pray for your kids, make time for yourself, even if it's just a daily walk away from everything, make time for date nights or trips with your spouse and don't be afraid to leave your kids (I was never good at that) and don't be afraid to be the "mean mom." It's okay to say no to something when everyone else says yes, even though it may make your child mad at you. Both you and your children will be thankful in the long run.

Your kids are only young once, so try to make the most of the time that you have with them before they start school. Give them a good foundation and it will help them the rest of their lives.

Looking back, what would you say was the greatest gift you gave to your kids?

I think my greatest gift that I gave to my kids was honesty. I have always been honest with my kids even though they may not like what I say, and I may not like how they respond. Some parents like to tell their kids what they want to hear, to try and make them feel better about a decision that they have made, but I've always tried to be honest with how I feel or what I think. I feel like I'm not doing them any favors if I lead them on to believe something that I don't.

If you could tell the world one thing, what would it be?

We are only on this earth for a short time, so live each day to its fullest, laugh as much as you can and love like there is no tomorrow.

"Knowing that someone loves you more than their self-image, more than any possessions, more than their own life – gives you the security to succeed and the security to fail. You'll be okay no matter what happens. That kind of love is such an immeasurable gift to a child."

Seth Phillips
IG: @DudeWithSign

Stacey Phillips is the mother of Seth Phillips, a social media influencer most known for his widely popular "Dude With Sign" Instagram account. Stacey is from Hawley, Texas, where she was the youngest of her parents' four children. Her father was in the Air Force, so Stacey spent her newborn years living near a West Texas Air Force base in Abilene. However, in an instance of extreme tragedy, her older sister, Tona, passed away when Stacey was 3 years old.

Following her sister's death, Stacey was forced to overcome a convoluted emotional challenge more intense than most will ever experience in their lives. She didn't let it stop her from living an enjoyable childhood. She was a strong student and held part-time jobs as a teenager. She wasn't sure of a future career but knew that she definitely wanted to one day become a mother. After graduating high school, she worked as a waitress at a local restaurant in Abilene and it was there that she met her future husband, Rob. They married in 1988 and had four children together – Chy Anne, Chelsea, Christine and

Seth – while also raising Rob's previous two daughters, Cassandre and Carissa. And just like that, Stacey was a mother of six.

Stacey and her husband were very involved in their children's lives. She taught each of them to read by the age of 3 and worked part-time at a dance studio in exchange for free classes for her daughters. Rob coached their youth sports teams. They were always encouraging the kids to pursue their interests. It seemed that Seth was born a comedian and in middle school he began making videos impersonating different personalities and other humorous videos that were shared over social media. He attended Midwestern State University for college, where he coined the moniker "Suga Seth" across the school's social scene. He graduated with a degree in Business/Marketing, but before committing to a career, he had to spend the summer traveling the country and world – spanning from 12 U.S. states to Australia, Vietnam, Thailand and Cambodia. His mother worried as he traveled alone weaving his way through countries on the other side of the world, but she knew Seth was brave and intelligent and had an unquenchable thirst for adventure. She had tried to convince him to read her travel books to familiarize himself with some of the countries he'd be visiting, but he preferred to arrive without any itinerary or expectations and be completely enthralled by new experiences. He would send her videos of his daily adventures and, whether he was road-tripping to Sydney with new Australian friends, riding a moped through bustling traffic-jammed streets with a Vietnamese woman, or trekking through Angkor Wat on a bicycle under monkey-filled trees in the rain, she knew he was creating lasting memories. Song tot, or "good living", became his theme for life. After returning home, he took a job in New York City writing comedy for social media. Then, he became, "Dude With Sign."

Seth's @dudewithsign Instagram account, which he co-founded with @Fuckjerry founder Elliot Tebele, features photos of him on the streets of his SoHo neighborhood holding up cardboard signs that display satirical messages. From his "Stop replying-all to company-wide emails" and "Charcuterie boards are just expensive Lunchables" signs to his "Register to vote" sign in advance of the 2020 election, Seth's work has become a smashing hit among the Millennial and Gen Z social media generations. Within four months, the account gained over 4 million followers and now has more than 7.5 million since its creation in September 2019. Seth is also a content creator for the board game What Do You Meme and the Instagram account @fuckjerry, a popular Instagram comedy account that has over 15 million followers. So far, the ripple effects of @dudewithsign have earned Seth numerous brand sponsorships, appearances on the *Ellen DeGeneres Show* and the *Tonight Show with Jimmy Fallon*, a front row seat at Dolce & Gabbana's Milan fashion show, a 2020 Super Bowl appearance and celebrity collaborations with Justin Bieber and Vanessa Hudgens.

In this chapter, Stacey reflects on the early signs of Seth's natural talent and his journey from a small town of 650 people to the streets of New York City.

Did your mother inspire you in any way? What kind of values did you take from her and instill in your own life as a mother?
She's the best mom on earth and such a loving person. She was an incredible cook. Many of our clothes were handmade in the latest fashions. She enjoyed donning us in trendy hairstyles. Our home was always clean and beautiful no matter the size of their bank account and our friends were always welcome there. We had parties, sleepovers, took wonderful family vacations and relatives filled our home over the holidays. My parents were always willing to take in the troubled friend or rejected family member who needed help. As the baby of the family, I

was lavished with attention. I was taken to a five and dime store after every doctor or dental visit to spend a dollar on inexpensive toys and candy. A dear family friend dressed as Santa and delivered magical Christmases to me each year. My dad built a treehouse for me that was the envy of every kid in my neighborhood. Our home was always filled with music, laughter and "I love you's" throughout the day. After finding out that my mother had suffered a very abusive childhood, I felt especially grateful for the beautiful one I experienced thanks to her. I know that abuse is often repeated throughout generations, but she credits her affection and devoted doting nature to her grandmother, Bessie Sconce. "Her deep unconditional love saved me" she confided. I can't help but wonder if it saved us all.

Aside from the normal mother-teenage daughter squabbles, my relationship with my mom has always been a close one. No matter where I go in this world, who I become, or what I do, I know without any doubt that she's going to love me. I can't mess that up. During low times in my life when I felt ashamed, depressed, or even disgusted with myself, she was always a source of comfort to me. If anyone ever wronged me, she was relentless in my defense. If I ever wronged someone, she was still relentless in my defense. I laughed during a recent phone conversation with her as she described dealing with someone who had made a slightly negative comment about a choice that I had made. She ripped the man apart with such soft-spoken class that he was speechless by the end. My tiny 84-year-old mother, who still has more energy, strength and beauty than most people half her age, giggled and assured me, "I've got your back." She has always had my back and it made a world of difference. Knowing that someone loves you more than their self-image, more than any possessions, more than their own life – it gives you the security to succeed and the security to fail. You'll be okay no matter what happens. That kind of love is such an immeasurable gift to a child and I'll be grateful to my mother as long as I live. It not only benefited myself but also my children, their children and generations to come. At times I think of it as "love strings" that run through families and bind them together. Unconditional love seems to be eternally rewarding and it breaks my heart that some people are deprived of it. Those who are, often grow up to feel hollow and empty and it's so unfair. Love makes all the difference.

When was the earliest indication that you thought Seth might have extraordinary talent?
His charm is undeniable and it has always seemed that he's instantly loved by everyone he meets. By the time Seth was in middle school, I knew he was going to be some type of entertainer. He loved to make others happy and could easily make an entire room full of people laugh. He won the "Funniest Boy" award all throughout high school and even had his own school holiday called "Hug Seth Day." He entertained audiences at his sisters' dance recitals, performing skits from Austin Powers, Risky Business and Napoleon Dynamite and went on to organize large entertaining events during college for his fraternity, Kappa Sigma. His kindness and compassion blended so well with his humor and made his joy infectious. He, like myself, has always been a genuine lover of people – all sorts of people. One of my favorite quotes is actually a Bible scripture: "Anyone can find the dirt in someone. Be the one that finds the gold." (Proverbs 11:27) Seth seems to have a natural inclination to easily see the gold in others.

How did you handle Seth's accomplishments and keep things in perspective?
The only advice I recall is asking him to remain true to himself. It's more than likely that he would have regardless, though. He currently has many friends who are models, celebrities and fashionistas, yet he still wears thrift store clothes. When he was backstage at the Ellen

Show, I asked him what he was wearing and he sent a picture of him in a plain t-shirt. I would have spent all week planning my outfit, but he's about as non-materialistic as they come.

All of my children have excelled and accomplished wonderful things, but so far only Seth has reached this level of notoriety. As his "Dude With Sign" fame began to grow, I did worry somewhat about how he would handle the pressure. He loves to please people, but it wasn't long before he started getting numerous requests to hold a sign for a certain cause or a friend's business or birthdays, weddings, engagements, so on and so forth.

Disappointing others suddenly became unavoidable and I knew it bothered him. It's difficult for a generous person to have to set boundaries and tell people no. The only other issue I recall discussing was regarding the desire to stay true to himself. He has done well, and I can't imagine that ever changing. I visited him in NYC recently and it was bizarre to walk around the city with him and hear people yelling, "It's Dude With Sign!" or "Hey Sign Dude!" He enjoyed stopping to chat with them and take photos while his sisters stood back and joked with his fans telling them, "He's really not that cool." They know he is, though. We're all super proud of him and his success and anyone who knows him agrees that he deserves every good thing that comes his way.

Any stories of adversity that Seth faced?
While in Vietnam, he was robbed by an Uber driver and needed to earn some money. Shortly thereafter, he saw an ad needing a person to teach English to young Vietnamese children. He applied and was given an address. He found his way there and walked into a house with chickens running around inside and an old man who silently directed him upstairs. Then, he entered a room full of excited, giggling children and after very brief instructions, he was left on his own to teach. He says it was one of his most gratifying experiences because it

strengthened his self-reliance and confidence in ways nothing had before.

If you were heavily involved, how did you make time for yourself?
I was heavily involved, and I really don't remember making time for myself until they graduated high school. Everyone warned me that an empty nest would devastate me since my whole life up to then had revolved around my children, but as much as I loved being a mother, I was actually thrilled to finally have some time to focus on myself. I wouldn't trade the memories of raising my children for anything, but I believe I did my job well and now I look forward to traveling, pursuing my own interests and enjoying my grandchildren.

As a mother, what were you good at saying no to?
I asked my children this question and they offered great responses. We were fairly lenient as parents since we lived in a small town where I knew all of their friends and usually their friends' parents and grandparents as well. Aside from the obvious objections to situations I feared might be dangerous or harmful, my children said I had no problem saying no to:

-   Friends coming over when their bedrooms were dirty was a no-no.
-   Saying no when they doubted themselves. They tell me "I'm great at the hype" and often joke about it, but I've always cherished the health of their self-esteems. If Seth was nervous about anything or questioned his ability against someone else, I'd tell him, "They have nothing on you. You're SETH PHILLIPS." A friend recently told me that he wished his mother would have encouraged him to be confident in that way but instead she was insistent that he always displayed humility. I also value humility but I know a

person can be both humble and confident. Humility and gratitude go hand in hand with compassion and I believe children acquire these qualities by helping people who are less fortunate and realizing that their circumstances could have easily been yours. My children weren't taught to believe they're better than others but that they are capable of doing phenomenal things with their lives.

What would you say were important qualities to possess to be the mother you were?
Patience, for sure, though mothers never feel they have enough. The ability to toss perfectionism right out the window and welcome chaos and unpredictability. Lastly, a sense of humor – the more twisted the better.

What were things you think you may have handled differently?
I would have disciplined myself to make sure I always got plenty of sleep. The times I look back on with regret were usually the result of irritability caused by sleep deprivation. I think most, if not every mother, remembers moments she's ashamed of – such as moments she lashed out and said things she shouldn't have said. Staying well-rested may be the best way to prevent them.

A few other changes: I would've bought less processed food. I would've recorded more memories in writing and captured more photos and videos. It's so easy today but it wasn't back then. I would've enjoyed more evenings with them outside under the stars just talking. My children are still, by far, my favorite people to talk to.

If you could name one characteristic you believe Seth inherited from you, what would that be?
He's a dreamer with big goals who loves people and new experiences and he can tear it up on the dance floor.

Did any times of adversity set you up for later success?

I distinctly remember making fun of two kids in high school on separate occasions. It's difficult for me to admit and I can only blame my adolescent insecurities, but those despicable moments have haunted me ever since. I apologized to those people at my first class reunion and assured them it had nothing to do with them and everything to do with my own issues. They were extremely receptive and forgiving and we're now great friends. Those experiences made me emphasize kindness and inclusion to my children. I wouldn't allow them to hand out birthday invitations at school unless every classmate was invited. I'll never forget one 16-year-old boy telling me that my daughter's birthday party was the first party he'd ever been invited to. The size of his smile as he jumped on the trampoline almost broke my heart.

Can you offer any advice to young or soon to be mothers/parents?

Just love them. Mistakes are unavoidable but unconditional love erases a multitude of mistakes. Also, never be more concerned with your image than the self-esteem of your child. I've seen so many parents who share negative things about their children to other adults right in front of them. The shame they're instilling by doing this is often the root of the problem. If you had friends over, would you openly scrutinize them or humiliate them? Use those opportunities to encourage and uplift and just love your children.

Looking back, what would you say was the greatest gift you gave to your kids?

Aside from unconditional love, I'd say compassion. The mission trips they went on to work with homeless people and disabled children around the country, building schools in Mexico, feeding orphans in India, or simply inviting every child in their class to their birthday parties so that nobody was left out – there are many ways to instill compassion.

If you could tell everyone in the world one thing, what would it be?

I think Mother Teresa said it best, "Spread love everywhere you go and let no one ever come to you without leaving happier."

What is your dream for Seth and his future from here?

I just want Seth and his sisters to be fearless in chasing their dreams, be loving and kind to others and be happy. Not anyone else's version of happy – strictly their own. They can hold cardboard signs or rule the planet or dance with three-toed sloths for all I care. They make the world a better place simply by their existence.

"I tried to never demand anything from my children. I wanted them to feel happy and appreciated. I feel that children respond better if you don't demand but ask. When they feel appreciated, they want to help you of their own free will, not because you made them."

Brianna Wiest
IG: @BriannaWiest
TW: @BriannaWiest

Lisa Wiest is the mother of Brianna Wiest, an American author, writer and poet known for her deep literary work on emotional intelligence. Lisa grew up on Long Island, NY, in a large family – one of five siblings all living in a household with both parents, her grandmother and aunt. Like any large family, life could be hectic at times, but Lisa never let her surroundings impact her focus on school. Her mother was a teacher, which fostered early childhood aspirations to one day become a teacher – and mom – herself. Lisa did just that, earning both undergraduate and Master's degrees in Education from Adelphi University before becoming an elementary school teacher, a role she's now held for 33 years. She's a devoted wife and mother of three – Brianna (28), Emmy (21), and Jake (11) – all raised on Long Island not far from where she grew up.

Brianna was first drawn to writing in high school. She majored in professional writing at Elizabethtown College in Lancaster, PA, while serving as editor-in-chief on the school's student newspaper. After graduating in three years, Brianna then moved to New York City and worked as an editorial director for the website *Thought Catalog*, where she produced thousands of bylined articles that amassed more than 70 million views. Her position with *Thought Catalog* provided an opportunity to publish three books of essays titled *101 Essays That Will Change the Way You Think, The Truth About Everything* and *The Human Element.* In 2015, she returned to Pennsylvania for a writer/copy editor position with *Fine Living Lancaster* magazine.

Throughout her brief career, Brianna has already published several books of poetry, prose and essays that explore the intricacies of emotional intelligence and mental health. Her bylines can be found in a variety of national publications, including the *Huffington Post, Forbes, USA Today, Medium, Teen Vogue,* and *Insider.* She has also contributed sponsored brand writing content for Smartwater® and the HBO series *Girls.*

Brianna's deep-rooted, lifelong mission has always been to help others in need. Except, at first, she didn't know exactly how to make a career out of it. In this chapter, Lisa explains how a gift for creative writing empowered her daughter to turn her passion into a profession.

Did your mother inspire you in any way? What kind of values did you take from her and instill in your own life as a mother?

I've called my mother three separate times today, so that might tell you something! I was very close to her and I still am! We live four miles from each other and speak every day – sometimes multiple times a day.

My mother was a teacher and I was inspired by her to pursue my own career and make it a focus in my life. I've been a teacher for 33 years and love what I do. As a mother, my first-and-foremost goal was to be caring and loving. I learned from my mom to go out of my way to make people feel comfortable and appreciated.

What kind of dreams and goals did you have when you were a kid? How much did they influence where you are today?

I wanted to be a teacher and mother from the time I was a little girl. I'm blessed that I knew what I wanted and that it came true. Better yet, I have loving, healthy and successful children.

When was the earliest indication that you thought Brianna might have extraordinary talent?

From an early age, Brianna would say that she was in this world to help others. It was the strangest thing, but she hung onto that belief. She didn't know how she would do it, but she knew she would. Nothing seemed right until she started writing in college and she flourished. She was a gifted writer from the start.

Did you have to do anything to foster Brianna's talent or was she always self-motivated?

Brianna and I read together from the time she was a baby. Education was always very important to us, but Brianna was always self-motivated. She knew she needed to figure out how she was going to create meaning in her life and she worked to find that niche.

Like I said, education has always been important to us as a family and I paid careful attention to the environment my kids were in. We sent them to a private high school that we knew would help foster a love of learning, integrity, a strong sense of curiosity, and hopefully, strong, independent people.

How did you handle Brianna's accomplishments and keep things in perspective?

My husband and I always acknowledged Brianna's accomplishments, but we only encouraged her to do her best. We didn't emphasize being *the* best or make a big deal about being superior to other kids.

If you were heavily involved, how did you make time for yourself?
I didn't always make time for myself, which in retrospect wasn't healthy or sustainable. That's why I encourage my children to focus on their wellbeing and put aside time where they can spend it in a way that's restorative for them.

Any stories of adversity that Brianna faced?
Brianna was always an old soul. She sometimes had trouble fitting in with kids her age because her thinking was often matured beyond her years. Brianna was oddly aware of herself and her impact on the world. She struggled with the knowledge that she wanted to have a meaningful impact on the world around her but didn't know how she would achieve it.

As a mother, what were you good at saying no to?
I didn't really have to say no much, it wasn't my style. I tried to set the example for my kids to make good decisions that would keep them happy in the long run. I feel blessed that they (almost) always made decisions I was proud of so I don't remember many times that I had to say no.

My biggest hope for my relationship with Brianna was that she would feel comfortable coming to me if she made a not-so-great choice and needed help. That was more important to me than trying to micromanage her behavior.

What would you say were important qualities to possess to be the mother you were?
As a mom, I'm loving, generous, and most importantly, easy going! I tried to never demand anything from my children. I wanted them to feel happy and appreciated. I feel that children respond better if you don't demand but

ask. When they feel appreciated, they want to help you of their own free will, not because you made them.

What were things you think you may have handled differently?

If I could redo it all, I think I would have encouraged Brianna to stop worrying so much about the future and spend more time being a child. She was driven and independent, which is why she's as successful as she is now, but if I could go back, I would help her spend more time having fun with other kids her age.

What is your relationship like now with Brianna?

Brianna and I are still very close, but we do live two hours apart which is hard for me. We get together and act just as silly and loud as we always were, but I do wish she lived closer. I miss having my baby right here with me. Brianna married a man that I truly love and we feel comfortable staying in each other's homes, which helps a lot. What's changed the most is that she now takes me to restaurants, shopping and is the one teaching me skills – especially about the online world. Everything comes full circle.

If you could name one characteristic you believe Brianna inherited from you, what would that be?

Brianna and I are both approachable people. We make it a point to be welcoming and that helps us foster a multitude of relationships. People are always around us, independently and as a pair, and that's important to us.

Did any times of adversity set you up for later success?

Well, because I still have an 11-year-old at home and don't want to repeat mistakes, I make sure to foster his childhood fun instead of laser-focusing on building his future. Jake's a serious hockey player, but it isn't healthy for that to be his whole life and it's my job to show him how to create balance for himself. I'm happy to say that Brianna has found balance in her adult life. She nurtures her friendships and enjoys life, even while working so hard.

How has Brianna grown from the adversity she has faced?

Brianna is ambitious and driven, but in her younger years, she had a tendency to throw herself into situations head-first. As she's grown, I can see how she's learned from that tendency and takes time to evaluate and plan before making a move, both in her career and personally.

How did you respond to situations that made you feel overwhelmed?

Run, yoga, pray and maybe most importantly, therapy.

Can you offer any advice to young or soon to be mothers/parents?

I believe that the most important part of mothering is creating and maintaining open communication. Never judge or critique too harshly but be understanding and open to their experiences and ideas. I think it backfires when you put too much pressure on a child. All kids are going to make mistakes as they learn what it means to be a person; the difference is whether or not they feel comfortable asking for your help cleaning up the mess when they make those mistakes. I guess this is a relationship-based approach. It isn't about trying to force a kid to be perfect but making sure they know they're always loved no matter what.

Looking back, what would you say was the greatest gift you gave to your kids?

I hope the greatest gift I've given my children is the confidence to believe that they don't have to put limits on what they can achieve! And to always remember that when working on these goals, to be sure they're helping others and society in their journey and not just themselves.

If you could tell everyone in the world one thing, what would it be?
The one thing I would tell the world is don't live life as if it's a dress rehearsal – live it as if it's opening night!

"I like to think my greatest gift was allowing my kids the freedom to explore anything that intrigued them and be there to support them while making sure they were safe."

Aquaria
IG: @AgeofAquaria
TW: @AquariaOfficial
Gina Palandrani
IG: @MamaAquaria

Gina Palandrani is the mother of Giovanni

Palandrani, an American drag queen, television personality and recording artist widely known by the stage name "Aquaria." Gina grew up just outside of Philadelphia in a town called Havertown with three much older siblings. Her parents divorced when Gina was 15, and after graduating high school, she moved to Los Angeles to see what sunny California had to offer.

A few years later, Gina decided to move back home to the Philadelphia area to work at her uncle's newly opened Greek restaurant. It was later on when Gina took up a job at the mortgage company that she met her husband David. They got married and had two children – Giovanni and Francesca – both of whom were born and raised in West Chester, Pennsylvania. Gina was a stay-at-home mom up until 2006, when the mortgage crisis hit, and she had to go back to work as a payroll manager until late 2019. And thanks to the spread of the coronavirus, she is currently unemployed but hopes to begin working with her sons' management firm, Voss Events, as part of the tour management crew.

Giovanni, now 24, has always been drawn to the

performing arts. In addition to taking dance classes in high school, he started experimenting with makeup after discovering tutorials on YouTube. Following his graduation, he enrolled in the Fashion Institute of Technology in New York. Even though he left after two semesters, Giovanni still carved a lane for himself within the city's fashion and drag community. Being taken under the wings of nightlife icons like Susanne Bartsch, it was there that Aquaria came to life and her meteoric rise came to fruition.

In 2018, Aquaria was introduced as one of 14 contestants for the 10th season of *RuPaul's Drag Race*. She became the youngest drag queen to win the competition. This same year, Aquaria saw many more successes, including a People's Choice Awards nomination for Competition Contestant of the Year. The following year, Aquaria made her second appearance in an issue of *Vogue Italia* and was also a model for H&M x Moschino's November 2018 Capsule Collection. Truly having an international fandom, she became an ambassador at the SM Store in the Philippines (a relatively conservative country when it comes to gender diversity and gender expression) speaking to young fans about what drag means to her, a visual representation of feeling, and the importance of it today and every day.

She has since signed to IMG Models and became the entertainment editor for *Dazed Magazine*. IMG has secured her great gigs - in 2019 Aquaria became the first drag queen to walk the red carpet at the Met Gala and was a model at Rihanna's Savage X Fenty Beauty Fashion Show during the Fall 2019 New York Fashion Week. Currently, you can find her producing her own digital drag shows for fans to enjoy during the pandemic.

In this chapter, Gina speaks about the importance of acceptance - sharing her unique perspective from raising an openly gay son and encouraging him to pursue his passions which lead to becoming an international drag icon.

Did your mother inspire you in any way? What kind of values did you take from her and instill in your own life as a mother?

I always remember my mom working, knowing the importance of being able to provide for me and my three older siblings. She was a hard worker and I believe her work ethic really rubbed off on me. My siblings and I always called her an "ever ready battery" because she just kept on going. Her foot could be in excruciating pain and she would just keep on going. That's one of many takeaways from her - work hard and keep going when times get tough.

She used to take me to the theater, she loved music, she loved art, she loved travel, fashion, flower gardening, painting, ikebana, photography, you name it - anything creative and adventurous. When Giovanni came along, she made an effort to introduce him to all her favorite pastimes. After retiring from working a full-time job for 30 years, she worked part-time as an usher at a performing arts theatre. She would take Giovanni to the shows, the first being Snow White. After the show, she made sure that Giovanni got pictures with the cast and autographs for his playbill - his first meet and greet, if you will.

Sadly, she passed away when Giovanni was 9. She never was able to see her own grandson's meet and greets, with her fans waiting hours for pictures and autographs. It might sound cliché, but I know she would be so proud and so accepting that her grandson has had such a successful career as a drag queen.

When was the earliest indication that you thought Giovanni might have extraordinary talent?

As parents, we tend to have a mindset that our kids are amazing at whatever they're doing. But in reality, they're usually growing and learning new skills or talents at the same pace as their peers. That being said, the first time I truly felt my son had a God-given talent was in the summer of 2010 when he was 15. Giovanni and his sister Francesca had been attending West Chester Summer Stage for a few years at this point and he really enjoyed the summer theater program. At the end of the third week of camp, the choreographer was very impressed with his dance abilities despite him not having any formal training. She suggested he join the dance studio where she taught, Chester Valley Dance Academy. She saw something in him and couldn't wait to see what he could do with some professional training. Most dance academies don't have many teenage boys in their programs, so the choreographer allowed him to train there for free as long as he took ballet – the foundation of all dance. Needless to say, I signed him up the next day! For the next three years, I drove him to classes four to five nights a week and I loved every minute of it, especially seeing how grateful he was for the opportunity – saying "thank you" each and every time we got back home.

I had two more "aha moments" before he graduated from high school. The next one happened when he was a junior, when he first began to paint his face (put on drag makeup) after school. If you ever saw me, you would know this is not a skill he learned from me! I was amazed by all the different drag makeup looks he would put on his face. The way he applied makeup, you would think he had years of professional makeup training.

The other moment came during Giovanni's senior year. I was surprised that in addition to his regular course selection, he chose an Advanced Studio Art class for which he did not have the required prerequisites. Clearly, the teacher saw something in him and allowed him into the class. His art was improving every day and by the time the Senior Art Showcase rolled around, he received the honored award of Best in Show for his portfolio from that year.

Did you have to do anything to foster Giovanni's talent or was he always self-motivated?

I think most parents want to expose their kids to as many activities as they can, as early as they can. David and I enrolled him in many extracurricular activities – sports, karate, flag football – to foster a strong sense of decision-making and give him the empowerment to choose a couple activities that he was most passionate about. We were super strict on ensuring that he completed any activity he started. If he hated flag football, that was fine, but he needed to finish out the season.

We gave Giovanni his grandfather's old keyboard and offered to enroll him in piano lessons. He refused. He wanted to learn everything on his own, it was a skill he took great pride in. He learned to play a song from Sunday school simply by listening to the notes and finding the corresponding key. I think he inherited an ear for music from both sides of the family. My father played bass violin and David's father played the organ. I love that even now he still loves music. He decided to take the guitar up during quarantine and plans on incorporating some melodies he wrote into future projects.

Even as Aquaria, she loves to work alone and independently. A few months ago, her management firm, Voss Events, offered to send her a crew to help her film a digital drag show that would include every element of an in-person drag show – perfect lighting, perfect audio, a large stage, a large array of music. Aquaria refused. She wanted to prove to herself that she could produce a digital show all on her own. That is not to say she doesn't like to collaborate with other creatives, but she just takes great pride in seeing something come to fruition simply because of her work and her work alone.

Everyone faces self-doubt, did Giovanni ever want to give up, and if so, how did you go about handling that?

As I mentioned earlier, David and I did not instill any

concept of "giving up." Giovanni could have hated flag football or hated the play I signed him up for, but he was going to finish that last game or that last performance. He wasn't going to compromise an entire team or an entire cast. I would like to think that since not giving up or not following through wasn't even a prerogative in our household, it helped shape Giovanni into a self-sufficient person. To my knowledge, he has not faced much self-doubt, but if he has, he probably wouldn't tell me. He would handle it alone and talk himself out of it. As Ross Mathews said on RuPaul's Drag Race, "Any self-doubt – knock it off!"

What would you say were important qualities to possess to be the mother you were?

Selflessness. Putting myself last on the list. Looking back, I guess I'd also have to say my most important quality was accepting my child for who he was - giving him unconditional love and making sure he knew it. By believing in him and trusting his judgement, I think this set him up for future success. He knew what he was doing, he has an old soul and he has always been above his years.

What were things you think you may have handled differently?

If I could go back, I would have made it more of a priority to sit with my kids every night before bedtime and simply listen to whatever they wanted to say. Any parenting book or magazine will mention this, it is one of a few recommendations that seems to be universal. I truly feel this is where I failed both of my kids. I spent a lot of time reading and singing at bedtime to Giovanni when he was a toddler. When his sister came along, his bedtime routine was taken away as my attention was focused on Francesca. Don't get me wrong, I continued to read to him at night when I could. I also enjoyed when he could read to me. But soon he didn't need me, he was a big boy.

That's about the time when I should've continued to come in and sit for a minute, just listening, but I rarely did.

One other thing I wish I could do over for my kids in their teenage years would be encouraging them to invite their friends to our house more often for dinner or sleepovers. But at that point, I was working about 50 hours per week and some weekends I was on-call. Needless to say, I was worn out by the end of the week, but I still wanted them to know that our doors were always open to their friends. These are two things I wish I had done better as a mom but que sera sera (whatever will be, will be).

If you could name one characteristic you believe Giovanni inherited from you, what would that be?

I feel Giovanni definitely inherited my work ethic, which in fact, I know I inherited from my mother! When Giovanni was born, I was very lucky to be able to take those early days off and stay at home with him, so I am sure he picked up on some of my habits - getting jobs done to the best of my ability, cleaning up completely. I now felt it my responsibility to take care of everything inside the house and in our backyard so my husband could focus on his job. Plus, I really enjoyed doing yard work, gardening and organizing etc.

I'm the type of person who works until the job is done. Again, part of the work ethic that I inherited from my mom. I try to do my very best at whatever I'm doing, nothing is ever done half assed! I always believed I could do anything I put my mind to. And come to think of it, that is Giovanni! I believed I could move a mountain if I had to! I could work seven days per week if that was what it would take to get the job done on time, which was easy for me because I usually was doing something I loved. It gave me such great satisfaction to look at what I alone had accomplished. As I'm writing these things down, it has put a big smile on my face and warmed my heart seeing what I've perhaps unknowingly given Giovanni, and now realizing just how important this one shared characteristic was and will continue to be to his success.

What is something you think the media or public has wrong about Aquaria?

There are two main things I think the public has wrong about Aquaria, both professionally and personally. Typically, when drag queens already have a large social media presence before coming onto RuPaul's Drag Race, people think they are just these "Instagram beauties" with nothing else there. This could not be further from the truth. Yes, Aquaria is a fabulous looking queen, but in her mind, being a drag queen requires the total package. She can dance, she can host, she can tell quick witted jokes, she can show young kids that it is okay to be different and that it is actually pretty cool to just be who you are!

Secondly, people have a misconception that Aquaria is some privileged, entitled, cocky diva. Something else that could not be further from the truth. Remember, Aquaria was the youngest contestant on Season 10 of the show, and what happens when you are the youngest? Your risk of getting walked all over, discounted and overlooked gets exponentially higher. Aquaria had no choice but to be confident and have a determined mindset if she had any chance of winning. Unfortunately, this came off as arrogant, but anyone who has seen or interacted with Aquaria since the show aired knows this is simply not the case. Just look at her Instagram account. She's always sharing fan art, promoting her friends' makeup lines, reposting her meet and greets with fans. People have great experiences when meeting Aquaria. Whenever she does a meet and greet, I like to scroll through Instagram looking at the pictures. All I ever see are captions and comments talking about how fun she is and how nice, taking time to speak to each and every fan.

Any stories of adversity that Giovanni faced?
Fortunately, Giovanni never expressed or showed any signs of being bullied in school. Sadly just a few years ago, I learned of some kids teasing him in elementary school and bullying him in middle school as he wrote about it for a school project. Again, I didn't know at the moment, he seemed to never allow what other people said or thought of him to get under his skin, so he never thought he needed to even mention the situation to me. I like to believe I planted that seed in his head by reading one of the Little Bill books titled *The Meanest Thing to Say*. It was a simple story with a strong message of how kids could stand up for themselves against bullies, brushing mean comments off each and every day.

As far as any bumps in the road getting him where he is today, I can only say that if any arose along the way, he always figured out a way to glide over them without stress or hesitation. He doesn't allow people or problems to distract him from the goals he has set for himself. Take the show, for example. Season 10 was full of drama, some of which Aquaria was involved in, but some of which was between other queens. All that noise and fighting in the work room would probably send most people over the edge, but not Aquaria. She knew she had to keep her eye on the prize, tuning out anything else on the show that could get in the way of her getting that crown.

Can you offer any advice to young or soon to be mothers/parents?
Simply strive to be the very best mom she can be. Trust your motherly instincts, you don't always have to follow what a book says is best for you. Every child is different, every parent is different, and sometimes trying to follow advice from ten different parenting books can do more harm than good.

Looking back, what would you say was the greatest gift you gave to your kids?

I like to think my greatest gift was allowing my kids the freedom to explore anything that intrigued them and be there to support them while making sure they were safe.

If you could tell the world one thing, what would it be?

We need to accept, support and, most of all, LOVE the children we've been blessed with.

"You may experience fatigue like you never have! Don't soldier on regardless: accept help! It's better to do things with your children - playing, walking, talking, crafting - than having a pristine house."

Charlie Carrel
IG: @CharlieCarrel

Jacqui Carrel is the mother of Charlie Carrel, a

celebrity professional poker player and CEO/Founder of Thrive, a charitable foundation. Jacqui is Jersey-English but spent her upbringing in several different countries due to her father's role in the British Army. The family lived in Africa, Germany, Belgium, Northern Ireland, Cyprus and England and eventually returned to the Channel Island of Jersey. Each place had their own unique cultures and values that shaped her view of the world. Jacqui was a focused student yet also found time to get outside and to be with friends. She studied Environmental Science at the University of Plymouth, graduating with honors in 1983, went on to gain a Postgraduate Certificate in Education and become a science teacher. Jacqui married in her late 20s and had two children – Francine and Charles ('Charlie') – in her early 30s.

When the children were young, their parents separated. Jacqui raised both children on her own while teaching at various schools (science, psychology, ICT and special needs) and college (ICT) and working part-time as an Open University tutor in biology. After developing an autoimmune disease, she left teaching and worked from home as a copywriter and search engine marketer in the early days of the internet. As Jacqui began to recover and wanting a new challenge, she re-trained and today works with clients worldwide through her own hugely successful BlockBuster Therapy to quickly eradicate anxiety, fear and phobias. She also works with businesspeople through her Business BlockBuster Programme to clear their blocks around imposter syndrome, money and visibility. She is an author of several books, all ghost-written and under her own name. Jacqui also creates and hosts workshops, seminars and courses.

To Jacqui, it's no surprise that her son has become one of the world's top rising poker players. He was inherently smart as a child with an aptitude for mathematics, chess and music. While living in Suffolk, England as a teenager, he first discovered online poker and devoted much of his life to it - spending hours upon hours studying every facet of the game through live play, courses, seminars and more. Then, in 2015, he took the professional poker scene by storm at the Grand Finale of the PokerStars European Tour in Monte Carlo. Charlie, 21 years-old at the time, beat 215 other players to bring home a net prize of $1.25 million.

Now 27, Charlie's fortune, fame and fanbase have all continued to grow in the six years since his come up first began. He has over 22K followers on Instagram, where he regularly posts clips and content from his latest tournaments and competitions. His career live tournament winnings have eclipsed $10 million – money he's using to directly help others in need. In November 2019, Charlie founded Thrive, which is striving to end homelessness in the U.K. by 2025 through an app that will enable users to donate money directly to people in need.

In this chapter, Jacqui discusses her experience molding Charlie's bright young mind and details the process it took to become one of professional poker's rising stars.

Did your mother inspire you in any way? What kind of values did you take from her and instill in your own life as a mother?

I adored her (and still do). She was strict, but scrupulously fair and always loving and kind. Mum was a very good nurse; in fact, she didn't retire until her early 80s! She is small, just 5'2, but tall men quickly learned not to patronize her! Big things come in small packages and she was (and still is) a bundle of energy and a never-ending fountain of kindness. She loved to play tennis and squash – and didn't like to play board games at all, but she would gracefully hide that from me, my brother and her grandchildren and play for hours with us. She is a good cook and would always prepare wonderful meals – and if my father, brother or I turned up with friends at mealtime, she'd welcome them with a smile, reach in the cupboard, add something and make it stretch to fit all appetites.

She inspired me in so many ways! With regards to being a mother, I learned:
-   To do my best for my children.
-   To do plenty of things with my children.
-   To welcome my children's friends into the house.
-   To eat and talk and have fun together.
-   To get out for a walk or sports daily, whatever the weather (this did not always go down well!).
-   To let my children make their own choices around what to wear, what subjects to study, what hobbies to enjoy and when to leave education.

When was the earliest indication that you thought Charlie might have extraordinary talent?

As an infant, Charlie used to watch me and Francine playing Snakes & Ladders; we played this partly for fun and partly to help Francine learn to count to 100. When Charlie learned to speak, we discovered he could already count to 100 and recognize the numbers.

I taught Charlie how to play chess when he was

young. At age 10, he gracefully asked if I'd mind not playing him anymore as I was too easy to beat! Charlie started playing poker for fun when he was about 14. As I had no clue how to play the game, I left him to it. His game turned more into a passion when he was 19. He had played an online game with a £10 pot; had he lost, he may never have carried on – but he won. Charlie kept a separate pot and only used that to play poker. Soon he was playing for many hours, honing his craft. He was banned from playing at the local pub because he kept winning!

Did you put any systems in place for Charlie to build the habits that lead to his success?
We did lots together around learning (making it fun), but the motivation to carry his talents further, mainly came from Charlie. The only exception was when he was in the Cathedral choir; three of the weekly practices were before school and it was not always easy to get him up in time!

How did you handle Charlie's accomplishments and keep things in perspective?
I was so proud of the children's accomplishments that I never felt a need to handle them. I kept them intellectually stimulated but also made sure to balance activities with downtime and 'being' time. Francine helped Charlie keep things in perspective in the only way that an older sibling can! They bounced off each other a lot.

If you were heavily involved, how did you make time for yourself?
Apart from a couple of years, I only worked part-time (or not at all during the period when I was very ill), so I could rest, read or see friends most days. When the children were younger, I had the evenings to myself too.

Any stories of adversity that Charlie faced?

Charlie was amazingly bright and shone in many areas, but he was badly bullied at middle school and for part of high school. Being on the autistic spectrum didn't help him here as bullies like to pick on people with 'differences' and vulnerabilities. The bullying was awful. At one point, I took it to the police. In the end, I requested that he move schools and the local authority agreed. It had a detrimental effect on his self-esteem, but he did not let that get in the way of his passions.

What would you say were important qualities to possess to be the mother you were?

- Love: Feeling and showing unconditional love for my children.
- Pride: Pride in my children and in all their achievements – and pride even when they tried but didn't quite achieve their goals; they still learned from what they had done.
- Acceptance and delight: Accepting and delighting in the ways that made them different.
- Support: While I didn't always like what the children wanted to do in terms of hobbies and subjects at school, I supported their right to do them and enjoyed their pleasure.
- Knowing the importance of family and friends: Our family unit was very important to me, so we spent plenty of time together reading, playing games, walking and chatting. I encouraged them to see their friends and our house was often full. We kept a stash of sleeping bags and duvets in the cupboard and behind the sofa so the children's friends could stay overnight at a moment's notice.
- Nutrition: I was determined my children would eat as well as possible overall. For a while, we had to have ready meals because I was too ill to cook, though I always added something green. While I steered them away from sugar and junk food, I

accepted those would be in their lives at times and I did my best to educate them in eating well.
- Education and learning: I was there for them to bounce ideas off of, but what educational path they chose was up to them. Charlie stayed on to do A levels in Physics, Maths and Further Maths; when his A levels finished, he taught himself A level Additional Further Maths. He attained top grades in them all. He was also interested in reading PPE (Politics, Philosophy and Economics). Throughout this time, Charlie worked tirelessly on honing his poker skills.

Charlie chose to read PPE at Warwick University – he left soon into the course because his studies were getting in the way of his burgeoning poker career! I remember people being shocked and saying he needed good qualifications to get a good job. I would reply, "Why does he need a good job?" The answer would always be along the lines of a good salary, to which I would say he was earning a lot more through poker – and that even if things went wrong or he got bored with the subject, he was intelligent enough to train in something else and do very well. I wasn't always keen on the hours he spent on the computer, but I supported his choices.

What were things you think you may have handled differently?
I'd like to have known then what I know now about talking/negotiating with a highly intelligent teenager who was on the spectrum and could not (at the time) read subtleties in my language and body language. It was very difficult at times and occasionally I'd end up shouting or crying and only then getting some results. I'm not proud of that but, as I said, I didn't have the tools then and sometimes I was so tired from my illness that I could barely stand. Now there are so many books, talks, therapies and courses out there – make full use of them.

Luckily, there are plenty of things I know I got right, so I've stopped beating myself up over my mistakes.

What is your relationship like now with Charlie?
Our relationship is lovely. We are very close and talk about all sorts. My biggest regret is that I don't see him as often as I'd like – and not at all at the moment with Covid-19 as we are in different countries. I am just so thankful for WhatsApp and Zoom so at least we can see each other online.

If you could name one characteristic you believe Charlie inherited from you, what would that be?
A huge and never-ending curiosity about the world and people.

How did you respond to situations that made you feel overwhelmed?
Go for a walk in nature and/or take photographs. I still do :)

Can you give any advice to young or soon to be mothers/parents?
- You may experience fatigue like you never had! Don't soldier on regardless. Accept help!
- It's better to do things with your children -- playing, walking, talking, crafting -- than have a pristine house.
- Always respect your children's thoughts and feelings even while maintaining boundaries around behavior, bedtimes, etc. What may appear childish or little to you is real to them and their thoughts and feelings are what matter.
- Remember, advice is just that: it's your life, your family, so listen to everything, read up on it and then make the choice that's right for you, not your friends.

- Here is a caveat – please listen to this advice: eat to nourish and sustain your body and emotional health and your child's growing body and brain, especially pre-pregnancy, during pregnancy and when breast-feeding. Eat real food, avoid processed foods, especially those that contain sugar, and get plenty of fats from oily fish, grass-fed meat, coconut, nuts and avocados.

Looking back, what would you say was the greatest gift you gave to your kids?
My unconditional love. And, as far as I'm concerned, it is their life to lead, not mine. So while I guided them away from bad choices and danger as best I could, I also gave unconditional support for their life-defining choices around education and career.

If you could tell the world one thing, what would it be?
Don't look back and regret what you *didn't* do – go for it!

Conclusion

James Clear, author of *Atomic Habits*, once wrote, "Asking what makes someone successful is like asking which ingredient makes a recipe taste good. It's not any single ingredient. It is the combination of many ingredients in the right proportions and in the right order - and the absence of anything that would ruin the mixture."

With 38 mothers from 10 states, 9 countries and 5 continents, this book contains a multitude of powerful ingredients. Now it is up to you to discern which elements are missing from your life and apply them accordingly. For easy access to some of the invaluable lessons and principles shared by our subjects, we have synthesized a short list:

Live in the moment

> Your time is the one resource you can never get back, no matter how much money or goodwill is accrued in a lifetime. The only antidote to that humbling fact is to consciously appreciate as many moments as possible — both good and bad. Worrying about the future or stressing over the past takes away from your ability to be present with your family. It speaks volumes that, of the few regrets our subjects have, nearly all of them regret not being more focused on the present moment, especially when their kids were young.

You cannot want it for them

> If your child doesn't possess an innate passion for the goals they pursue, no amount of objective

success will be fulfilling. Encouragement and support are critical to fostering achievement but forcing dreams upon your children eventually culminates into unhealthy relationship and resentment. A degree of autonomy during early years is important. Longitudinal studies tracking learners confirm that overbearing parents erode intrinsic motivation.[3]

Embrace mental health

Going to therapy does not mean you are a failure, or you are mentally weak. Just like your physical well-being, mental health requires constant attention and care. Hiring a professional to help guide you and your children provides immense benefits for all personal and professional pursuits.

Encourage educated risks

One way to stifle personal growth is by living perpetually within your comfort zone. However, on the other hand, stepping into a completely unknown situation can have catastrophically discouraging consequences. Many of our subjects discussed a healthy combination of encouraging loved ones to do their research, finding the courage to take chances and learning from their experiences. Oftentimes a result of this is a confidence your child finds organically, which leads to continued growth. Organic confidence that comes naturally from within is much more

---

[3] Angela Duckworth, *Grit* (Simon and Schuster, 2016) 107.

powerful in the long run compared to a forced sense of confidence from parents who constantly reassure children how great they are.

Unconditional love and support

Unconditional love is a foundational pillar to parenting. Don't be afraid to express it and express it often. There are dozens of examples of unconditional love in this book, but no one articulated it better than Stacey Phillips, "Knowing that someone loves you more than their self-image, more than any possessions, more than their own life, gives you the security to succeed and the security to fail. You'll be okay no matter what happens. That kind of love is such an immeasurable gift to a child."

Make time for yourself

Sometimes as a parent we lose ourselves in our children. We are constantly worrying about their health, education and reputation before realizing one day that our identity is gone. Remember that if you're encouraging your child to be an independent person, they need to see the same example from you. Whether it's going for a walk, meditating for 10 minutes a day, or getting in some daily exercise, we all need to find whatever it is that helps us be the best version of ourselves.

If you start something, finish it

Every parent wants to ensure their children enjoys participating in extracurricular activities. There are numerous options to choose from, so it's no surprise how easily some kids bounce from one activity to the next. Our subjects did not encourage that behavior in their children. While they didn't have rigid long-term expectations, they always made sure their child finished what they started.

You'll never be perfect

Mistakes are unavoidable. As parents, apologizing to children and admitting when we're at fault is an uncommon, but important trait. Embrace the uncomfortable conversations with your loved ones. The quicker they understand you're not perfect, the better off your relationship will be.

Focus on what you can control

There are so many things out of your control: your friends' approach to parenting, the passions your children gravitate towards, whether their coaches or teachers like you, etc. It is easy to get caught up in the countless things that we find ourselves worrying about on a daily basis. You'll be doing yourself a huge favor by simply noticing what is within your sphere of influence. Worry less, relax more. As Janet Lavelle so wonderfully put it - "control the controllables."

Lead by example

Your children are perceptive. If you are telling them one thing and practicing another, they will notice. By showing up every day and being a consistent presence, you demonstrate in the most powerful way what it means to be true to yourself.

> Trust your instincts and ignore anything that goes against that little voice in your head.

It is our hope that you have taken something positive from this book. Whether that means as a mature parent empathizing with some of the things you read and using it to reflect on your own parenthood journey – or as a young parent finding useful mental models and acquiring new perspectives to help guide you in life's unpredictable adventures – or, if you're a young adult and raising a family isn't necessarily in your view for the time being, we hope you will feel better prepared if and when that day comes thanks to these 38 admirable mothers.

We would love to connect with you to hear any ideas about how we can enhance the material for the next edition. Who should we include? What should we ask them? We view this as a community project and greatly appreciate any sincere feedback. You can reach us at Creatrix.blog or on Instagram @Creatrix_book.

Bonus To see sneak peaks of future volumes, featured chapters, and podcast episodes, go to Creatrix.blog to sign up for free exclusive content.

@Creatrix_book
www.creatrix.blog